The Siege of Tsingtau

For Scotty

My old pal: Peter William Scott

11 May 1948–27 November 2016

Death drives an Airflow Chrysler on the streets of man
A hit and run driver cruising since the world began

The Siege of Tsingtau

The German–Japanese War 1914

Charles Stephenson

Pen & Sword
MILITARY

First published in Great Britain in 2017 by
Pen & Sword Military
an imprint of
Pen & Sword Books Ltd
47 Church Street
Barnsley
South Yorkshire
S70 2AS

ISBN 978 1 52670 292 0

A CIP catalogue record for this book is available from the British
Library

Typeset in Ehrhardt by
Mac Style Ltd, Bridlington, East Yorkshire
Printed and bound in Malta by Gutenberg Press Ltd

Pen & Sword Books Ltd incorporates the imprints of Pen & Sword
Archaeology, Atlas, Aviation, Battleground, Discovery, Family
History, History, Maritime, Military, Naval, Politics, Railways, Select,
Transport, True Crime, Fiction, Frontline Books, Leo Cooper,
Praetorian Press, Seaforth Publishing and Wharncliffe.

For a complete list of Pen & Sword titles please contact
PEN & SWORD BOOKS LIMITED
47 Church Street, Barnsley, South Yorkshire, S70 2AS, England
E-mail: enquiries@pen-and-sword.co.uk
Website: www.pen-and-sword.co.uk

Contents

List of Maps

Introduction

Perhaps uniquely in terms of European 'Great Power' royalty, Archduke Franz Ferdinand, the heir to the throne of the Hapsburgs, had a wife that protocol dictated he couldn't normally be seen with. Despite Sophie Chotek, the Duchess of Hohenberg, having been described as 'one of the cleverest and most accomplished women in Austria-Hungary', she was considered too socially inferior to sit at the 'top-table' of the Imperial Court and most certainly wasn't to be generally observed on the arm of the heir presumptive.[1] It was then ironic that on one of the few occasions that the couple were actually together in public they became immortalised for what happened to them. The place was Sarajevo, capital of Bosnia, the territory recently (1908) annexed by Austria-Hungary, and the date was 28 June 1914. News of the event flashed around the world. As is well known, the assassinations with, according to Austria-Hungary, the complicity of the Serbian government led to war; Austria-Hungary made a declaration of such with Serbia on 28 July 1914.

But what might have been the Third Balkan War quickly escalated into a general European conflict. The reasons why this happened are still debated, but there is little controversy in arguing that it became a worldwide war, indeed the First World War retrospectively, when Germany, France and the United Kingdom became embroiled. This was so because those polities had extra-European empires. So, for example, when the UK declared war with Germany on 4 August 1914, and with Austria-Hungary some eight days later, so did the rest of the British Empire. This included the self-governing dominions; as the then Canadian Prime Minister (Sir Wilfred Laurier) had stated the matter in 1910: 'When Britain is at war, Canada is at war; there is no distinction.'[2] There was little or no distinction with respect to the other dominions either; this was so even in South Africa where the war between the British Empire and the Boers had only ended twelve years earlier and many Boers still preserved anti-British sentiments. The colonial territories that were without representative government had even less discretion in the matter.

Austria-Hungary had no extra-European territory, but Germany most certainly did though this is often forgotten.[3] France too had vast oversea territories. Thus it was that peoples in several far-flung parts of the globe found themselves automatically at war whether they liked it or not. There was though one other state, one massively distant from the main fronts of the conflict in Europe, which actively chose to become involved. That state was Japan. Indeed Japan sent Germany an ultimatum on 14 August 1914 which went unanswered, and then declared war on 23 August. The same declaration was made on Austria-Hungary on 25 August.[4] It was the case that Japan was formally allied to the UK, but the terms of that alliance did not automatically bring Japan in on the UK's side.

One of the aims of this book is to explain why Japan chose to declare war on the Central Powers in the manner she did in 1914, which necessitates examining Japanese and German colonial expansion in East Asia and the Pacific, and the (eventually realised) potential for conflict this induced.

The main focus however is on the conflict itself; the German-Japanese War of 1914. Despite a state of war between Japan on the one hand and Germany and Austria-Hungary on the other existing until 1919, 1914 is emphasised simply because that was when the vast majority of the actual fighting took place. There is of course a major caveat to insert here; the Imperial Japanese Navy despatched the 10th and 11th destroyer flotillas under Admiral Sato Kozo to the Mediterranean in March 1917 for convoy escort and antisubmarine work, and they saw some action.[5] In the main however Japan elected only to deploy forces in the Far East and Pacific regions. This was despite the hopes of their allies, who tried and failed to get a much greater level of commitment to the European theatre. To the UK and France the various 'colonial' campaigns were sideshows, and the only direct military clash between Japan and Germany was a fairly minor version of even that categorisation.[6] This was not the case for Japan, who committed serious resources, an army corps and virtually their entire navy, to ensure a quick and decisive victory. The story of that campaign forms the core of this book, and the text proceeds more or less chronologically; those who wish only to read about the actual fighting might wish to skip the first couple of chapters.

This is not a book aimed at the academic end of the spectrum. There are no theoretical frameworks within which the tale is constructed, nor are there any new or startling conclusions. It merely attempts a narrative history from, mainly, primary sources pertaining to the campaign, whilst providing the context within which it came about using, mostly, secondary sources. The book is then targeted at the intelligent general reader and not the professional historian.

Having said that, I have been careful in correctly attributing the sources used, including those in Japanese. A full bibliography is provided, but chief amongst the latter are four volumes that were published by the General Staff of the Japanese Army (*Rikugun Sanbo Honbu*): Taisho 3 Nen Seneki Shoken Shu (Collection of Reports and Observations on the War of 1914) in two volumes published in 1915; and *Taisho 3 Nen Nichi-doku Senshi (The German-Japanese War of 1914)* in two volumes published in 1916. These works were put together as staff studies and are incredibly detailed; they give day-to-day accounts of the movements of all the Japanese formations involved and reproduce the various orders issued at all levels. They are not easy reads in any sense of the term, but have been invaluable in providing information from the Japanese side. I am grateful in the extreme for the help provided by certain individuals in translating them, but who wish to remain uncredited. It must though be emphasised that any errors in the process are my responsibility and mine alone.

There are of course minefields to negotiate when dealing with the Chinese and Japanese languages, and then converting them into English or German. Perhaps one example will suffice. The city at the centre of this story is, under the current official system of Romanising Chinese (*Hanyu Pinyin*), named *Qingdao* and it sits on *Jiaozhou Bay*. However, the former system of rendering the language into English (Wade-Giles) meant the city was known as *Tsingtao* and the bay upon which it sat dubbed variously as *Kiaochow*, *Kiauchau* or *Kiao-Chau*. A different system (Lessing-Othmer) was eventually devised for the German language, and this validated the formulation whereby *Tsingtau* was situated on the shores of *Kiautschou*, or *Kiaochau*, Bay.

There is of course no way of pleasing everyone in these matters, and this book isn't meant to be about arcane disputations over transliteration. However, since these places, and others, have to be called *something* I have opted to go for the German variation as it was usually expressed in 1914. The area in question was effectively German territory at that time, albeit only because it had been obtained from China by extortion, and such a method at least provides a degree of consistency. Apologies in advance to anyone that might take issue with this.

Once again it gives me pleasure to thank a couple of people who have greatly helped in the putting together of this work; Charles Blackwood and Michael Perratt. Charles drew the excellent maps whilst Michael applied the acid test to a volume of this sort; is it intelligible and accessible to the intelligent lay reader? Happily he thought so.

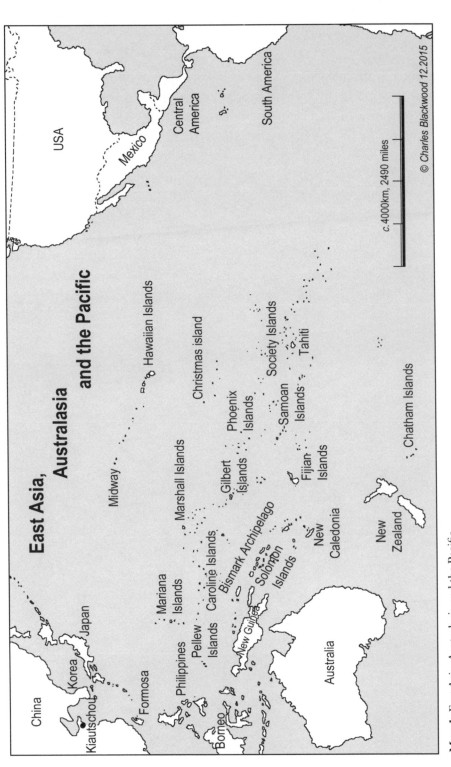

Map 1: East Asia, Australasia and the Pacific.

Chapter 1

'… A Transaction in the Old Prussian Style'

P ut at its most basic, the Japanese decision to declare war on Germany in 1914 had its roots in German imperialist expansion into the East-Asian and Pacific regions. This was a policy that began under the rule of Otto von Bismarck in 1884, despite his arguing a decade earlier that 'colonies […] would only be a source of weakness, because colonies could only be defended by powerful fleets, and Germany's geographical position did not necessitate her development into a first class maritime power'.[1]

The reasons for Bismarck's change of mind need not concern us here, but a large area of territory was acquired; the 'Protectorate of German New Guinea' consisted of Kaiser Wilhelm's Land (*Kaiserwilhelmsland*) (the north-eastern part of New Guinea), the Bismarck Archipelago (the Admiralty Islands, Duke of York Islands, Mussau Islands, New Britain, New Hanover, New Ireland, the Vitu Islands) and the German Solomon Islands (Buka Island, Bougainville), totalling a land area of some 240000km^2, of which Kaiser Wilhelm's Land accounted for the majority at 179000km^2. These parts eventually, following acquisitions in later years and the reorganisation of German colonial administration in the Pacific in 1906, became known as the 'Old Protectorate'.

There was a further addition in 1886 with the acquisition of the Marshall Islands. These had been Spanish territory, but had been somewhat neglected by their 'owner' and both the UK and Germany had begun diplomatic moves to safeguard their interests in the area. This had taken the form of a joint note to Spain refusing to acknowledge her sovereignty over the Caroline and Palau islands. On 24 September 1885 Bismarck proposed referring the matter to the arbitration of the Pope, Leo XIII, which was accepted by all parties. The Pope announced his findings on 22 October in a masterful judgement that succeeded in mediating all the conflicting claims, and Germany and Spain, the UK having withdrawn from the dispute, signed

2 The Siege of Tsingtau

an agreement at the Vatican on 17 December 1855. The agreement meant that Spain's claim to the Caroline Islands was formally recognised, though Germany's right to establish naval stations and trading posts there was conceded, whilst Germany's claim to the Marshall Islands was agreed. This territory, consisting of the Ratak Group in the east and the Ralik Group in the west, numbers overall some 353 individual islands, which have a total land area of about 400km². A German protectorate was formally declared on 13 September 1886.

On 16 April 1888, following an agreement on delineation with the UK – the Anglo-German Convention of 1886 – that placed the territory within its purview, Germany annexed the island of Nauru. This tiny island, with a total area of some 21km², was placed, administratively, within the Protectorate of the Marshall Islands.

The Marshall Islands were, like German New Guinea, also to be run by a private company, though in a 'condominium' arrangement with the German government. The agreement was signed on 21 January 1888 granting the Jaluit Company (Jaluit-Gesselschaft AG), which had been created a year earlier by the same two companies that had formed the New Guinea Company – Robertson & Hernsheim and the German Trading and Commercial Company, a trading monopoly and obliging it to underwrite administrative duties in the islands. This meant that whilst the German government appointed officials to administer the territory, the Jaluit Company paid their salaries and all associated administrative costs. This was not a particularly onerous duty; by 1906 the total number of administrative staff had doubled from its original number, and amounted to four personnel. The downside, from the administrator's point of view, was that the company regarded the Marshall Islands very much as its own colony.

Whatever the economic worth, or lack thereof, of the territories thus acquired (by 1899 'nine million marks had been buried, like the dead, in the soil of Kaiser Wilhelmsland.' they formed a colonial empire which it was deemed necessary to protect.[2] Accordingly, and as the Iron Chancellor had foreseen, there arose a pressing need, as viewed from the German Admiralty, for a permanent base in the Pacific area to accommodate the vessels of the East Asian Cruiser Division.

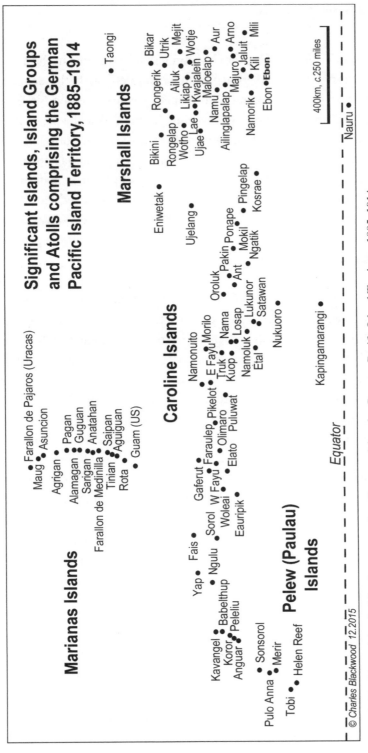

Significant Islands, Island Groups and Atolls comprising the German Pacific Island Territory, 1885–1914

Marianas Islands

- Farallon de Pajaros (Uracas)
- Maug
- Asuncion
- Agrigan
- Pagan
- Alamagan
- Guguan
- Sarigan
- Anatahan
- Farallon de Medinilla
- Saipan
- Tinian
- Aguiguan
- Rota
- Guam (US)

Caroline Islands

- Namonuito
- Gaferut
- Sorol
- W Fayu
- Faraulep
- Pikelot
- E Fayu
- Morilo
- Olimaro
- Elato
- Puluwat
- Truk
- Kuop
- Nama
- Losap
- Namoluk
- Lukunor
- Etal
- Satawan
- Oroluk
- Pakin Ponape
- Ant
- Mokil
- Ngatik
- Pingelap
- Kosrae
- Nukuoro
- Ujelang
- Yap
- Fais
- Ngulu
- Woleai
- Eauripik
- Kapingamarangi

Pelew (Paulau) Islands

- Kavangel
- Babelthup
- Koror
- Peleliu
- Anguar
- Sonsorol
- Pulo Anna
- Merir
- Tobi
- Helen Reef

Marshall Islands

- Taongi
- Bikini
- Rongerik
- Bikar
- Rongelap
- Ailuk
- Utrik
- Wotho
- Likiap
- Mejit
- Ujae
- Lae
- Kwajalein
- Wotje
- Namu
- Maloelap
- Aur
- Ailinglapalap
- Majuro
- Arno
- Namorik
- Jaluit
- Ebon •Ebon
- Kili
- Mili
- Eniwetak
- Nauru

400km, c.250 miles

Equator

© Charles Blackwood 12.2015

Map 2: Significant islands, island groups and atolls comprising the German Pacific Island Territory, 1885–1914.

A precursor to that Cruiser Division had been formed in the early 1880s, and its importance had grown commensurately with the acquisition of colonial territories. It became a permanently constituted unit in September 1894 following the outbreak of the Sino–Japanese War the previous August. Contemporary practice designated a division as a four-ship unit under the command of a Rear Admiral; the first holder being Paul Hoffman who took up position in November. The four warships in the command comprised three 'Carola' class iron flush decked corvettes, *Alexandrine*, *Arcona* and *Marie*, and the 'Irene II' class protected cruiser-corvette *Irene*. Hoffman's orders enjoined him to protect German interests in the region generally, and to seek out potential sites for a permanent base.[3]

Both the composition of the Cruiser Division, the 'Carola' class vessels were obsolete when constructed, and the lack of dedicated facilities greatly hampered the operational efficiency of the unit. It was however easier to increase the potency of the division by attaching more powerful vessels to it, *Alexandrine* and *Marie* being replaced by the 'Kaiser' class central battery ironclad *Kaiser* and *Prinzess Wilhelm*, sister of *Irene*, in January 1895, than it was to establish a permanent base. Hoffman's successor, from 1896, was Alfred von Tirpitz, and as he was to later put it: 'The lack of a base hampered us because the sole factor of power [...] was our flying squadron [*sic*], and the existence of this depended upon the Hong-Kong docks and consequently upon the favour of Britain'.[4] These docks, Tirpitz noted, had to be booked nine months in advance and 'our Eastern Asiatic Squadron [*sic*] could be rendered useless on the slightest provocation by [their] refusal.'[5] Alternative facilities in Japan and China had been refused to Hoffman during the Sino–Japanese conflict.[6]

Though Tirpitz was later to claim that he came to the conclusion that Kiautschou Bay was the ideal site for a German naval base, the matter was undecided when he was recalled to Berlin to become Navy Secretary and begin planning a German battle-fleet. The future Grand Admiral handed over his command to the next most senior officer in the squadron, Captain Hugo Zeye, and returned to Berlin in March 1897.[7]

Tirpitz's successor was Rear Admiral Otto von Diederichs, a former instructor of naval history and strategy at the Kiel Marine Academy.[8] Diederichs left Berlin on 1 May 1897, finally arriving at Shanghai on 10 June whereupon he was compelled to wait three days pending the arrival of the divisional flagship *Kaiser*. During this sojourn he discovered he was sharing the hotel with a colleague; the chief of engineering at Kiel, Georg Ludwig Franzius, who was later to design the 128m-span transporter bridge at the seaport constructed in 1909–10. Franzius had been despatched to China to survey the various locales deemed potential sites for Germany's proposed naval base, and had, in May 1897, decided that Kiautschou offered the best prospects on a number of counts, including the potential for economic development.

The economic potential of the area had already been discovered, and enumerated, by the German geologist, geographer and explorer Ferdinand Baron von Richthofen. The uncle of the 'Red Baron' of Great War fame, and 'the most important Western researcher on China of his time', Richthofen had undertaken several far-reaching journeys through China during the 1860s and 70s, with the results being recorded in a massive six-volume work that appeared between 1877 and 1912; the final volumes posthumously.[9] The area had become directly known to Germany, or at least Prussia, in 1860 when three Prussian warships, *Arkona*, *Frauenlob* and *Thetis*, had anchored in Kiautschou Bay as part of an attempt, successful as it turned out, to open trade links with China. The resultant treaty, giving the parties most favoured nation status, was dated 2 September 1861.

Following his return to Germany in August, Franzius therefore recommended Kiautschou as the best site for the base.[10] There was, as far as Germany was concerned, one potential problem; it was possible that the Russians had a prior claim through the concept of 'first anchoring', though this entire principle was dismissed retrospectively by Tirpitz. If this principle were adhered to, he stated, it would mean that 'England could claim not only Tsingtau, but the whole world, because Englishmen had at one time or another anchored everywhere.'[11] That the Chinese might have an opinion on the matter was not a factor that featured in the calculation. Whilst the various organs of the German government, Foreign Office, navy and Kaiser, were now singing from the same, metaphorical, hymn sheet, there was another grouping, singing from a literal hymn sheet, that held more or less identical views and sought to implement them; the German missionaries of the Society of the Divine Word. There were a number of different German missionary groupings in Shantung (Shandong) province and Esherick, who has studied the matter deeply, categorises them thus:

'Protestants were on the whole a good deal less disruptive than the Catholics [...] and of the Catholics, none were more disruptive than the new order which entered the field in the 1880s – the German missionaries of the Society of the Divine Word (S.V.D.)'.[12] Otherwise known as the Steyler Mission, the local head of this organisation was Johann Baptist von Anzer, who had been in China since 1879. He was appointed Bishop of Shantung in 1886, and he has been described as 'the most powerful and most vigorously colonialist' of all the German missionaries in the province.[13] Anzer had a close relationship with the German Foreign Office, and in March 1896, he complained to them that the Chinese, due to their perception of Germany's weakness, no longer respected him.[14] Indeed, it has been argued, his policy during his tenure up until 1897 was designed to engineer German military intervention through provoking an incident with the indigenous population.[15]

This policy was ultimately successful when, on 1 November 1897, two German missionaries, Richard Henle and Francis Xavier Nies, were hacked to death by a band of twenty to thirty armed men at Yen-chu-fu in Shantung province.[16] When this news reached Berlin the Kaiser sprang into action, writing to the Foreign Office on 6 November:

I have just read in the press the news of the attack on the German Catholic Mission in Shantung, which is under my protection. Full atonement for this must be exacted through vigorous intervention by the fleet [...] I am now quite determined to give up our excessively cautious policy, which is already regarded as weak throughout East Asia, and to use all severity and if necessary the most brutal ruthlessness towards the Chinese, to show at long last that the German Kaiser is not to be trifled with, and that it is a bad thing to have him as an enemy [...][17]

The 'vigorous intervention by the fleet' came in the form of an order he commanded be transmitted to Diederichs. It read: 'Proceed at once [to] Kiautschou with your whole squadron, occupy appropriate positions and places there and then exact full atonement in the way which seems the most appropriate to you. The greatest possible vigour is ordered. The goal of your voyage is to be kept secret.'[18] Diederichs was at Shanghai with two of his vessels, *Kaiser* and *Prinzess Wilhelm*, when he received the order on 8 November. He replied to the head of the Navy High Command, Admiral Eduard von Knorr, that he would 'immediately proceed against Kiautschou with [the] greatest energy'.[19] Two ships of the division were unavailable to him; *Arcona* was in dock at Shanghai and *Irene* similarly indisposed at Hong Kong. He could however call upon the services of the 'Bussard' class light cruiser *Cormoran*, which had been assigned to East Asia but was not formally a member of his command, though the vessel was upriver of Shanghai, at Wuhan (Wuchang) and could not join him immediately.[20] Nevertheless, even with this attenuated force Diederichs calculated that he could carry out his orders and, observing secrecy as per his orders, proceeded to sea with *Kaiser* on 10 November leaving the other two vessels to rendezvous with him later.

Meanwhile in Berlin the Reich Chancellor, Hohenlohe, had been throwing cold water on the operation by putting some of the realities of the situation to the Kaiser:

If Your Majesty [...] wishes to give the squadron commander orders to take action at once, it might be necessary to choose somewhere other than Kiautschou, as in order to occupy Kiautschou in accordance with the agreement reached between Your Majesty and the [Czar] at Peterhof, Russian consent would have to be sought.[21]

Still in full flow, and at this time undeterred by diplomatic considerations, Wilhelm telegraphed to the Czar, seeking approval for the operation he had set in motion, and justifying it by recourse to a 'conversation' he recalled having taken place:

Chinese attacked German missions, Shantung, inflicting loss of life and property. I trust you approve according to our conversation Peterhof my sending German squadron to Kiautschou, as it is the only port available to operate from as a base against Marauders. I am under obligations to Catholic party in Germany to show that their missions are really safe under my protectorate.[22]

He received the following reply:

I am very grateful that you informed me personally. Regret attack by Chinese on German Catholic missions under your protectorate. Cannot approve nor disapprove your sending German squadron to Kiautschou as I lately learned that this harbour only had been temporarily ours in 1895–1896. I feel anxious lest perhaps severity may cause unrest and insecurity in Eastern China and widen the breach between Chinese and Christians.[23]

The Kaiser, taking this as approval of his behaviour, fired off messages to his Chancellor, stating 'we must use this excellent opportunity without delay, before another great power provokes China or comes to her aid! Now or never;'.[24] He also communicated with his recently appointed Foreign Secretary, who was in Rome:

Our conversation about [Kiautschou] […] at the end of which you said that it was high time to stiffen up our tepid and vacillating policy in the Far East, has had a quick result, quicker than we imagined. Yesterday I received official information of an attack, with murder and robbery, on the German missionary station at Yen-chu-fu in Shantung. So the Chinese have at last given us the grounds and the 'incident' which your predecessor, [Baron Adolf Marschall von Bieberstein] so long desired. […]

The message to the Admiral contains instructions to proceed at once to [Kiautschou] and seize it, threaten reprisals and act with energy. [25]

He also reported the misgivings of the Reich Chancellor:

Today the Chancellor informed me that this intention would be a breach of the Peterhof Agreements, and that it must first be ascertained how the Russian Government would feel towards this enterprise. [...] However humiliating it may be for the German Empire to be obliged almost to obtain permission in St. Petersburg to protect and avenge the Christians in China who are committed to its care, and also to help itself to a spot which it refrained from occupying three years ago out of excessive modesty – and to which there could have been no objection.[26]

Foreign Secretary Bernhard von Bülow was also apprised of the Czar's anxieties vis-à-vis severe action causing a rift between the Chinese and Christians, but these concerns were utterly dismissed by the Kaiser:

I do not share this anxiety. Thousands of German Christians will breathe a sigh of relief when they hear that the German Kaiser's ships are near by, hundreds of German traders will exult in the knowledge that the German Reich has won a firm foothold in Asia, hundreds of thousands of Chinese will tremble when they feel the iron fist of the German Reich bearing down on their necks, and the whole German Reich will rejoice that its government has done a manly deed [...] but let the world learn the lesson once and for all from this incident, that where I am concerned: Nemo me impune lacessit ('No-one provokes me with impunity' – coincidentally (?) the motto of the British Royal Family in Scotland).[27]

The 'Peterhof Agreements', so called, mentioned by Hohenlohe were the outcome of diplomacy that had attended the Kaiser's visit to Russia, accompanied by the Chancellor and Bülow (then Acting Secretary of Foreign Affairs), from 7–10 August 1897. Whilst on this visit the Germans had stayed at Peterhof, a site located southwest of the Russian capital St Petersburg. This 'palace, fountain and park ensemble' was commenced at the behest of Peter the Great in 1714.[28]

We only have what transpired between Czar and Kaiser at several removes, but it seems as if the Kaiser, at least to his own satisfaction, received the approval of the Czar for Germany to take Kiautschou. Sergius Witte, at the time the Russian Finance Minister and later the constitutional prime minister of the Russian Empire from 1905–6, put it thus in his memoirs:

During the German Kaiser's stay at Peterhof there occurred an incident which was destined to have the most far-reaching effects upon the course of Russian history. It was afterwards related to me by Grand Duke Alezey Alexandrovich. Once when the two emperors were driving alone out in the country, so [the Czar] told the Grand Duke, the German Kaiser asked his host whether Russia had any use for the Chinese Port of Kiautschou. He added that he would like to occupy that port and use it as a base for German shipping, but that he did not wish to take the step without his, [the Czar's] consent. [The Czar] did not tell the Grand Duke whether or not he actually gave his consent to the occupation of Kiautschou. What he did say was that his guest had placed him in an awkward position and the whole incident was extremely distasteful to him. I have but little doubt that [the Czar], who is exceedingly well-mannered, found it impossible to refuse his guest's request point-blank and that the latter interpreted this attitude as indirect approval and implied consent. Some time later, Count Muraviev [Russia's Foreign Minister from 1896 until his death in 1900], in discussing with me my opposition to the occupation of Port Arthur, let the cat out of the bag. He admitted that we had, in his words, 'rashly given our consent to the step which Germany had taken'.[29]

Whatever the Czar had agreed with Wilhelm, or what Wilhelm thought he had agreed, the Russian government was, as Hohenlohe had warned, not acquiescent in the German manoeuvre. This was demonstrated on 10 November 1897 when the Kaiser was apprised of the views of that government via a telegram from the German Chargé d'affaires in St Petersburg. This set out the views of Count Muraviev as expressed to the diplomat:

As regards Russia's right to Kiao–chau Bay, he had at the time (during 1895–96) received from China not only the right to use the harbour, but also the droit du premier mouillage, i.e., a promise that if the harbour was to be handed over to a foreign Power, Russia should under all circumstances be assured of the preference.

For the safeguarding of these rights the Russian Commander of the squadron in the Far East had been commanded to send Russian ships into that harbour, the moment that any German ships entered it. But the Russian ships would not participate in our action in obtaining satisfaction for the murder of the missionaries. [...] Count Muraviev, deplored the Imperial Government's step. The result would be that the British, and perhaps even the French, would send ships into Kiautschou Bay, and this could not be prevented; so that what would happen would just be what least suited both our interests; the harbour would become open first to England, and then to all nations. Moreover it was an open question what China's attitude would be towards a forcible seizure of the harbour. Finally Count Muravieff said that so far he had discussed the matter with no one.

The Russian Minister thus declares clearly enough that the Emperor Nicholas' Government has no intention of letting any other Power have Kiautschou, but wishes to take it itself, supposing China loses it.[30]

The last sentence was annotated by Wilhelm 'The direct contrary of what he and his Master both said to me at Peterhof.' The German Foreign Office now became alarmed at the turn events were taking, with Friedrich von Holstein, the Political Secretary, warning the Chancellor on 9 November: '[...] the Russian declaration is so brutally explicit that it scarcely seems necessary to give the Kaiser any advice. He alone will know whether he wants war with Russia or not. We shall now have to be very careful with our action in China.'[31]

Hohenlohe was alarmed at the potentiality for the dispute to escalate into conflict, particularly if the Kaiser once again decided to intervene personally with the Russians. 'Things really look very bad' was the message he sent to Wolfgang von Rotenhan the Under-secretary of State at the Foreign Office on 10 November. He seemed not to think however that there was any imminence of war, provided nothing was done to inflame the situation: 'The Russians are [only] trying to frighten us. I cannot believe that the [Czar] will declare war on us because of Kiautschou Bay.' The peril, as he perceived it, was his headstrong monarch: 'There is a danger that [the Kaiser] will send a telegram to the [Czar] at once. And what will it say?'[32] It is perhaps remarkable that the Kaiser remained, by his standards, cool and collected and did not send an inflammatory telegram to the Russians. His logic was explained to the Foreign Office on 11 November:

Count Muraviev's note corresponds perfectly to the character of this mendacious gentleman [...] We should attempt to come to an arrangement with Russia to acquire the rights to Kiautschou, if necessary by purchase. Even Russia will yield to a fait accompli, and will certainly not start a war on account of Kiautschou, as she needs us in the East.[33]

It was, in any case something of an academic debate, because Otto von Diederichs, having received his orders, could not be recalled once he had sailed on 10 November. The *Kaiser* rendezvoused with *Prinzess Wilhelm* and *Cormoran* at sea on 12 November, the latter two vessels having departed without arousing suspicion as to the nature of their mission, and set course for Tsingtau, arriving in Kiautschou Bay on the morning of 13 November. Diederichs determined on a reconnaissance of the area and accordingly landed at Tsingtau under the guise of a friendly visit later that day. His observations convinced him that even though there was a significant Chinese force in the vicinity, numbering some 3,000 men manning artillery positions and other fortifications, he could succeed in his mission. The Chinese had first become aware that Kiautschou Bay was a vulnerable point on the coast in 1891, and established and maintained the 3,000-strong garrison thereafter.[34] The most notable artillery position had been constructed on a 128m promontory that overlooked the bay, the coast and surrounding territory.[35]

The efficiency of this force was however judged to be low by Diederichs, who had also noted that their artillery, which should have covered the proposed landing site, was not operable.[36] Accordingly he re-entered Kiautschou Bay on the morning of 14 November 1897 and, at 08:00hr local time, set about landing a party of some 700 officers and ratings. Within an hour, and without fighting, these had gained several strategic points and put the telegraph out of commission. Backed by the guns of the three vessels in the bay, an ultimatum was delivered to the local Chinese commander in the terms of: remove all your forces within three hours.

Faced with the superior force embodied in the guns of the warships, the Chinese withdrew and at 14:20hr the German flag was hoisted. A twenty-one-gun salute, a symbolic demonstration reserved for the most imposing occasions, was ordered in commemoration of the bloodless victory.

Diederichs, having made a speech to the Germans, then, essentially, declared himself governor of the area and issued instructions to the inhabitants of the area occupied to the effect that they should continue as normal. He cautioned them that opposition was futile.[37]

The pretext for all this was of course the murder of Henle and Nies on 1 November, and, at least ostensibly, the German government was awaiting a reply from the Chinese government on the matter. Indeed on 11 November Hohenlohe had advised the Kaiser that no occupation of Chinese territory should take place until such time as a reply arrived and was deemed unsatisfactory.[38] Perhaps realising that events might be spiralling out of control, Wilhelm accepted this advice. Accordingly he had a telegram despatched, via Admiral Hans von Koester, to Diederichs on 13 November telling him to suspend operations against Tsingtau and, if they had already taken place, to ensure that his occupation was deemed temporary.[39]

Diederichs had not received this message, and was unable to do so until, so as to enable him to report the success of his mission, he ordered the repair of the telegraph. Upon having the message decoded he could only reply that he had already proclaimed German occupation on a permanent basis and that going back on this was impossible.[40] Presentation of this fait accompli seems to have settled the matter in Berlin, and Knorr telegraphed him the following day offering congratulations and informing him that his proclamation remained in effect.[41]

This news overjoyed the Kaiser, who made it perfectly clear on 15 November that he stood four-square behind Diederichs, and indeed wanted to go further. He argued that the demands to China should be set 'at such a level that they cannot be fulfilled and therefore justify further seizure' and that 'permanent occupation of [Kiautschou Bay] is to be envisaged'. He also reiterated his mantra that he had the support of the Czar:

His Majesty remarked that he stood by the fact that [the Czar] had given telegraphic approval. Two years ago the Czar had already expressed his agreement to Germany taking a port in China, while thanking him [the Kaiser] for our support for Russian policy in the Far East [...] His Majesty therefore does not believe that there will be a war with Russia [...][42]

The reference to the Czar's agreement of 'two years ago' was another example of Wilhelm's 'personal diplomacy'. The posthumously published memoirs of Hohenlohe record a diary entry of 11 September 1895 following the Chancellor's meeting with the Russian monarch:

> As regards the East Asiatic question [the 'Triple Intervention'], the [Czar] expressed his satisfaction that we had acted in concert with him, and was pleased when I told him that were guided therein by the desire of manifesting our good relations with Russia. [...] The [Czar] then said that he had written in the spring to our [Kaiser], saying that he would have nothing against our acquiring something in that quarter, so as to have a fixed depot or coaling station. I told him that the [Kaiser] had mentioned this to me under the seal of secrecy [...].[43]

Despite this apparently unshakeable belief in the 'agreements' he had reached on a personal level with a brother emperor, the Kaiser still had to reckon with the Russian government, which continued to protest. As Hohenlohe wrote to the German Ambassador to the UK: 'A stiffening, if only temporary, of our relations with Russia is to be expected, since His Majesty the Emperor is not disposed to let Kiautschou go, whilst the exchange of views between here and St. Petersburg, of which you know, show that Russia takes a lively interest in that spot [...]'.[44] On 18 November Hohenlohe informed Wilhelm that the Czar placed a somewhat different interpretation on the telegraphic exchange that had occurred on 7 November: 'The tone and content of the Russian document leave no room for doubt that the Czar has been persuaded to take the view that [the Kaiser] intended to make improper use of his telegram, to the detriment of Russian rights, which it had never been [his] intention to relinquish.'[45]

The Kaiser seemed unconcerned, and to a suggestion of the Chancellor that delaying tactics be resorted to, and that the Czar should be informed that Russian warships would be welcome to share Kiautschou Bay with the German Navy, he noted: 'Completely agree [...] Their famous right of *premier mouillage* will in no way be infringed by our occupation and later seizure. Russians can stay anchored there until they are blue in the face. But that cannot prevent us building a coaling station and docks there.'[46]

This inflexible attitude took material form in the arrangements to despatch reinforcements to the area, one additional warship at first and then a second division as well as a specially put together detachment of naval infantry and artillery personnel (*Matrosenartillerie-Abteilung Kiautschou*) to garrison the territory. If the response of the Russian government was shouldered aside, then that of the Chinese was to be ignored completely. Wilhelm made this very clear in a message to the Foreign Office of 24 November:

> That the Chinese know exactly what we want is certain; that they will wage war is highly unlikely, as they have neither ships nor money and the number of troops in Shantung is not great. The fact that Heinrich is being sent and the second division formed must of course be mentioned [in a telegram to China], as everyone knows it and it shows that the Imperial House does not for a moment hesitate to risk the lives of its members for the honour of Germany.[47]

The 'Heinrich' mentioned in the document was the Kaiser's younger brother, Prince Heinrich of Prussia, a naval officer since 1877. On 23 November Diederichs had been promoted to Vice Admiral and his command formally rose from the status of a division to that of a squadron, the second, four-ship, division of which was to be commanded by Prince Heinrich.[48] Wilhelm publicly announced this in a speech to the Reichstag of 30 November.[49] Meanwhile, on 26 November, Wilhelm had again written to Hohenloe displaying impatience with what he perceived as the slowness of the German government's response:

> In about three weeks the *Kaiserin Augusta* will arrive in China; Prince Heinrich and the rest of the ships not until February [1898]. So that the crews do not remain away from their ships any longer than absolutely necessary, the moment has now come to form the colonial force, charter the steamer and embark them as soon as possible. I expect an answer tomorrow morning so that I can give my orders. No one is in any doubt about our intentions. A longer delay is impossible. That it is not for Russia to say anything in Kiautschou is as clear as daylight.[50]

That the Kaiser had been engaged in personal rule was made evident to the Chancellor when *Generallieutenant* Heinrich von Gossler, the Prussian Minister of War, told him that he had received an order to put together a force to form the garrison, including artillery batteries. 'I know nothing about the despatch of the batteries' he conceded to his diary, noting further that 'if things continue as they are we shall have a war with China'.[51]

In fact the Kiautschou garrison was to be formed from naval personnel and resources, for two main reasons. First, the navy was an Imperial institution, whilst the federal states of the German Empire retained, at least nominally, control of their own armies. Secondly, the territory was, uniquely amongst German overseas territory, to be run by the navy rather than the Colonial Office.[52]

The Imperial German Navy had a body of personnel, trained as infantry and more or less ready to depart for overseas duty, in the form of I and II Naval Battalions (*See-Bataillons*) stationed at Kiel and Wilhelmshaven respectively.[53] On 3 December 1897 Admiral Knorr ordered a new unit, III Naval Battalion, to form by amalgamating the existing units. Accordingly, by the morning of 13 December 1897, the four companies at Kiel had amalgamated into two companies: the 1st and 3rd Companies of I Naval Battalion now formed the 1st Company III Naval Battalion, whilst the 2nd and 4th Companies formed the new 2nd Company. These two enlarged companies then travelled to Wilhelmshaven, where by a similar process the II Naval Battalion had formed companies 3 and 4.[54]

The Battalion and its auxiliaries boarded the steamer *Darmstadt* of the Nord-Deutscher Line and in the afternoon of 16 December, embarked on their voyage halfway around the world.[55] They arrived on 26 January 1898, and the next day Wilhelm issued an edict authorising the Imperial Navy to take charge of the administration of the area.[56] This force was augmented on 4 February when the steamship *Crefeld*, carrying 300 personnel of the Marine Artillery Detachment and a battery of field guns, also arrived.[57] On 1 March, the Kaiser issued another decree, stating:

> At the head of the military and civil administration of the territory of Kiautschou will be a naval officer with the title of Governor. [...] The Secretary of the Navy Office has the right to inspect the naval infantry

and the marine artillery in connection with the military garrisoning of the protectorate of Kiautschou.[58]

Thus was established the system whereby the German Protectorate of Kiautschou was to be governed and defended, somewhat pre-empting the formal confirmation of the seizure by the Sino-German 'Lease Agreement' that was not signed until 6 March 1898. It ran:

Article I

With the intention of both fortifying the amicable relations between China and Germany and strengthening the military readiness of the Chinese Empire, His Majesty the Emperor of China agrees to the following: while reserving all rights of sovereignty within a radius of fifty kilometres (100 Chinese li) from Kiautschou Bay, measured at high tide, His Majesty promises to allow the free march of German troops through this zone at all times, to refrain from any measures or directives in this zone without the prior agreement of the German government, and to place no obstacles in the way of any necessary regulation of these bodies of water. His Majesty the Emperor of China reserves the right to station troops and to take other military measures in this zone in cooperation with the German government.

Article II

With the intention of fulfilling the justifiable request of His Majesty the German Kaiser, who wants Germany, like other powers, to have a place on the Chinese coast to repair and fit out ships, to store materials and supplies, and to maintain other related facilities, His Majesty the Emperor of China shall lease both sides of the entrance to Kiautschou Bay to Germany for a provisional period of 99 years. At an opportune time, Germany shall undertake to build fortifications in the leased area to protect both the planned structural works and the entrance to the bay.

Article III

To prevent any conflicts, the Imperial Chinese Government will not exercise sovereign rights in the leased area for the duration of the lease. It will surrender such rights to Germany for the following area:

1. On the northern side of the entrance to the bay: the area comprising the spit bounded to the northeast by the line drawn from the north-eastern corner of Potato Island to Loshan Harbour;
2. On the southern side of the entrance to the bay: the area comprising the spit bounded to the southwest by the line drawn to Tolosan Island from the south-western tip of the inlet southwest of Chiposan Island;
3. Chiposan Island and Potato Islands;
4. The entire water area of the bay up to the high water mark;
5. All Islands lying off Kiautschou Bay as well as those needed for its defence from the sea, including Tolosan, Chaolian Dao, etc.

As regards the area leased to Germany and the fifty-kilometre zone around the bay, the supreme parties to this agreement reserve the right to define the boundaries more precisely in keeping with local conditions. This task will be carried out by commissioners appointed by both sides.

Chinese military and merchant vessels shall be granted the same privileges in Kiautschou Bay as those conferred on ships of other nations that are on friendly terms with Germany. The entry, departure and mooring of Chinese ships in the bay shall be subject to no restrictions other than those that the Imperial German Government shall deem necessary to impose at any time on the ships of other nations by virtue of the sovereign rights transferred to it.

Article IV

Germany agrees to place the necessary navigation marks both on the islands and in the shallows in front of the entrance to the bay.

No duties shall be levied on Chinese military and merchant vessels in Kiautschou Bay, with the exception of those to which other vessels are subject for the purpose of maintaining the necessary port and quay facilities.

Article V

If Germany at a subsequent date expresses the desire to return Kiautschou Bay to China before the expiration of the period of the lease, China shall compensate Germany for its outlays and provide Germany with a more suitable location.

Germany agrees never to sublease to another power the area it has leased from China.

As long as the Chinese living in the leased area abide by the law and local regulations, they shall at all times enjoy the protection of the German government. The Chinese residents may remain in the leased area provided their land is not claimed for other purposes. If property owned by Chinese residents is used for other purposes, the owners are entitled to compensation. Concerning the reinstatement of the Chinese customs stations once located outside the area leased to Germany but within the agreed-upon fifty-kilometre zone, the Imperial German Government intends to reach an agreement with the Chinese Government on ways to regulate both the customs border and customs revenue in a manner that protects all China's interests; it also reserves the right to enter into additional negotiations on this matter.[59]

On 27 April the Kaiser issued a Supreme Decree noting that the Chinese government had 'transferred possession of the area off Kiautschou Bay […] to Germany, and we hereby place this area under imperial protection on behalf of the Empire'.[60] Via then 'a transaction in the old Prussian style' Germany had its place in the sun.[61]

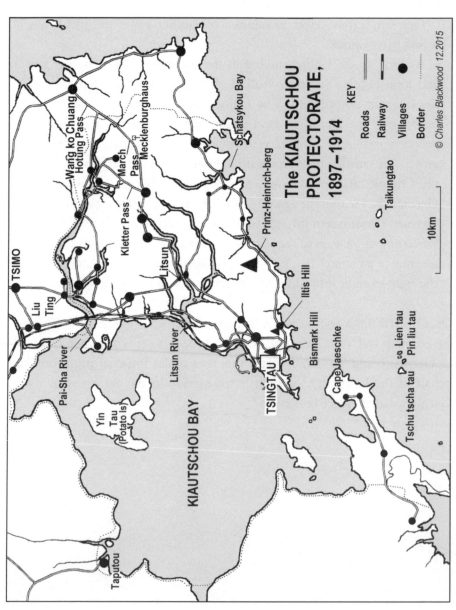

Map 3: The Kiautschou Protectorate, 1897–1914.

Chapter 2

Expansion

K iautschou was not the last territory Germany was to obtain in the Far East, though it was to be the last acquired by force of arms, or at least at first hand. The German interest in acquiring further territory coincided with an unrelated struggle between a long-established imperial power and an up and coming one; the Spanish-American War of 1898. A number of factors influenced the American decision to go to war against Spain, including the Cuban struggle for independence, American imperialism and, the ostensible trigger, the sinking of the US warship *Maine* in Havana harbour on 15 February 1898.

The US declared war on 29 April, but two days earlier Commodore George Dewey of the US Navy sailed, from China, in command of his Asiatic Squadron. His orders, from Secretary of the Navy John Davis Long, were to attack the Spanish Navy in the Philippines. Dewey's squadron arrived at the mouth of Manila Bay on the night of 30 April and he planned to enter and attack whatever Spanish warships he found there the next morning. It was a mission fraught with potential difficulties, including coastal defence batteries mounted on the islands of Corregidor and El Fraile covering the entrance, and the probability that that entrance was mined. Undeterred by these dangers, and in the full knowledge that he could do nothing to repair any damage caused to his squadron, Dewey entered the bay on the morning of 1 May 1898. There were no mines and the coastal artillery was ineffective, so by daybreak the squadron was well inside the bay and advancing towards the city of Manila.

The Americans dubbed the subsequent events as the Battle of Manila Bay, the Spanish termed it the Battle of Cavite (*Batalla de Cavite*), and it was an extraordinary affair. By 12:30hr the Spanish squadron had ceased firing and the Spanish colours flying onshore were struck and replaced by the white flag of surrender. The Spanish commander, Admiral Patricio Montojo y Pasarón, ordered those of his ships remaining afloat to be scuttled, and the Americans burnt several of those that failed to disable themselves in this manner.

Dewey had won a famous, and decisive, victory; Spanish naval power in the Pacific had been utterly destroyed in a morning, with around 380–400 fatalities, whilst the American squadron had not had a single man killed, and only 7 wounded, none of them seriously. There was no significant damage to any of the vessels either. The next day the Americans took over the naval facilities at Cavite, and thus gained access to a dockyard that would be essential in maintaining the squadron so far from the continental US.

However, and despite his unequivocal victory, Dewey now found himself beset with difficulties. He had only a few hundred men to deploy militarily, yet garrisoned in Manila was a Spanish force numbering some 13,000. These were, in theory, able to manoeuvre and might conceivably have marched on Cavite to dispossess Dewey. The Spanish Army in the Philippines had been fighting an insurrectionist movement for several years, and it was in order to bolster this insurrection, and thus 'assist me in my operations against the Spanish' as Dewey put it, that he had the exiled leader of the insurrection, Emilio Aguinaldo, brought back to the Philippines from Singapore.[1] Aguinaldo landed on 19 May and immediately rallied the insurgent forces behind him, then began the task of rounding up the Spanish garrisons in the islands. Manila though was still held by the Spanish. Aguinaldo believed, as of course did his followers, that what they and the Americans were fighting for was Filipino independence. He was only to be disabused of this notion at a later date.[2] For the moment he was useful in the absence of any US Army forces, which were not expected to arrive until June or July. The principal potential problem facing the US forces was that Aguinaldo might capture Manila before they could get their troops there.

Dewey also faced difficulties, or perceived difficulties, on the naval front from two directions. Most immediately, two German warships, *Irene* and *Cormoran*, arrived at Manila Bay on 6 and 9 May respectively. On 10 May the commanders of the two vessels called on the Spanish Governor-General and Admiral Montojo in Manila.[3] Rumours began to circulate to the effect that Germany would join with Spain and attempt to defeat Dewey's squadron. The rumour mill was fed still further on 6 June when the German liner

Darmstadt sailed into the bay carrying some 1,400 German seamen. These were not however a landing party, but rather relief crews for the German East Asiatic Squadron that had been sent to Manila Bay to relieve a portion of the crews of *Irene* and *Cormoran*. The *Darmstadt* having departed on 9 June, three days later SMS *Kaiserin Augusta* arrived with Otto von Diederichs on board. The German vessels at Manila were further augmented by the arrival of *Kaiser* on 18 June and *Prinzess Wilhelm* two days later.[4]

The German warships at Manila Bay constituted a powerful squadron, probably as powerful as the US force, and Dewey was profoundly suspicious of them, outnumbering, as they did, the contingents of Japan, France and the UK.[5] What, with perspective, can now be viewed as minor incidents assumed frightening proportions contemporaneously; incidents such as Diederichs' visits to the Spanish Governor-General and the apparent refusal of the German squadron to acknowledge the proclaimed US blockade. These incidents were much magnified by the popular American press.

Subsequent scholarly research has established that the 'confrontation' between Diederichs and Dewey was, largely, the product of the stressful situation Dewey found himself in following his destruction of the Spanish ships.[6] He was, literally and figuratively, the man on the spot and his communications with his superiors were both slow, 'I was three days from any working cable station', and difficult since he was unable to make use of the Manila–Hong Kong cable.[7] Any decisions he made could have had the most profound repercussions. It is hardly surprising then that the arrival of Diederichs, who was senior to him, was irksome in itself, but given that the German admiral was also known as the recent occupier of Kiautschou, and therefore as an accomplished annexationist at the head of a powerful force, then that Dewey was suspicious is hardly surprising.

The German Foreign Office, under Bernhard von Bülow, had no wish to antagonise the Americans as Bülow was later to claim: 'I only approved of sending our fleet to Manila to protect Germany's great economic interests there. Any enmity against America was distant from our minds.'[8] This position is confirmed by contemporaneous documents; on 14 May he had informed the Kaiser that the Filipinos would be hardly likely to acquiesce in exchanging 'the Spanish yoke' for another set of European masters, and presciently he foresaw that to subject them against their will to such foreign rule would probably be no easy task. He cautioned Wilhelm against any 'imprudent move' whilst remaining hopeful that territory would be gained through diplomatic means.[9] The German consul in Manila, Dr Friedrich Kruger, was instructed to 'remain negative' if approaches were made with a view to Germany becoming entangled in Philippine issues, and he was also told to 'observe unobtrusively and report any signs that may indicate that one or another power, for example England or America, is attempting to establish itself permanently through negotiations with the insurgents'.[10]

Diederichs' instructions from Admiral Eduard von Knorr were also clear as to what he was there to achieve; his remit was to 'protect German interests', 'obtain a clear and correct picture' of what was happening and 'develop a personal appraisal of the Spanish position'.[11] Diederichs' actions during his time at the bay are evidence that he did not exceed these instructions as, for example, when the Spanish Governor-General asked him to mediate a truce between the Spanish military and the insurgent forces, and Diederichs declined as this would breach German neutrality.[12] Diederichs also considered that the blockade Dewey had declared was in fact illegal, inasmuch as it was ineffective.[13]

The relevant, indeed only, piece of International Law pertaining to blockades was the 16 April 1856 Declaration of Paris.[14] This had stated that 'Blockades, to be binding, must be effective – that is to say, maintained by a force sufficient in reality to prevent access to the coast of the enemy.'[15] Though the US was not a signatory, and there was in any event no international body that could enforce it, the US declared that it would respect the principles of the declaration during hostilities with Spain.[16] Spain too declared its intention to abide by the declaration, but also gave notice that it would reserve its right to issue letters of marque.[17]

Whatever the legal niceties, and however irritating Dewey found the German presence, the two squadrons did not come to blows, and in truth there was probably very little chance of that really happening. Neither commander was a fool, nor a knave, so it seems likely that some of the reports that found their way into the US public domain, both during and after the war, were much exaggerated.

Real, rather than fictional, fighting was something Dewey had to worry about in terms of Spanish naval reinforcements arriving. A relief expedition set off from Cadiz on 16 June, commanded by Rear Admiral Manuel de la Cámara y Libermoore. The core of this relief consisted of the second-class battleship *Pelayo* (1888) and the 'Reina Regente' class cruiser *Carlos V* (1898). There were also three destroyers and, in order to reinforce Spanish forces in the Philippines, six vessels carrying troops and supplies. This armada set out on 16 June from Cadiz and, intending to pass through the Suez Canal, reached Port Said on 26 June with the aim of coaling. The British/Egyptian government however was dogmatic concerning enforcement of neutrality laws, and procrastinated to such an extent that it took over a week for the expedition to transit the canal.[18]

By sending their last naval reserves to the Philippines the Spanish government knew it was leaving itself open to naval attack, and that this might become a reality was brought home in no uncertain terms by the Battle of Santiago de Cuba, fought on 3 July 1898. It was another decisive victory, and the destruction of the Spanish Navy in the western Atlantic meant that the Americans could now, if they wished, deploy their heavy ships on operations against mainland Spain. Indeed US propaganda and misinformation techniques had made an apparently convincing case that a US naval force would cross the Atlantic and attack the Spanish mainland and other holdings such as the Canary Islands.[19] On 7 July Cámara was ordered to return home.[20]

With the recall of the relieving force the Spanish government had no cards left. Accordingly, on 26 July it asked France to mediate with the US and Jules-Martin Cambon, Ambassador to Washington 1897–1902, opened negotiations with William R. Day, the US Secretary of State, both 'possessing for this purpose full authority from the Government of the United States and the Government of Spain'.[21]

Cambon and Day negotiated a 'Protocol of Agreement' that was transmitted to Madrid for scrutiny, and, having been accepted on 11 August, was signed by both men the next day. There were six articles, but the key points were that Spain relinquished 'all claim of sovereignty over and title to Cuba' (Article I) and ceded to the US 'the island of Porto Rico and other islands now under Spanish sovereignty in the West Indies, and also an island in the Ladrones [Mariana, or Marianas, Islands] to be selected by the United States' (Article II). The position as regards the Philippines was less clear cut: 'The United States will occupy and hold the city, bay and harbour of Manila, pending the conclusion of a treaty of peace which shall determine the control, disposition and government of the Philippines.' (Article III).

Articles V and VI stipulated that peace negotiations would commence in Paris 'not later than October 1, 1898' and that 'Upon the conclusion and signing of this protocol, hostilities between the two countries shall be suspended' respectively.[22] Because of the distances involved word only reached Manila on 16 August of the armistice terms, by which time they were rendered somewhat academic; the city had surrendered to the Americans at 17:45hr on 13 August.[23] This academic point was, however, to cost the US $20 million. During the formal peace negotiations that began at Paris on 1 October the Spanish were justified in pointing out that because Manila had surrendered after the armistice had been signed, when under the terms of that armistice the US should have stopped all operations, the conquest did not count. In recognition perhaps that the Spanish point had some validity, the US offered financial compensation, which the Spanish accepted, and on 10 December 1898 the US and Spain signed the Treaty of Paris. The final form of the Treaty, whilst otherwise not differing greatly from the terms set out in the Protocol (Article II specified the 'island in the Ladrones' was to be Guam), demonstrated in no uncertain terms the change of heart that had occurred within the US administration vis-à-vis the Philippines. Article III stated that 'Spain cedes to the United States the archipelago known as the Philippine Islands [...] The United States will pay to Spain the sum of twenty million dollars ($20,000,000) within three months after the exchange of the ratifications of the present treaty.'[24]

Historians have achieved little in the way of consensus as regards when and why McKinley came to the decision to change his Philippines policy to one of annexation, though the President was later to claim that it was arrived at by supernatural means.[25]

Whatever the metaphysical input into the decision, there is little doubt that it was palatable to the European Great Powers. When the war started the Great Powers had accepted US intervention in Cuba, but Dewey's victory in Manila Bay raised the conflict from regional to global dimensions. The

UK, France, Germany and Russia, and of course Japan, then became very interested in the fate of the Philippines. The Europeans were particularly concerned about the implications should the war proliferate, and the conflict spread to the eastern side of the Atlantic; potential US naval bases in, say, the Canaries or Balearics were not a prospect to be contemplated with equanimity. Accordingly they sought to encourage the peace process.[26] Had the US decided not to annex the Philippines then it seems probable that one or more of them, alone or in combination, would have claimed the archipelago or portions of it. Germany, or at least the Kaiser, seems to have been a firm proponent of acquiring territory there. Bülow records receiving a message from him in April 1898: 'Tirpitz is as firm as a rock in his conviction that we must have Manila and that this would be of enormous advantage to us. As soon as the revolution has torn Manila from Spain we must occupy it.'[27]

It seems unlikely that Alfred Tirpitz was particularly fixated on Manila in 1898; that was the year he was campaigning for the first of his Fleet Acts to be adopted by the German Empire. In any event, once it became clear that the US intended to annex the Philippines, Germany set out a more realistic goal; that of acquiring the Spanish Pacific islands. Indeed it was with US and British knowledge and approval that Germany approached Spain to open negotiations.[28] Spain, if shorn of the Philippines, would, in all likelihood, have had no end of difficulty in attempting to administer these remote and scattered territories. In any event, provisional agreement was reached in September 1898 that, subject to the final terms of the negotiations (the islands would remain under Spanish control until the treaty with the US was concluded) that were due to start in Paris on 1 October, they would be transferred to Germany.[29] The price was settled on 12 February the next year; 16.6 million Marks (*c.* 25 million pesetas or $5 million).[30] The exchange was embodied in the Spanish-German Treaty of 30 June 1899 (*Tratado hispano-alemán de 30 junio de 1899*).[31]

President McKinley was able to include in his 1899 State of the Union Address his approval of the transaction: 'Subsequent to the exchange of our peace treaty with Spain, Germany acquired the Caroline Islands by purchase, paying therefore $5,000,000. Assurances have been received from the German Government that the rights of American missionaries and traders there will be considerately observed.'[32] Bernhard von Bülow records that he was also able to report positively on the matter:

> The acquisition of the Caroline and Marianne Islands turned our possessions in the western Pacific into a connected whole. With the Bismarck Archipelago and Kaiser Wilhelm Land in the south, the Marschall, Caroline, and Pelew Islands in the centre, and the Mariannes in the north, we now had a firm basis for our economic and general political development in Oceania. I was able also to point out in the Reichstag that the acquisition of the Carolines had in no way disturbed our good relations with Spain. For Spain they represented only fragments of a crumbled building, for us they were pillars and buttresses for a building with a future.[33]

Prince Heinrich thought that whilst the new German territories might have been of minimal economic value, they would nevertheless have value for the German Navy. Not only would it be possible to construct more coaling stations, but, because of their existence, they would 'help to increase our navy in general, as well as our squadron out here'.[34] These islands and island groups acquired by Germany were located within the region known as Micronesia (from the Greek 'small islands'). The term originated with the French explorer and navigator Jules Dumont d'Urville, who, in 1832, proposed differentiating the various island groups in the Pacific that had previously been aggregated as Polynesia. Henceforth, Micronesia described those islands inscribing an arc across the northern and central Pacific, whilst Melanesia (black islands) became the term for those to the north and east of Australia, including New Guinea, the Bismarck Archipelago, Fiji, the Solomon Islands and the Pelew (Palau) Islands. Polynesia then became the term for those islands roughly within the triangle Hawaii, New Zealand and Easter Island.[35] Micronesia in general has been described as resembling 'a handful of chickpeas flung over the sea'.[36] The German territories in particular as 'a "cloud" of islands, stretching east and west between the parallels of 4° and 12°30′ North, and the meridians of 134° and 172°30′ East'.[37] In terms of distance, the area covered was over 3700km east–west and 2200km north–south, the extremities being Tobi (Hatohobei) and Mili

Atoll in the Palau and Marshall Islands respectively, and the uninhabited volcano of Farallón de Pájaros in the Marianas and Kapingamarangi Atoll in the Carolines.[38]

In material terms the newly gained island territories were worthless; they were 'show colonies' acquired merely to boost Germany's prestige as a world power.[39] This was not a fact kept particularly well hidden at the time; indeed the precarious financial position of German New Guinea had been exemplified by the 'nationalisation' of that territory. The administration of the territory had been in the hands of the German New Guinea Company until the Imperial Government had been forced to take over the administration, appointing Rudolf von Bennigsen as governor on 1 April 1899.[40] The vice-governor, Albert Hahl, assumed the governorship in 1902 and put the economic status of the newly acquired islands quite clearly to the Reichstag the same year:

Admittedly, Germany is unlikely to gain much economic advantage from this island territory. But I still think we can achieve a highly idealistic purpose there. This is to preserve the Polynesian [...] and gradually civilising them. Germany should hold tight to the idea that this purpose alone is enough to justify keeping and administering these islands.[41]

The Carolines and Marianas were, for administrative purposes, sub-divided into three districts; the Eastern Carolines, the Western Carolines including Palau (Belau), and the Marianas. Initially there were two district officers (*Bezirksamtmann*) stationed at Yap and Saipan under the vice-governor at Ponape. The whole was under the overall governance of the governor of German New Guinea based at Herbertshöhe in Neu Pommern (New Britain) in the Bismarck Archipelago. The vice-governorship was abolished in 1902 upon the then holder of the post, Albert Hahl, being elevated to gubernatorial level.[42] This entire area had, up until 1911, a total administrative workforce, spread across the three centres, of fourteen personnel, including three seamen for the government schooner.[43]

The territory acquired from Spain was not the last such to come to Germany however. That honour, if such is the correct term, went to German

Samoa, a territory retrospectively dignified by Bülow as 'one of the finest brilliants in our colonial diadem'.[44] Samoa is the native name of a group of volcanic islands in central Polynesia long known as the 'Navigators Islands'. The two largest islands are those in the western part of the archipelago, Savaii (Savai'i) and Upolu, the latter gaining some fame in Europe in the late nineteenth century for being the final home and last resting place of the Scots author Robert Louis Stevenson.

The eastern portion of the archipelago consists, in the main, of Samoa's third largest island, Tutuila, and the three islands of the Manu'a Islands Group, Ofu, Olosega and Tau (Ta'u), located some 110km east of Tutuila. The unusual circular atoll of Swains Island is some 320km to the north of Tutuila and Rose Atoll, the easternmost of the Samoan islands, is located some 144km to the east of Tau.

European and American traders began visiting the islands during the 1830s, when, politically, they were divided into a number of competing chieftainships. The various traders, mainly British, American and German, began backing, and arming, various of these factions in their disputes with each other, hoping thereby to achieve dominance if 'their' client won. The 1889 'Final Act of The Berlin Conference on Samoan Affairs', whereby the UK, the US and Germany all agreed to recognise Samoan independence, brought this process, immensely destructive in every sense of the word, to an end, at least temporarily. Under the terms of the 'Berlin General Act', as it became known, the Samoan king would be 'advised' by the consuls of the three powers.[45]

Problems arose when the succession came into question, and the election of a new king, according to the laws and customs of Samoa, was contested by force of arms. As President McKinley put it in his State of the Union Address in December 1899:

The active intervention of American and British war ships became imperative to restore order, at the cost of sanguinary encounters. In this emergency a joint commission of representatives of the United States, Germany, and Great Britain was sent to Samoa to investigate the situation and provide a temporary remedy. By its active efforts a peaceful solution was reached for the time being, the kingship being abolished and a provisional government established. Recommendations unanimously made by the commission for a permanent adjustment of the Samoan question were taken under consideration by the three powers parties to the General Act. But the more they were examined the more evident it became that a radical change was necessary in the relations of the powers to Samoa.[46]

The 'radical change' referred to was embodied in the 'Tripartite Treaty' of 2 December 1899, between the three powers. Under the Treaty, Germany assumed control of the western Samoan islands and the US took over the eastern islands. The UK relinquished any claims and was compensated by German territory in the Solomons; the former German Solomon Islands (*Nördliche Salomon-Inseln*) territories of Santa Isabel, Choiseul and Ontong Java Atoll (Lord Howe Atoll), as well as the Shortland and Treasury archipelagos in the Bougainville Strait.[47] Thus came into existence the territory of German Samoa, the possession of which Admiral Tirpitz had deemed of great importance, and the last acquirement of colonial territory by Imperial Germany in the Pacific.[48]

In administrative terms, as well as geographically and politically, the German Pacific colonies, Kiautschou excepted, were at the periphery, and they largely escaped any close supervision from Berlin. They were also neglected in terms of defensive measures; there were no colonial troops or military forces in the territories and no defences were constructed on any of the islands. The administrators of the various territories, islands and groups of islands were largely left to manage their domains in their own way.[49]

One advantage that accrued to Germany through possession of the islands was the ability to build stations at strategic points in order to expand the German Wireless Network. Until the advent of dependable wireless systems, intercontinental telecommunication relied on submarine telegraph cables. These were laid across oceans and provided a reliable means of communication between far-flung points. The UK, with a vast and distant empire to communicate with, was in the forefront of deploying this technology – consisting of copper cores insulated with gutta-percha (a resin from the *Isonandra Gutta* tree) and externally protected by steel wire braiding.

Accordingly the UK became preponderant in ownership; over half the world's cable network was British in 1908. Aware of the vulnerability to their communications this implied, Germany began, in 1906, constructing an alternative system based on wireless technology. The hub of this system was the powerful Nauen Transmitter Station near Berlin with, from 1911, a range of some 5000km.[50] The receiving station was some 30km away, at Geltow near Potsdam, in order that the power of the transmitter did not overload the system.

Operated by Telefunken, a joint venture of Siemens and AEG, the German Wireless Network expanded throughout the various colonial territories. In the Pacific, the main radio station, with a range of some 1900km, was constructed at Yap, the island being chosen because of its cable link with Tsingtau and the US. Other stations were constructed at Apia (Samoa), Nauru, Bitapaka (Rabaul, Kaiser Wilhelm's Land), Anguar and Tsingtau. All these station were able to transmit a signal from between 1200 and 2000km, and thus gave coverage throughout Germany's colonial sphere in the Far East.[51]

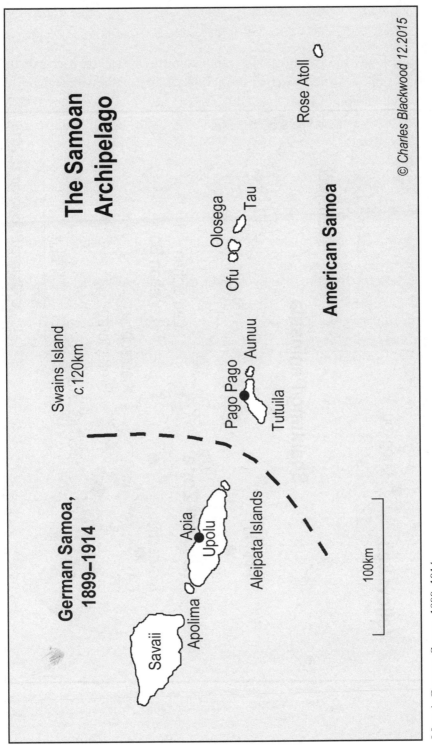

Map 4: German Samoa, 1899–1914.

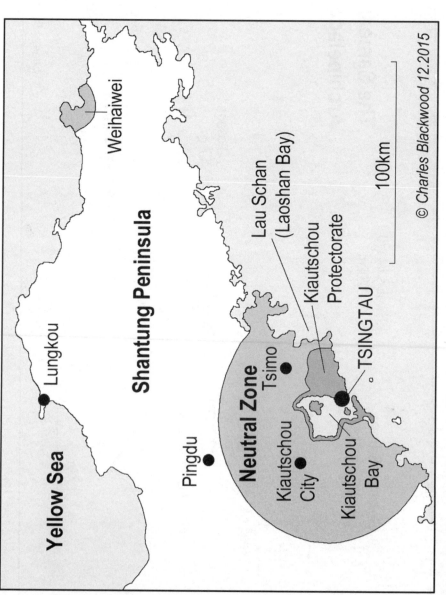

Map 5: The Shantung Peninsula: the Kiautschou Protectorate, the Neutral Zone and Weihaiwei.

Chapter 3

Strategic Realignment

On 12 February 1902 it was announced, simultaneously, in the UK and Japan that a treaty of alliance existed between the two states. This, the Anglo-Japanese Alliance of 1902, had actually been signed on 30 January but had not been publicly announced so that the 'Great Powers' of Germany, Russia and France could be informed.[1] The US was also notified prior to the alliance being made public.

Both parties embarked on the alliance out of self-interest and as a measure to counter prospective and real Russian expansionism, which Germany and Austria-Hungary sought to divert eastwards. This, if realised, meant potential conflict with Britain across the Raj's northern borders, particularly in Afghanistan, and with Japan, particularly in Manchuria and Korea.

The British Admiralty, at the time under the political leadership of William Waldegrave Palmer, the 2nd Earl of Selborne, First Lord of the Admiralty 1900–5 and son-in-law of the Prime Minister, the 3rd Marquess of Salisbury, was keen on the alliance, not least for reasons of economy. Sir Michael Hicks Beach, the Chancellor of the Exchequer from June 1895– July 1902, had to finance the Second Boer War of October 1899–May 1902, and refused extra finance for the Royal Navy, which was required in order to maintain a margin of superiority over any potential enemies. Selborne railed against financial constraints, writing in 1903:

> This is a simple question of national existence. We must have a force which is reasonably calculated to beat France and Russia and we must have something in hand against Germany. We cannot afford a three Power Standard but we must have a real margin over the two Power Standard and this policy the Cabinet has definitely adopted.[2]

Russia and France had been allied since 1894, a combination that Russia had entered into following the lapse of the Reinsurance Treaty with Germany in 1890. The exact terms of the Franco-Russian Alliance were secret, but the existence of the alliance was generally known. Franco-Russian relations were cemented further by the extension of the alliance in 1899. The alliance was essentially defensive in character and directed against Germany and its co-signatories of the Triple Alliance, Austria-Hungary and Italy. It bound Russia to come to the aid of France, with all her available forces, should France be attacked by Germany, or by Italy supported by Germany, and France to aid Russia, again with all available forces should Russia be attacked by Germany, or by Austria supported by Germany. It did not bind France to come to Russia's aid in the event of an attack by another power, which was what occurred during February 1904 when Japan launched the Russo-Japanese War, the conflict lasting until September 1905.

This was perhaps fortunate for the UK, as articles two and three of the Anglo-Japanese Alliance required neutrality if either signatory became involved in war with another power, but 'support' should either signatory became involved in war with more than one power. Arthur Balfour, who was to succeed his maternal uncle, the 3rd Marquis of Salisbury, as Prime Minister upon the latter's retirement in July 1902, had commented on the danger this feature might cause when the alliance was being considered by the Cabinet: 'we may find ourselves fighting for our existence in every part of the globe against Russia and France'.[3]

As one of the non-combatant powers allied to one of the warring states, the French government greatly feared that a collapse of their ally would leave France isolated in Europe, and facing Germany alone. A further factor involved the French banking system; this had underwritten most of the money that Russia had borrowed to wage the conflict and was becoming strained.

The UK also had an interest in the conflict being halted before one side or the other suffered irreparable damage. There was a financial aspect, inasmuch as the government had supported the loans required for the Japanese to wage the war, but also because the UK, for strategic-political reasons, had become 'officially friendly' with a state, France, whose ally, Russia, was at war with Britain's ally, Japan. On 8 April 1904 Lord Lansdowne, the British Foreign Secretary had, along with Paul Cambon, the French Ambassador, signed what became known as the *Entente Cordiale*. Although ostensibly the *Entente* was about extra-European matters respecting Egypt and Morocco, the friendly relations now entered into between the two states had their genesis in the behaviour of, and worries about, Imperial Germany. These were of long standing as regards France, but fairly recent in the case of the UK; the public revealing of *Weltmacht*, in 1896, and the First and Second Navy Laws, of 1898 and 1900 respectively, being factors in the equation; described as being tantamount to a declaration of 'cold war' against the UK.[4]

Japan, though it was unable to inflict a decisive defeat on Russia militarily, destroyed their enemy's navy at Tsushima on 27–8 May 1905. If we recall Selborne's comments in 1903 concerning Britain's naval position it may be adjudged just how much improved the international strategic naval situation was vis-à-vis Britain in 1905; with the Russian fleet destroyed and France's friendly 'something in hand against Germany' amounted to virtually the entire Royal Navy. Indeed, Tsushima totally vindicated British policy in relation to Japan, inasmuch as Russia's naval threat had been annihilated decisively at no cost whatsoever to Britain.

The 1905 Anglo–Japanese agreement contained some significant changes from the earlier, 1902, version and was therefore new, rather than a simple extension of the old. The most significant of these changes was the geographical extension, to cover British India, and the pledge of mutual assistance if either party was attacked by a single power. The clauses in question stated it thus:

Preamble

The Governments of Great Britain and Japan, being desirous of replacing the Agreement concluded between them on the 30th of January 1902, by fresh stipulations, have agreed upon the following Articles, which have for their object:

a. The consolidation and maintenance of general peace in the regions of Eastern Asia and India;
b. The preservation of the common interests of all Powers in China by insuring the independence and integrity of the Chinese Empire and the principle of equal opportunities for the commerce and industry of all nations in China;

c. The maintenance of the territorial rights of the High Contracting Parties [viz., Britain and Japan] in the regions of Eastern Asia and of India, and the defence of their special interests in the said regions:

Article I
It is agreed that whenever, in the opinion of either Great Britain or Japan, any of the rights and interests referred to in the preamble of this Agreement [i.e., items a, b, c above] are in jeopardy, the two Governments will communicate with one another fully and frankly, and consider in common the measures which should be taken to safeguard those menaced rights or interests.

Article II
If, by reason of an unprovoked attack or aggressive action, whenever arising, on the part of any other Power or Powers, either Contracting Party should be involved in war in defence of its territorial rights or special interests mentioned in the preamble of this Agreement, the other Contracting Party will at once come to the assistance of its ally, and will conduct war in common, and make peace in mutual agreement with it.[5]

The UK had originally, in the negotiations leading up to the signing, wanted to specify that in the event of a threat to the borders of the Raj, Japan would send a certain number of troops. This did not, in any explicit form, make it into the final form, though it could have happened under the 'communications' referred to in Article 1. A change of mind took place however, one not necessarily originating in the change of administration, when, in December 1905, the Conservative Balfour government fell and was replaced by the Liberal government headed by Sir Henry Campbell-Bannerman. Rather it arose from a process, largely contained within the Committee of Imperial Defence, whereby the implications of pursuing such a policy became apparent. The following memorandum, of 4 November 1905, summarises the harmful effects that British pride would suffer if such an event were to occur:

It is recommended that we [...] should not ask Japan to send troops to India, first, because the number of men that can be employed across the north-west frontier is limited by the means of transport and supply; and secondly, because to ask for assistance to ward off attack by a single adversary would [...] be highly detrimental, if not absolutely fatal, to our prestige throughout the Asiatic continent.[6]

This potential threat to British Imperial 'prestige' was removed on 31 August 1907, when the UK and Russia signed the Anglo-Russian Entente. Though overtly about Persia, the treaty explicitly recognised existing special interests:

[...] each of them [the UK and Russia] has, for geographical and economic reasons, a special interest in the maintenance of peace and order in certain provinces of Persia adjoining, or in the neighbourhood of, the Russian frontier on the one hand, and the frontiers of Afghanistan and Baluchistan on the other hand [...][7]

Two months previously, on 10 June, Russia's ally France had signed an *entente* with Japan, bilaterally guaranteeing an 'open door' policy vis-à-vis China and the maintenance of the status quo in, and security of, the territory in the Far East where each had 'special interests'. The French also agreed to assist Japan with loans, the injurious financial effects of the war with Russia still being much in evidence.

A rapprochement between Russia and Japan had also taken place with the 'Secret Convention' signed at St Petersburg on 30 July 1907, whereby Russia acknowledged Japanese 'special interests' in Korea and Japan recognised Russian 'special interests' over Outer Mongolia (present-day Mongolia). This convention was the first of three such over the period 1907–12 whereby the two powers defined their respective spheres of influence in, and fixed the status quo regarding, Northeast Asia, including Korea, Manchuria and Inner Mongolia.[8]

These various changes in international relations, combined with Japan's annexation of Korea on 22 August 1910, meant that the whole basis upon which the 1905 treaty had been structured was changed.[9]

There was a further factor; the US. There were several areas of friction between Japan and the US, one being Japanese policy and behaviour towards China.[10]

Another revolved around the potential threat the Imperial Navy posed to the American position in the Philippines.[11] Conversely, of course, a US fleet strong enough to defend that archipelago was also a potential threat to Japan. The US fleet was growing and under the presidency of Theodore Roosevelt an extrovert foreign and defence policy was adopted; the most enduring physical legacy of which is surely the Panama Canal. Politically he formulated the 'Roosevelt Corollary', which stated that the US would intervene in Caribbean affairs when 'chronic wrongdoing, or an impotence which results in a general loosening of the ties of a civilised society' by governments made it necessary, as an addition to the 'Monroe Doctrine'.[12]

In naval terms one of Roosevelt's best known acts involved the creation and voyage of the Great White Fleet. As Assistant Secretary to the Navy he had, the year before the US annexed Hawaii in 1898, instructed naval planners to develop contingency plans for fighting Japan in the Pacific; at this time however the US Navy had no organised fleet in the Pacific.[13] He also inaugurated a campaign to modernise the navy by constructing a fleet of the most powerful warships. The visible manifestation of the success of this campaign came with the despatch, on 16 December 1907, of almost the entire US battle fleet from Hampton Roads on a circumnavigation of the globe. The capital units of the Great White Fleet, as it came to be known, comprised sixteen battleships organised into four divisions of four ships each. The only heavy units that did not sail, apart from four coast defence ships, comprised one battleship under repair and one battleship not yet ready for deployment, though both the latter vessels joined the fleet at a later date. The fleet returned to Hampton Roads on 22 February 1909 having steamed some 70000km. The object of this mighty display of power projection was several-fold, including learning the art of such matters on the part of the US Navy and, undoubtedly, a signal to Japan, which the fleet had visited from 18–25 October 1908.

This Mahanian concept incarnate, the 'Mahan–Roosevelt legacy' as one authority has termed it, of the big battle fleet demonstrating command of the sea was of course rather similar to the ideas pursued by Admiral Tirpitz and William II.[14] Indeed the latter had established the High Sea Fleet as a command in February 1907.[15] According to Mahanian precept, command of the sea could only be established by keeping a fleet massed so as to be able to confront and destroy an enemy fleet. This to him was a cardinal point; if the establishment of the US Naval War College 'had produced no other result than the profound realization by naval officers of the folly of dividing the battle-fleet, in peace or in war, it would by that alone have justified its existence and paid its expenses'.[16]

The implications of growing US naval power, and the inevitable potential for further friction with Japan this entailed, were most obvious in respect to Japan's formal ally, the UK. It was however highly unlikely that the UK would ever go to war with the US. One of the palpable restraints in this regard related to Canada. As Roosevelt had pointed out to Mahan in 1897, 'Canada was a hostage to British good behaviour.'[17] That this was indeed the case was recognised equally by the British. An Admiralty Memorandum of February 1905 is explicit on the point:

In the event of an occurrence so much deprecated as the rupture of friendly relations with the United States, the position of Canada is one of extreme danger, and, so far as the navy is concerned, any effective assistance would be exceedingly difficult. Generally, the more carefully this problem is considered, the more tremendous do the difficulties which would confront Great Britain in a war with the United States appear. It may be hoped that the policy of the British Government will ever be to use all possible means to avoid war.[18]

Canada might have been a guarantee of good British behaviour vis-à-vis the US, but it, and the other British Dominions in the Pacific, had concerns of their own relating to Japan, particularly given Japanese naval expansion. The rapturous welcome given by the public to the Great White Fleet in its visits to New Zealand and Australia are, it is argued by some scholars, evidence of this; America being seen as a potential ally against possible Japanese ambitions.[19] Indeed it has been argued that Australia's Prime Minister, Alfred Deakin, to show Australia's potential enemies the might of their 'American friends', engineered the visit of the fleet.[20]

Britain's empire had evolved politically, a notable point being the extension of Dominion status to the self-governing colonies. Canada (1867), Australia (1901), New Zealand (1907), Newfoundland (1907) and the Union of South Africa (1910) formed this group, sometimes, and for obvious reasons, sometimes collectively referred to as the 'White Dominions'. The Dominions had more or less full internal control, but foreign relations and defence were still conducted through the UK government, though Canada created a Department of External Affairs in 1909.

Defence, and the problems therein, of the Dominions varied greatly; Canada and Newfoundland were unique in that they were completely at the mercy of their powerful neighbour, the US, but by the same token were protected by that neighbour; the US would not have tolerated any foreign incursions into their territory. South Africa was geographically remote and possessed what were probably the most powerful military forces on the continent. Military forces capable of meeting them on a level could only have come from Europe by sea, and there was the Royal Navy to take care of that.[21]

Australia and New Zealand were a different story, and were hypothetically vulnerable to a power that could exercise power projection into the South Pacific. The Royal Navy was tasked with providing maritime defence via an 1887 agreement that the, then, colonies should contribute to the Royal Navy in return for the permanent stationing of a squadron in the region.

However with the necessity to concentrate in North European waters in order to counter the German High Seas Fleet the ability to offer a high level of naval protection became problematical.[22] It was this problem, although originally with respect more to France and Russia than Germany, which had led to the original Anglo-Japanese Alliance, but following Japan's victory in 1905, the Australasian Dominions now viewed Japanese naval power as the greatest threat. This was in contrast to the British view, as, for example, enunciated by Admiral Sir John Fisher in 1906: 'Our only probable enemy is Germany. Germany keeps her *whole* Fleet always concentrated within a few hours of England. We must therefore keep a Fleet twice as powerful concentrated within a few hours of Germany.'[23] Fisher had become First Sea Lord in 1904 and remained in the post until the beginning of 1910, towards the end of which period the British Admiralty proposed an ingenious idea for maintaining British naval power in, particularly, the Far East and Pacific Ocean areas; the Imperial Dominions would raise and pay for the necessary forces.

There had been attempts on the part of the British government to extract larger contributions from the colonies, above all those that were self-governing, towards the cost of naval defence since the 1887 agreement. These efforts however met only with relative success; the colonial politicians knew that the British would maintain the Royal Navy as a global force in any event.[24]

What brought matters to a head were statements made in the British House of Commons on 16 March 1909 by Prime Minister Asquith and First Lord – the Cabinet Minister in political charge of the Royal Navy – Reginald McKenna during the presentation of the 1909–10 naval estimates. Parliament was asked to sanction funding for three dreadnought battleships and one dreadnought cruiser (battlecruiser) to be laid down before the end of the year. However, contingent funding was also sought for another four similar vessels to be laid down no later than April 1910, unless, in the meantime, Imperial Germany agreed to negotiations limiting naval expansion. This increase in the estimates was sought because the Admiralty believed, based on intelligence reports and calculations on potential capacity, that the tempo of German dreadnought construction was increasing, to possibly encompass six units per year. It seemed, as one authority has put it, that 'for the first time since the ironclad revolution a foreign naval power had the capacity to build capital ships as fast as Great Britain'.[25] As McKenna told the House of Commons, 'we do not know, as we thought we did, the rate at which German construction is taking place'.[26]

No agreement on the limitation of capital ship production with Germany was reached, and this, together with the knowledge that Austria-Hungary and Italy were undertaking dreadnought construction, meant that Parliament was asked for, and approved, the funding for the additional vessels on 26 July 1909.[27] This matter caused a great deal of domestic political controversy for the British government, and there was undoubtedly an excess of overreaction and panic surrounding the matter, but early on in the affair assistance was offered by some of the Dominions. On 22 March the government of New Zealand offered to bear the cost of the immediate construction of one of the dreadnought battleships, as well as one of the additional vessels if necessary, an offer that was 'gratefully accepted' by the British government. The Canadian House of Commons passed a resolution on 29 March, approving 'any necessary expenditure designed to promote the speedy organisation of a Canadian naval service in co-operation with and in close relation to the Imperial Navy'. A similar offer came from Australia on 15 April, stating that 'whereas all the British Dominions ought to share in the burden of maintaining the permanent naval supremacy of the Empire, so far as Australia was concerned this object would best be best attained by the encouragement of naval development in that country'.[28]

In view of these offers, representatives of the four Dominions (Australia, Canada, Newfoundland and New Zealand) and the Cape Colonies (the Cape, Natal, Orange Free State and Transvaal were in the process of becoming the Union of South Africa) were, on 30 April, invited 'to attend a Conference […] to discuss the general question of the naval and military defence of the Empire, with special reference to the Canadian resolution and to the proposals from New Zealand and Australia'. There was however a change of government in Australia on 2 June, when Andrew Fisher of the Australian Labour Party was replaced by Alfred Deakin of the newly formed Commonwealth Liberal, or Fusion, Party. This led to a further offer on 4 June; Australia would fund a dreadnought for the Royal Navy, 'or such addition to its naval strength as may be determined after consultation in London'.[29]

When the Dominion representatives arrived in London they were not expecting to undertake much more than the finalising of details regarding the offers already made. They were therefore surprised to discover that the Admiralty had formulated a quite different idea, though one of long, if somewhat secret, gestation. As the Admiralty Memorandum stated it:

If the problem of Imperial naval defence were considered merely as a problem of naval strategy it would be found that the maximum output of strength for a given expenditure is obtained by the maintenance of a single navy with the concomitant unity of training and unity of command. In furtherance, then, of the simple strategical ideal the maximum of power would be obtained if all parts of the Empire contributed, according to their needs and resources, to the maintenance of the British Navy.

It has long been recognised that in defining the conditions under which the naval forces of the Empire should be developed, other considerations than those of strategy alone must be taken into account. [...]

The main duty of the forthcoming Conference as regards naval defence will be, therefore, to determine the form in which the various Dominion Governments can best participate in the burden of Imperial defence with due regard to varying political and geographical conditions. [...]

In the opinion of the Admiralty, a Dominion Government desirous of creating a navy should aim at forming a distinct fleet unit; and the smallest unit is one which, while manageable in time of peace, is capable of being used in its component parts in time of war. [...]

The fleet unit to be aimed at should, in the opinion of the Admiralty, consist of the following:

1 Armoured cruiser [of the] new 'Indomitable' class, which is of the 'Dreadnought' type
3 Unarmoured cruisers ('Bristol' class)
6 Destroyers
3 Submarines

[and] with the necessary auxiliaries, such as depots and store ships etc.

Such a fleet unit would be capable of action not only in the defence of coasts, but also of the trade routes, and would be sufficiently powerful to deal with small hostile squadrons should such ever attempt to act in those waters.

[...][30]

This was a complete volte-face in respect of Admiralty policy, which had previously sought to restrict Dominion naval forces to those only capable of flotilla defence via small vessels such as destroyers, torpedo boats and, latterly, submarines. What was now being proposed was something approaching an early twentieth-century version of the later concept of the carrier strike group, with a powerful capital ship and attendant vessels forming a balanced and powerful force capable of power projection.

Here then was a method whereby Imperial communications, principally in the Pacific, might be safeguarded whilst a superior fleet could still be retained in the waters around the British Isles. As will be argued later, retaining 'two or three' battlecruisers in the Pacific would not have made intolerable inroads into the strength of Jellicoe's Grand Fleet, as it became, and that ship type was in fact detached as and when required without noticeable harm. The fleet units as visualised could have combined to form a larger fleet, but the concept allowed them to work primarily as individual units, as was made clear. The potential enemy against which they might be expected to operate was patently not the Japanese fleet. Not only was Japan a British ally in 1909, but a combination of units comprising even, say, four battlecruisers would have been an inferior force if pitted against a Japanese fleet with dreadnought battleships.

The potential enemy that the battlecruiser-centred fleet units were conceived as deterring or countering were hostile cruisers conducting commerce-raiding activities. Indeed the Australian sailor Captain William R. Creswell, later Vice Admiral Sir William, who had attended the 1909 Conference, stated in November 1909 that the force would be powerful enough to ensure the safety of Australia's commerce against hostile cruisers, while the possibility of these cruisers threatening ports would be 'so remote as to be hardly worth considering'.[31] It is the case that such vessels could, in 1912, have, theoretically, been ships from a number of nations, but realistically those in question were the East Asiatic Cruiser Squadron based at Tsingtau.

Defence matters generally, and the relationship between the UK and the British Empire on one hand, and Japan on the other, were to feature in the Imperial Conference of 1911 held in London; one of a series of Colonial and, after 1907, Imperial Conferences held between 1887 and 1937. These conferences were the principal means of high-level consultation between representatives from the various component parts of the British Empire, discussing, amongst other subjects, economic and military co-operation.

At the 1911 conference, the UK's Foreign Secretary from 1905–16, Sir Edward Grey, briefed the representatives of the Dominions on Anglo-Japanese relations. Grey, who had made the defence of France against German aggression the central plank of British foreign policy, consulted them on a renewal of the Anglo-Japanese Alliance.

The Japanese had, in January 1911, asked the UK for a renewal, and implicit renegotiation, of the 1907 treaty.[32] There were undoubtedly several factors in this approach, including the Japanese fear that the British might not renew the alliance at the end of the timescale specified in 1907.[33] This factor was also influential as regards Sir Edward Grey:

> If the alliance were to be terminated in 1915, Japan would be left with free hands without restraint and we could not control her and her fleet might array against us in the Pacific or allied with that of some other Power. These are changes that are unpleasant to contemplate and I believe that in 1914 it will still be our policy to be in alliance with Japan.[34]

Another factor was the Anglo-American Arbitration Treaty, proposed by the US in the autumn of 1910. This had been the brainchild of President William Howard Taft, Roosevelt's successor. As an ex-jurist, who went on to become a Supreme Court Judge, Taft was a convinced proponent of the peaceful resolution of international problems via arbitration. His State of the Union Address, on 6 December 1910, had contained references to this vis-à-vis the UK and France.[35]

The existence of these arrangements allowed the UK a significant get-out, for Grey negotiated a clause, Article IV, in the agreement whereby, without naming the US specifically, the renewed Anglo-Japanese Alliance would not apply to a country that had a treaty of general arbitration with either of the contracting countries. On 13 July 1911 the third alliance was signed for a further ten years, lasting until August 1923, with the unanimous approval of the Dominions.

The UK, embroiled in the naval race with Germany, saw the alliance as a bulwark ensuring the security of the Pacific Dominions and colonies, whilst the Japanese viewed it as a safeguard against isolation. That the existence of the alliance might exercise a restraining influence upon Japan was echoed by the public utterances of Japan's Foreign Minister, Hayashi Tadasu. He emphasised this in the *Japan Times* on 22 July 1911:

> The value and importance of the Alliance will be unchanged, nor is there any doubt of its long continuance. The only point against which Japan must guard is a wantonly aggressive policy. On the contrary, she must always adhere to a peaceful policy and endeavour to make the most of what she has gained so far, and to promote her interests and development in a manner consistent with a pacific policy. If Japan should adopt a policy of wanton aggression, the continuation of the Anglo-Japanese alliance would be out of the question.[36]

Whilst the governments of Australia and New Zealand had supported the 1911 version of the Anglo-Japanese Alliance, and thus the existence of an alliance in general, there were elements of opinion in both countries that were at odds with this viewpoint; put simply, they feared Japanese ambitions. As one scholar has put it: 'Australians were not comforted when British officials and politicians, such as Winston Churchill, pointed to the Anglo-Japanese alliance as the protector of British interests in the Pacific. The alliance was with Australia's main perceived potential enemy.'[37]

Japanese naval expansion, though nowhere as great in scope as that of the UK and Germany, was nevertheless significant both in terms of quality and quantity. In 1906 the battleship *Satsuma* was launched, a design that pre-empted the UK's *Dreadnought*.[38] The vessel had been designed and built in Japan, though many of the components were imported from the UK, and the Japanese shipbuilding industry was increasingly becoming self-reliant and independent of foreign, particularly British, yards. The UK had constructed all Japan's major warships up to the *Satsuma* and her sister *Aki*, and Japan was to revert to British expertise only once more, when the battlecruiser *Kongo*, of extremely advanced design, was ordered from Vickers at Barrow-in-Furness in 1911.

Japanese determination to acquire a fleet capable of more than just regional power projection was of particular concern to the US, which had both commercial interests and territories in the Western Pacific to protect, particularly, in the latter category, the Philippines. Indeed, Theodore Roosevelt opined in 1907 that the archipelago formed 'our heel of Achilles. They are all that make the present situation with Japan dangerous.'[39] That the US was a likely potential enemy had been accepted by Japan since the end of the Russo-Japanese War, and, apparently for the first time, such a naval conflict was 'gamed' during the 1908 fleet manoeuvres.[40] The US Navy, on its part, had evolved a strategy for projecting its power across the ocean and fighting Japan; War Plan Orange.[41] It was not however until 'the-war-after-the-next-one' that the potential of US–Japanese conflict was to be realised.

Chapter 4

A Moment of 'Supreme Opportunity'

On 28 June 1914 the 'damned silly thing in the Balkans' set in train the 'July Crisis'.[1] This led to the outbreak of war at the end of July and beginning of August, though British involvement was far from automatic. Sir Edward Grey, who served twice as Foreign Secretary, first from 1892–95 in Gladstone's final administration and then from 1905–16 in the Campbell-Bannerman and Asquith administrations, had in 1906 authorised secret 'discussions' between the General Staffs of France and the UK, but he kept these hidden from his Cabinet colleagues, and the full import of them even from the Prime Minister. Winston S. Churchill, whilst concluding that Grey's 'Entente with France and the military and naval conversations that had taken place since 1906, had led us into a position where we had the obligations of an alliance without its advantages', also opined that the policy was, in all essentials, correct.[2] Lloyd George was less sanguine (at least long after the event) arguing that:

> During the eight years that preceded the war, the Cabinet devoted a ridiculously small percentage of its time to a consideration of foreign affairs. [...] Nothing was said about our military commitments. There was an air of 'hush hush' about every allusion to our relations with France, Russia and Germany. [...] We were made to feel that, in these matters, we were reaching our hands towards the mysteries, and that we were too young in the priesthood to presume to enter into the sanctuary reserved for the elect.[3]

A.J.P. Taylor considered that Grey '[...] followed a resolute line [...] but he consulted the cabinet very little, and he informed the public hardly at all'. He also argued that whilst Grey repudiated the phrase the 'Balance of Power' he was 'concerned about the European Balance in a way that no

British foreign secretary had been since Palmerston'.[4] Grey later justified his policy by arguing that:

> We must be free to go to the help of France as well as to stand aside [...]
> If there were no military plans made beforehand we should be unable
> to come to the assistance of France in time [...] We should in effect not
> have preserved our freedom to help France, but cut ourselves off from
> the possibility of doing so.[5]

This was, as Taylor commented, a good argument, but it failed to take into account that if the arrangements were secret and non-binding they could not have the effect of deterring Germany. However, it was politically impossible for Grey to publicise his diplomacy because of the risk that it would have divided the Cabinet, the Liberal Party and probably the country.

As the crisis deepened Grey was unable to give a clear warning to Germany that, in the event of a war, Britain would fight on the side of France and Russia. Whether or not this would have made any difference remains the subject of scholarly argument. It was only after his attempts to convene a conference of all the Great Powers had failed that he warned the German Ambassador to London, Prince Lichnowsky, on 29 July, that Britain could not remain uninvolved in any general European war: 'it would not be practicable to stand aside and wait for any length of time'. This warning was however contradicted by information received by the Kaiser the day before from his brother, Prince Heinrich. This was to the effect that George V had told him that the UK would endeavour to stay neutral.[6] War was, by this time, probably inevitable in any case. Austria-Hungary had issued a declaration of war against Serbia on 28 July, causing Russia to order partial mobilisation. This was followed by full mobilisation on 31 July. Germany declared war on Russia the next day, and on France on 3 August.

The British government had still to decide what to do, and two Cabinet meetings were held on Sunday, 3 August. The last of these decided to issue an ultimatum concerning Belgian integrity, which was the issue around which the Liberal government and Party could, mostly, unite; two Cabinet ministers resigned, John Burns and John Morley. At 11:00hr London time on 4 August 1914 the UK declared war on Germany.

With British participation the war became a worldwide conflict, particularly since the British declaration automatically committed the dominions and colonies. This was not necessarily unpopular in the Pacific territories; the Australian Labour Party leader, the political veteran Andrew Fisher, as part of an ongoing election campaign put it thus on 31 July 1914:

All, I am sure, will regret the critical position existing at the present time, and pray that a disastrous war may be averted. But should the worst happen after everything has been done that honour will permit, Australians will stand beside our own to help and defend her to our last man and our last shilling.[7]

Fisher's party won the subsequent election and he became Prime Minister for a third time. Australian involvement in the conflict was of vital importance to the prosecution of the conflict in the Far East against Germany; the largest and most powerful force in the area available to the British Empire was the Royal Australian Navy (RAN).

At the outbreak of war the effective offensive strength of the RAN, the fleet unit as agreed at the 1909 Conference, consisted of the 1911 'Indefatigable' class Battle-Cruiser *Australia* (Flagship), the 1912 'Chatham' class light cruisers *Melbourne* and *Sydney*, and the 1905 'Challenger' class light cruiser *Encounter* (the latter being an ex-Royal Navy vessel given to the RAN pending the completion of the Australian built 'Chatham' class light cruiser *Brisbane*). There was also an obsolete 1900 'Pelorus' 3rd Class Protected Cruiser *Pioneer* and three 'River' class destroyers *Parramtatta* (1910), *Yarra* (1910) and *Warrego* (1911), together with two modern (1914) E-class submarines *AE1* and *AE2*. This mainly modern and unquestionably powerful force was under the command of Rear Admiral Sir George Patey RN, and was more than a match for the East Asiatic Cruiser Squadron.

Commanded since December 1912 by Vice Admiral Maximilian Graf von Spee, the core of the German force comprised the two modern Armoured Cruisers *Scharnhorst* (1907) and *Gneisenau* (1908). The other main fighting units of the force consisted of a quartet of Light Cruisers: *Dresden*, *Emden*, *Leipzig* and *Nürnberg*. This squadron, together with the, albeit sparse, infrastructure created in the German Pacific colonies made for a potent threat. As the Australian Official History has it:

> A powerful [...] fleet [...]; it had bases and coaling facilities at carefully selected points, with which it could communicate by wireless. As long as it remained [...] and could maintain communication with its bases in the islands, it was obvious that the position was one fraught with endless possibilities for Australia and New Zealand.[8]

However the presence on the Southern Pacific of the Australian flagship acted as a severe deterrent on Spee, who was to write in his diary on 18 August 1914: 'The *Australia* is my special apprehension – she alone is superior to my whole squadron.'[9]

Not in any way distinctly superior, other than in numbers, was the other major force deployed in the Pacific by the Royal Navy; the China Squadron under Vice Admiral Sir Martyn Jerram. The main components of this force were the Flagship, the armoured cruiser *Minotaur* (1906), the name ship of her class, *Hampshire* (1903), a 'Devonshire' class armoured cruiser, *Newcastle* (1910), a 'Bristol' class light cruiser, and *Yarmouth* (1911), a 'Weymouth' class light cruiser.[10] Despite this lack of superiority it was the China Squadron that had the task of dealing with the German squadron and its base in the event of war.

Knowing full well that Jerram's force as constituted was not assured of despatching Spee's – Jerram had warned he might be unable to take on the squadron without reinforcements in 1913 – the Admiralty had arranged for the RAN to provide strong support in the shape of the flagship, upon which occasion Patey would hoist his flag as admiral of the Australian Squadron in the *Encounter*. The British were able to direct the disposition of *Australia*, and indeed any RAN resources, under arrangements entered into at the Imperial Conference of 1911. There it had been agreed that operational control of the RAN ships would revert to the Admiralty in time of war:

> On the receipt of a pre-arranged cablegram from the Imperial authorities, the Australian Government would place the [...] naval services of the Commonwealth directly under the control of the

Admiralty. The sea-going fleet would then become a squadron of the Imperial Navy, taking orders either direct from London or from the British officer under whom they were placed.[11]

When the Admiralty's 'war warning' telegram was despatched on 28 July 1914, Jerram was at Weihaiwei with all his vessels other than *Newcastle*, which was visiting Japan. However, rather than steam directly towards Tsingtau, some 320km away, he was directed to concentrate at Hong Kong, a further 1600km to the south, in order to assemble his squadron around the 'Swiftsure' class pre-dreadnought battleship *Triumph* (1903), which was refitting there. This was, perhaps, an excessively cautious manoeuvre as *Triumph* was only marginally better armed, 4×10in and 14×7.5in guns, than Jerram's armoured cruisers, but was a great deal slower with a maximum speed when new of some 19 knots. Jerram said later that he nearly disobeyed the order entirely, annoyed that a 'definite plan of action formed in peacetime after mature consideration' could be 'thrown to the winds by one peremptory telegram'.[12] In any event the need to make this detour far from the object of the exercise probably allowed the *Emden* to escape from Tsingtau and certainly, unless they parted company with the battleship, precluded any realistic chance of the China Squadron attempting to pursue Spee.

There are perhaps two points worth considering in relation to this episode. It may be recalled that HMS *New Zealand* had, as per Asquith's statement to the House of Commons on 26 August 1909 regarding the recently concluded Imperial Conference on Defence, been originally earmarked for the fleet unit based on China. Churchill had viewed this deployment with disfavour, disclaiming that 'The employment of a ship like *New Zealand* in China is not to be defended on any military grounds', and had subsequently ensured that the vessel deployed to British waters in 1913. How different the course of events in 1914 might have been if Jerram were able to deploy such an overwhelming force against the East Asiatic Cruiser Squadron and Tsingtau is unknowable. All that can be said with certainty is that it would have greatly increased the efficiency and fighting strength of the China Squadron, rather than reducing it as *Triumph* did.

The second point relates to the Admiralty orders to concentrate on the old battleship. This is in many ways a portent of similar orders to

Sir Christopher Cradock, the commander of the South American Squadron, later in the year. Prior to his disastrous engagement at Coronel in November, Cradock was told to keep his squadron concentrated around HMS *Canopus* (1898), another venerable pre-dreadnought, with a similar thickness of armour though larger calibre, but not necessarily longer ranged, guns than *Triumph*. It seems highly unlikely that either of these vessels, which were very slow in comparison with armoured cruisers, would have proved the slightest use in combat with Spee's much faster and almost equally well-armoured vessels had such an eventuality come to pass. Churchill seems to have had a blind spot, evident even before he became First Lord, regarding the ability of heavily gunned, though old and slow units, to deter and deal with lighter gunned, newer and faster enemy warships. His faith in *Canopus*, in respect of Cradock's command, and *Triumph*, in respect of Jerram's, reflect this in 1914, whilst in July 1910 he had resisted the deployment of battlecruisers in the Far East, arguing, in direct contradiction of Fisher's belief and policy, that 'older battleships or smaller cruisers could perfectly well discharge all the necessary naval duties'. He was, no doubt, disabused of this view following the Battle of Coronel.[13]

Churchill was later castigated for seeking, in the first volume of *The World Crisis*, to place the blame for the defeat at Coronel on Cradock, whom he accused of disobeying orders by engaging Spee without *Canopus*. As one reviewer of Churchill's work put it, the outcome of the Battle of Coronel 'came about partly through a lack of precision in the orders sent to Cradock and partly through an exaggeration, on Churchill's part, of the fighting and steaming capabilities of the *Canopus* [...]'. He went on to argue that the pre-dreadnought 'possessed the same armour as that of *Good Hope*, which proved impotent against the modern 8-inch [210mm] guns of von Spee, and she carried guns which were not only of an antiquated mark (only 35 calibres), but which were quite outranged by von Spee's eights'.[14] Perhaps it is just as well that neither *Triumph* nor *Canopus* was put to the test.

Australia meanwhile had remained in Australian waters, not, as has been argued on occasion, because of a reluctance on the part of the Australian government to conform with British wishes, but because it had been discovered that Spee was not anywhere near Tsingtau but rather was 'somewhere within range of Australian wireless – i.e., not more than 1,500 miles away'.[15]

Accordingly the capital ship, and attendant vessels, under the command of Patey, patrolled off New Britain from 11–13 August in search of the enemy cruiser squadron, before joining HMAS *Melbourne* and proceeding to New Caledonia on 21 August 1914 on missions of occupation. First these vessels, together with the French 'Gueydon' class armoured cruiser *Montcalm*, and the Royal Navy ships HMS *Psyche*, HMS *Philomel* and HMS *Pyramus*, in 'Australia's first coalition operation'[16], escorted a New Zealand Expeditionary Force of 1,400 troops to take German Samoa, which surrendered without a fight. Following this the Australian ships formed escort to the Australian Naval and Military Expeditionary Force, whose object was to take Rabaul, the seat, from 1910, of the governor of German New Guinea.[17] These expeditions had been sanctioned, indeed encouraged, by the Colonial Office in London, which had communicated with the Australian government on the matter on 6 August 1914 via the Governor General Sir Ronald Munro-Ferguson.[18] Colonial Secretary Lewis Harcourt had stated:

> If your Ministers desire and feel themselves able to seize German wireless stations [...] we should feel that this was a great and urgent Imperial service. You will, however, realise that any territory now occupied must be at the disposal of the Imperial Government for purposes of an ultimate settlement at conclusion of the war.[19]

On 18 August a further communication was sent by Harcourt: 'In connection with the expedition against German possessions in Pacific, British flag should be hoisted in all territories occupied successfully by His Majesty's forces and suitable arrangements made for temporary administration. No formal proclamation of annexation should however be made without previous communication with His Majesty's Government.'[20] The taking of this territory, whilst unquestionably sanctioned by 'His Majesty's Government', was also certainly congenial to the Australians, for Australia, or rather the precursor states, had long coveted much of the territory occupied by Germany.[21] In 1864, 1874, 1878 and 1879, New South Wales, with the co-operation of Queensland, had strongly urged that possession should be taken of the northeast coast of New Guinea, but the Imperial government refused its consent. In 1883 the Queensland government had annexed that part of New Guinea, and adjacent islands, which fell between the 141st and 155th meridian, but again the British government demurred. It though did take action in 1884, when a British protectorate was proclaimed over the south coast of New Guinea and neighbouring islands. Thus the occupations, or at least the undercurrent to them, have been classified by some as 'sub-imperialism'.[22]

Whatever the rationale behind the expeditions however they were overwhelmingly successful through being able to apply overwhelming superiority; as Rear Admiral Patey had put it in a letter of 11 September 1914 to the Governor of German New Guinea:

> I have the honour to inform you that I have arrived at Simpsonshafen [Simpson Harbour] with the intention of occupying Herbertshöhe, Rabaul, and the Island of New Britain.[23]
>
> I will point out to Your Excellency that the force at my command is so large as to render useless any opposition on your part, and such resistance can only result in unnecessary bloodshed.[24]

Patey was not indulging in hyperbole, and, although there was some resistance and a small number of casualties on both sides, the 'Terms of Capitulation of German New Guinea' was signed on 17 September 1914. It was of course the presence of HMAS *Australia* that alone rendered it possible for the despatch of the expeditionary forces to the German possessions in the southern Pacific, and as it turned out the lack of the vessel with the China Squadron had little effect; far more formidable forces had joined the Allied cause.

The British Foreign Office had been informed of Japan's position as regards Germany, on 3 August 1914, via a telegram from the British Ambassador in Tokyo, Sir Conyngham Greene. The Japanese offered to assist the UK in the Pacific, but left it 'entirely to [the British] Government to formulate the reason for and nature of the assistance required'.[25]

Grey had, on 1 August, informed Japan via Inouye Katsunosuke, their Ambassador to London, that British participation in the European war was probable, but had argued that he did not consider it 'likely' that the British would 'have to apply to Japan under our alliance'. He informed the British representative in Tokyo of his discussion the same day:

> I told the Japanese Ambassador to-day that the situation in Europe was very grave. We had not yet decided what our action should be, but under certain conditions we might find it necessary to intervene. If, however, we did intervene, it would be on the side of France and Russia, and I therefore did not see that we were likely to have to apply to Japan under our alliance, or that the interests dealt with by the alliance would be involved.[26]

He modified this stance somewhat two days later, when he had communicated to the Japanese the view of Sir Walter Langley, an Assistant Under-Secretary of State for Foreign Affairs. Grey had asked Langley 'whether the present situation in any way affects the Japanese under the 1911 Agreement and whether we have anything to ask them'. The reply he received set out the parameters of the issue as perceived by the Foreign Office secretariat:

> The only ways in which the Japanese could be brought in would be if hostilities spread to the Far East, e.g., an attack on Hong Kong by the Germans, or if a rising in India were to take place.
>   There seems no reason to say anything about India, but it might be as well to warn the Japanese Government that in the event of a war with Germany there might be a possibility of an attack upon Hong Kong or Weihaiwei when we should look to them for support.
>   The Japanese are no doubt quite alive to this possibility, but perhaps under Article 1 of the agreement we should communicate with them.[27]

Grey obviously considered this position to be in accordance with his own views, authorising the despatch of a telegraph to Japan without further reference to him.[28] The message sent stated that 'if hostilities spread to [the] Far East, and an attack on Hong Kong or Weihaiwei were to take place, we should rely on [Japanese] support'.[29] Greene had meanwhile elicited from the Japanese Foreign Minister the official position held by Japan:

[...] the Imperial Government will await an intimation from His Majesty's Government as to what action they have decided to take before defining their own attitude, which will be based thereon.

Japan has no interest in a European conflict, and his Excellency [Kato, the Minister for Foreign Affairs] notes what you say as to the Anglo-Japanese Alliance, but, if British interests in Eastern Asia should be placed in jeopardy – as say, for instance, by a German attack on Hong Kong or by any other aggressive act – His Majesty's Government may count upon Japan at once coming to assistance of her ally with all her strength, if called on to do so, leaving it entirely to His Majesty's Government to formulate the reason for, and nature of, the assistance required.[30]

This placing, as it seemed, of Japanese interests behind those of the UK was very much to Grey's taste, as can be readily discerned from a perusal of his messages already quoted. He reinforced his appreciation of the position that he perceived Japan as adopting during a meeting he held with Inouye on 4 August 1914. He sent a report of the conversation to Greene in Tokyo:

I asked the Japanese Ambassador today to thank Baron Kato most cordially for his generous offer of assistance. I told the Ambassador how much I had been impressed by the way in which Japan, during the Russo–Japanese war, demanded nothing of us under our alliance with her except what was strictly in accord with the Treaty of Alliance; indeed, he had asked almost less than at one time it seemed she might have been entitled to have from us. I had thought that a fine attitude of good faith and restraint; and now we in turn should avoid, if we could, drawing Japan into any trouble. But, should a case arise in which we needed her help, we would gladly ask for it and be grateful for it.[31]

On the same day he received from Greene a telegram containing the response to one of his earlier messages:

Your telegram of 3rd August [(35865) No. 549.] was laid before the Cabinet this morning, and Minister for Foreign Affairs desires me to say that in the special eventualities referred to, namely: An attack on Hong Kong and Weihaiwei or a similar concrete act of aggression the Imperial Government will be ready at once to support His Majesty's Government if called upon, as explained in my telegram [(35666) No. 571]. In the hypothetical cases, such as a capture of a British merchant ship or a case involving, perhaps, a question of Chinese or Russian territorial waters, the Imperial Government would wish to have the opportunity of considering it and consulting with His Majesty's Government before taking definite action.

Secret.

His Excellency tells me that 2nd battle fleet of four large cruisers, to which volunteer fleet may be added, is lying ready at Sasebo for immediate action if required, while a cruiser has been stationed at each of the ports of Nagasaki, Fusan, and Chemulpo to meet possible eventualities.[32]

Unless and until such eventualities materialised however, the only assistance the the UK government sought was, in effect, that of having the Japanese Navy act as support to the Royal Navy. This is made clear in a note sent by Grey via Greene on 5 August:

HM Government would gladly avail themselves of the proffered assistance of Japanese Government in the direction of protecting British trading vessels from German armed merchant cruisers, whilst British warships are locating and engaging German warships in Chinese waters [...] it would be of the very greatest assistance to HM Government if they [Japanese] would be good enough to employ some of their warships in hunting out and destroying German armed merchantmen in China. British Government realise that such action on the part of Japan will constitute declaration of war with Germany, but it is difficult to see how such a step is to be avoided.[33]

A declaration of war with Germany was, unknown to Grey it seems, very much at the forefront of Japanese political thought. Indeed Greene had reported to him on 2 August that 'Japanese vernacular papers are now discussing the possibility of Japan being invited to support her ally in defence of her interests in the Far East. The view generally taken seems to be that Japan will gladly accept responsibility.'[34]

Indeed the Japanese cabinet, without waiting to be invited, accepted the responsibility at an emergency cabinet meeting on 7 August. This meeting resolved to declare war and also decided that Japan would not restrict itself to the secondary role allotted by the UK. Japan would however negotiate with the UK as to the form of its declaration of war against Germany.[35] The *Genro* and the Emperor swiftly ratified the cabinet decision.[36] This information was sent to the Japanese Ambassador to the UK on 9 August and communicated to Grey the next day:

> Having once declared war, [Japan] cannot confine her actions to the destruction of [German] merchantmen alone. To attain the object common to the two allied powers, as far as Chinese waters are concerned, namely the destruction of Germany's power to damage the interests of Japan and Great Britain in Eastern Asia, Japan will have to use every possible means. Besides, taking into consideration that employment of Japanese men-of-war for the purpose of destroying German armed merchantmen may be regarded as an act limited in scope and to have been necessitated by the temporary convenience of Great Britain, the Japanese Government are of the opinion that the reasons for Japan's participation in the war should be made on the broad grounds as stated in the Agreement of Alliance, and they should take such action as the development of events may dictate. [...] The Japanese Government will therefore state in the declaration of war [...] that, as the consequences of aggressive action by Germany, the British Government finding that the general peace is threatened in Eastern Asia, and that the special interests of Great Britain are in jeopardy, have requested the support of Japan, to which she has acceded.[37]

The ambassador also made plain Japan's desire that the declaration of war should be so phrased as to convey that it had been made at Britain's request: '[The Japanese Government] also wish that Britain will [...] make a statement which will not conflict with that of [Japan]'.[38] Grey replied to this message on 11 August: '[...] in the absence of any present danger apparent to Hong Kong or British concessions I cannot say the special interests of Great Britain in Eastern Asia are so seriously menaced as to make it essential to appeal to the Alliance on that ground alone'.[39] However, he went on to point out that:

> [...] I recognize that Japan has interests also to be considered [...] I agree therefore to a statement that the two Governments having been in communication with each other are of opinion that it is necessary for each to take action to protect the general interests contemplated by the Anglo-Japanese Alliance. It should also be stated that the action of Japan will not extend to the Pacific Ocean beyond the China Seas nor extend beyond Asiatic waters westward of the China Seas, or to any foreign territory except territory in German occupation on the continent in Eastern Asia. This is important to prevent unfounded misapprehension abroad.[40]

This was despite a reassurance received the day before that Japan had no intention of undertaking operations affecting China: '[...] lest a declaration of war on the part of Japan [...] give rise to the impression that extensive operations affecting China may take place [...] [Japan's actions would be limited to] the destruction of German power in these regions for which no extensive operations are required'.[41] Even though from this distance in time it looks like mere semantics, British ambivalence had the potential to embarrass Japan as reports of an imminent declaration of war had leaked, or been leaked, into the public domain and military preparations had been undertaken. Grey's Cabinet colleague, Winston Churchill, the First Lord of the Admiralty, was, as his biographer put it, 'alarmed' when he sighted Grey's 11 August telegram.[42] He wrote immediately to the Foreign Secretary:

> Your [...] [s]tatement [I cannot say the special interests of Great Britain in Eastern Asia are so seriously menaced as to make it essential to appeal to the Alliance on that ground alone] is not borne out by our information [...]

I must say I think you are chilling indeed to these people. I can't see any half-way house myself between having them in and keeping them out. If they are to come in, they may as well be welcomed as comrades. This last telegram is almost hostile. I am afraid I do not understand what is in your mind on this aspect – though I followed it so clearly till today. [...]

This telegram gives me a shiver. We are all in this together & I only wish to give the fullest effect & support to your main policy. But I am altogether perplexed by the line opened up by these Japanese interchanges.

You may easily give mortal offence – which will not be forgotten – we are not safe yet – by a long chalk. The storm has yet to burst.[43]

Under this pressure Grey modified his telegram, and wrote to Churchill later that day stating that he thought 'it is all right now with Japan'. Whatever the policy of the Foreign Office with respect to Japan, Churchill was keen on them becoming allies, indeed he sent a message of his own to the Japanese Minister of Marine, Admiral Yashiro, on 13 August, welcoming him and his service as 'brothers in arms': 'On behalf of the Board of Admiralty I express the warm feeling of comradeship & pleasure with which the officers & men of the British Navy will find themselves allied in a common cause & against a common foe with the gallant & seamanlike Navy of Japan.'[44] This message, it may be noted, was sent some five days before Japan sent any ultimatum to Germany and ten days before her declaration of war. If Churchill can be accused of jumping the gun to some extent, and being somewhat at odds with Foreign Office policy, then perhaps he may be absolved by noting that any discussion taking place in London pertaining to Japanese actions against Germany in the Pacific were academic.

Japan could see for itself the prospects that the European 'Great Powers' being at war with each other opened up, particularly recognising 'the advantages of raising Japan's status through obliterating German bases from East Asia' and the 'gains which Japan could make in the Pacific and in China, especially in Manchuria'.[45] Abe Moritaro, the head of the political bureau of the Foreign Office, had, during 1912 and 1913, composed a number of memoranda on the subject of Japanese relations with China urging a moderate approach lest Japanese intervention succeed only in uniting the Chinese and causing an anti-Japanese backlash. For being associated with political moderation Abe was assassinated.[46]

Foreign Minister Makino Nobuaki took a somewhat different line, and in a memorandum composed just prior to him leaving office in April 1914 he had advocated direct intervention as the only means of protecting Japan's position in relation to China.[47]

The situation, and Makino's solution to it, thereafter came within the purview of Kato. The problem with direct intervention was that it would inevitably draw in the other Great Powers, including perhaps Japan's ally, the UK, which, despite the alliance, was not necessarily overly sympathetic to Japanese attempts to broaden its influence in China.[48] This problem would be greatly mitigated of course if the powers were occupied elsewhere. The outbreak of war in Europe thus gave Japan a 'one in a million chance' both to secure her existing position and extend her economic and political influence by taking control of Germany's possessions and investments.[49] Japan's entry into the war was thus opportunist; as Inoue Kaoru, the senior member of the *Genro*, put it: 'August 1914 was a moment of "supreme opportunity" for Japan.'[50]

The prospects of territorial expansionism on the part of Japan had, naturally enough, not only exercised Grey in the UK, but were also of great concern to the US government. Indeed the US proposed that Germany and Japan accept the neutralisation of 'foreign settlements' (specifically treaty ports) in order to 'protect the interests of the United States in China'.[51] They were particularly concerned about the effect on trade and commerce, as well as Chinese territorial integrity, if and when Japan went to war.

On 14 August Robert Lansing, the counsellor for the Department of State and an authority on International Law, wrote to Secretary of State William Jennings Bryan, of the 'persistent reports and rumours [...] that Japan intends to declare war upon Germany'.[52] Recognising the motivation that existed behind the Japanese position, and their likely response to US pressure, he proposed to Bryan that the US should wait until after hostilities occurred before 'with perfect propriety' approaching 'all the belligerents simultaneously'.[53] He hoped that by adopting this method Japan would find it difficult to ignore the approach, and he also made mention of the last point of the Root–Takahira Agreement:

Should any event occur threatening the *status quo* as above described or the principle of equal opportunity, as above defined, it remains for the two governments to communicate with each other, in order to arrive at an understanding as to what measures they may consider it useful to take.[54]

The day after Lansing had composed his note the Japanese, as he had predicted, presented their ultimatum to Germany via a note from Prime Minister Okuma Shigenobu:

We consider it highly important and necessary in the present situation to take measures to remove the causes of all disturbance of peace in the Far East, and to safeguard general interests as contemplated in the Agreement of Alliance between Japan and Great Britain.

In order to secure firm and enduring peace in Eastern Asia, the establishment of which is the aim of the said Agreement, the Imperial Japanese Government sincerely believes it to be its duty to give advice to the Imperial German Government to carry out the following two propositions:

(1) Withdraw immediately from Japanese and Chinese waters the German men-o'-war and armed vessels of all kinds, and to disarm at once those which cannot be withdrawn.
(2) To deliver on a date not later than September 15th, to the Imperial Japanese authorities, without condition or compensation, the entire leased territory of Kiaochau, with a view to the eventual restoration of the same to China.

The Imperial Japanese Government announces at the same time that in the event of its not receiving, by noon on August 23rd, an answer from the Imperial German Government signifying unconditional acceptance of the above advice offered by the Imperial Japanese Government, Japan will be compelled to take such action as it may deem necessary to meet the situation.[55]

At the same time as the note was delivered to Germany, Kato Takaaki, Japan's foreign minister, informed George Guthrie, the US Ambassador to Japan, that 'Japan sought no territorial aggrandizement nor other selfish ends through war' and reassured the US that any action taken would not infringe upon the interests of other powers.[56] This reassurance was, perhaps, somewhat undermined when Japan totally rejected any measure that would have prevented it taking and occupying Kiautschou; Germany's attempts to retrocede the lease to China, in effect to hand back the territory, was nullified when the Japanese warned that they would not recognise any such transaction.[57]

The US was also approached to accept the lease, but refused; as John Van Antwerp MacMurray, Secretary of the US Legation in Peking from 1913–17, put it 'such a course would do more to provoke war than to avert war'.[58]

Bearing the above points in mind then, it appears that the message sent to Japan from the US government on 21 August vis-à-vis Kiautschou rather made a virtue out of a necessity:

> [The US] notes with satisfaction that Japan, in demanding the surrender […] of […] Kiautschou, does so with the purpose of restoring that territory to China […] Should disturbances in the interior of China seem to the Japanese Government to require measures to be taken by Japan or other powers to restore order, the Imperial Japanese Government no doubt desire to consult with the American Government before deciding on a course of action [in accordance with the Root-Takahira Agreement of 1908].[59]

Sir Edward Grey meanwhile had been explaining to Walter Hines Page, the US Ambassador to Britain from 1913–18, that the Japanese action had not been coordinated with the British. Page explained Grey's position in a message of 18 August 1914: 'Sir Edward Grey has explained to me confidentially that the Japanese government acted on their own account when they sent their ultimatum to Germany. They did not confer with the British government about it but only informed the British government after they decided to send it.'[60]

If Grey, as Churchill had pointed out in his message of 11 August, was indeed cool ('chilling') towards the Japanese entry into the conflict, then the First Lord had no such inhibitions; where Grey saw potential trouble Churchill saw only potential. Shortly after Japan's formal declaration, he was badgering Grey on the subject of utilising their great naval strength on the Allied side, writing on 29 August 1914:

> Now that Austria has declared war on Japan, and in view of the general situation, including the attitude of Turkey, it would seem only fitting that the Japanese Government should be sounded as to their readiness to send a battle squadron to co-operate with the Allied Powers in the Mediterranean or elsewhere. The influence and value of this powerful aid could not be overrated. It would steady and encourage Italy, and would bring nearer the situation, so greatly desired, of our being able to obtain command of the Baltic. There is reason to believe that the Japanese would take such an invitation as a compliment.[61]

Churchill was, it seems, mistaken, as no ships at all were forthcoming, never mind a battle squadron, which in the contemporary Royal Navy consisted of eight battleships. Indeed, to move forward in time somewhat, it was not until 1917 that the Japanese Navy sent any assistance to the European theatre with the deployment of an old though large armoured cruiser, *Nisshin*, and eight destroyers under Admiral Sato to the Mediterranean.[62]

To return to 1914 however, Japan wasted no time in deploying her powerful naval assets in support of her ally in the Far East. The modern battlecruiser *Kongo* was immediately dispatched to patrol the sea-lanes in mid-ocean and three days later, on 26 August, the battlecruiser *Ibuki* and 2nd class light cruiser *Chikuma* were ordered to Singapore, at the UK's request, to provide support in the search for German commerce raiders, particularly the *Emden*.[63] Whilst *Chikuma* stayed in the area patrolling unsuccessfully as far south as Ceylon, the *Ibuki* was soon despatched (18 September) back eastwards to begin the task of escorting troop convoys, carrying ANZAC contingents, from Australia and New Zealand to the Middle East.[64] In a like manner French convoys, containing contingents from French Indo-China, were also escorted.[65] The first of these voyages, ten transports from

Ellington, New Zealand, was undertaken on 16 October and they were to continue throughout the war.[66]

The hunt for German commerce raiders, the original task that Sir Edward Grey had foreseen for the Japanese Navy, was not neglected however, and the battleship *Satsuma*, together with the 2nd class light cruisers *Yahagi* and *Hirado*, were sent to watch the sea lanes around Australia.[67] The force in the Indian Ocean was greatly strengthened during October in an effort to hunt down German forces, and it became an important command under Vice Admiral Sojiro Tochinai; ultimately employing two Battlecruisers, *Ibuki* and *Ikoma*, three Armoured Cruisers, *Tokiwa*, *Yakumo* and *Nisshin*, and three lighter cruisers, *Hirado*, *Yahagi* and *Chikuma*.[68] On 1 November 1914, in response to a British request, the Japanese Navy assumed temporary responsibility for all Allied naval activity in the Indian Ocean east of 90 degrees longitude and remained in command for the rest of the month.[69]

The appearance of one such potential German raider, SMS *Geier*, at the US port of Honolulu on 15 October 1914 resulted in the despatch of the battleship *Hizen* and armoured Cruiser *Asama* to intercept the vessel should she try to leave.[70] The US government prevented any such action however by interning *Geier* on 7 November, whereupon the two Japanese vessels joined the armoured cruiser *Izumo*, which had been there since the commencement of hostilities, searching off the coast of South America.[71]

The Japanese also began seizing the German island colonies, and at the risk of disrupting chronological progression it is worth examining this process.

The scattered groups of German islands had been largely left unmolested, apart from operations to disrupt various strategically placed radio stations. For example, HMS *Hampshire* attacked the station at Yap on 12 August, and a party landed from HMAS *Melbourne* on 9 September similarly dealt with the installation at Nauru. The occupation of the islands, though they should have been unopposed from a military point of view given the terms of capitulation signed on 17 September 1914, was prevented by a lack of available warships. The 'guarantee' of no military resistance' did not however apply to Spee and the East Asiatic Cruiser Squadron, and Patey, conceiving his primary duty was to keep his assets concentrated in order to destroy this force, was unwilling to detach units for escort work.[72] He therefore recommended that no unescorted expeditions should venture outside the relatively safe waters around New Guinea until such time as Spee had either been dealt with or at least his whereabouts were known.[73] SMS *Scharnhorst* and SMS *Gneisenau* had been sighted at Apia, Samoa on 14 September, but it was only in early October that intelligence indicated with a degree of liability that Spee was heading for the west coast of South America; consequently, no Australian military effort had been undertaken against the islands prior to this.[74]

However, the Japanese Navy in its search for Spee and other German vessels had begun, during early September, to extend their patrols further into the areas of the former German possessions. Harcourt telegraphed to Munro-Ferguson on 10 September:

> Please inform [the Australian Government] very confidentially that it is very likely that Japanese ships [...] may cruise in the Pacific round the Marianne and Caroline Islands in order to hunt down the German squadron which is believed to be in those parts and which, unless it is attacked, will prey upon British and Japanese shipping in Pacific.[75]

On 7 October a Japanese vessel visited Yap at the request of the British in order to ascertain the status of the radio station supposedly destroyed on 12 August. It found evidence that repairs had been affected, and also discovered the German survey vessel, SMS *Planet* in the vicinity.[76] *Planet* scuttled herself to avoid capture, with the crew going ashore, but this episode led the Japanese to land forces to prevent further occurrences of the kind. They communicated their thoughts on the matter to the UK on 10 October:

> [The Japanese Foreign Minister] asks whether [the] Australians propose to take Yap [...] and station a guard there, in which case [the] Japanese squadron will be instructed to hand over the place; but if not, [the] Japanese Admiralty consider it necessary in view of the strategical importance of the island, that it should be occupied by a British or Japanese force.[77]

This message was passed on to Australia on 13 October, in a telegram from Harcourt to Munro-Ferguson:

[The] Japanese Government state that, in [the] course of searching Western Pacific islands for enemy vessels and bases, squadron called Yap on October 7th and landed marines to investigate wireless telegraph and cable stations there. They found that both had been repaired and used by Germans and since destroyed again. They have temporarily occupied it but they are ready to hand it over to an Australian force. On account of strategical importance island must be occupied by some force. Your Ministers will remember that it was originally intended that they should send force to occupy Yap, and they will no doubt agree that it is desirable to relieve Japanese as quickly as possible of the task of holding the island. Japanese Government have therefore been informed it is intention of your Government to occupy Yap, and I am communicating with Admiralty as to provision of transport. Please ask ministers to arrange in communication with Admiral Patey details of force to be sent. It need not be large and could presumably be detached from force already in occupation of German possessions.[78]

This message was replied to on 17 October 1914 in a message from the Australian Naval Board to the Admiralty, stating that, with regard to the British request for the occupation of Yap:

[...] Military force can now be provided from Simpsonhafen for this purpose. Vice-Admiral commanding cannot at present spare Encounter, also Encounter cannot well enter Yap or Ponape. Fully appreciate pressing importance of occupation of Yap by British force. Pending despatch of proposed expedition to make effective occupation of islands could China Squadron detach vessel [to] relieve Japanese care of Yap[?] Consider desirable to fit out small expedition with Commissioners to report on Government organisation, trade, food supplies, wireless communication, and naval requirements and to take possession Pelew, Marshall, Caroline, and Marianne islands. These islands all included in terms of surrender by Governor Simpsonhafen. Propose to mount four-inch guns in *Fantome* and *Komet* and send these vessels with a small supply ship carrying troops and stores also a collier round islands as soon as situation will permit. *Fantome* and *Komet* can be manned by

Australian Navy. If Pioneer or Encounter available by time expedition ready and any probability of meeting superior force of enemy one or both might be attached to expedition. On account of great distance recommend arrange this cruise round islands in preference to isolated expedition to take possession of single islands.[79]

Whatever discussions and decisions the British and Australians may have been having, the situation was, on the part of the Japanese, developing its own dynamic, which was altering their perspective somewhat. Greene had communicated the changing situation as he perceived it to Grey on 12 October, explaining that Japanese public opinion, as evidenced by press reports, was moving in favour of Japan acquiring the islands for itself. Although arguing that such a proposition was 'premature', he noted that the government was being accused of subordinating Japanese interests to those of her ally. He went on:

It appears to me that it would be at once political and graceful if we offered them some signal mark of our confidence, which would vindicate their policy in the eyes of the nation and would assure us [of] their further assistance, should we require it. I submit that this object would be attained [...] [if we] refrain from requesting at the present juncture the transfer to Great Britain of any islands which Japan may occupy for strategic reasons.[80]

The requirement for 'further assistance' from Japan was very much in the mind of Churchill, who, as has been noted, viewed the Japanese Navy as, potentially, a powerful reinforcement for the Allied effort. Accordingly he was very much against in any way antagonising them, particularly by attempting to displace them from territory they already occupied. As he put it in a private letter to Harcourt of 18 October:

We have no cruiser available for Yap at the present time and much inconvenience would be caused by changing existing arrangements. There appears to be no military reason which requires us to eject the Japanese at this juncture. I do not gather that the Australasian Governments are pressing us to act. On the contrary, it would seem that we are pressing them. The Admiralty would strongly deprecate any action towards Japan which would appear suspicious or ungracious. We are deriving benefit from their powerful and generous aid. They have intimated that their occupation is purely military and devoid of political significance and there I trust we may leave the matter for the present.[81]

This rather defensive missive is understandable if it is considered that the various missions undertaken by Japan, whether or not at the instigation of the British Admiralty, had led to a situation whereby, it could be argued, the Admiralty had been conducting something of a foreign policy of its own vis-à-vis Japan. Churchill was perhaps keen to play down the political significance of the consequences, because they were profound.

Typical of the 'powerful and generous aid' provided by the Japanese Navy was their taking, at the instigation of the British Admiralty, of the administrative centre of the Marshall Islands, Jaluit Atoll.[82] This was the site of a German coaling station, with a large reserve of the commodity, and on 22 September the Admiralty informed their Australian counterparts that a Japanese squadron would be at the atoll 'about a week later'.[83] This was in response to a report, inaccurate as it turned out, that Spee and his entire squadron, complete with colliers and store ships, were at the Marshall Islands on 15 September.[84] Germany had established a coaling station at Jaluit prior to colonising the territory, having negotiated a treaty with the indigenous population as long ago as 1878. Following the German takeover it had become the capital of the Marshall Islands protectorate, and the commercial centre of eastern Micronesia. After taking possession of Enewetak (Eniwetok) Atoll on 29 September, units of Vice Admiral Tanin Yamaya's 1st Southern Squadron, based around the cruisers, *Asama*, *Kurama* and *Tsukuba*, seized Jaluit on 3 October 1914. By the middle of the month Japan had taken possession of most of the, now, ex-German islands north of the equator, excluding Guam which was a US possession.[85]

Nobody, least of all the Japanese, seems however to have informed either the British Foreign or Colonial Offices, the latter sending a message to Australia on 13 October urging the despatch of the expedition to take the islands 'as soon as possible'.[86] Neither knowledge of Japanese activities, nor the sense of urgency evidenced by the British Colonial Office, seems to have been communicated to Australia; a joint naval/military conference was convened on 26 October to co-ordinate plans and strategy for taking the islands north of the equator. The result of this meeting was the ability to reply to another query from the British government of the next day: 'With reference to your [...] telegram dated 13 October re. Yap etc. [A] force consisting of 200 men [is] being organised to garrison [the] principal islands. Particulars as to dates, convoy, etc., will be cabled later on.'[87]

The Australian military raised a force, known colloquially as 'The Druids' or the 'Tropical Force', more correctly, the Third Battalion of the Naval and Military Expeditionary Force. This unit contained a significant proportion of over-age men including 'a surprisingly large proportion [that] wore the ribbons of the South African War'.[88] By 13 November this force was assembled at Liverpool, NSW, ready to embark on a chartered vessel of the Eastern and Australian Line, and the following day instructions were issued to the expedition leader, Commander Samuel Pethebridge, who was also given the military rank of colonel on 21 November.[89] His instructions were unambiguous: 'The Government desire you to proceed with the troops being sent to occupy the islands recently held by Germany north of the equator.' They went on:

Your mission will be:

(a) To visit the various islands and possessions in the Pacific Ocean, recently held by Germany, and to be occupied by Great Britain.
(b) To place such troops in occupation as may be available, thus relieving any members of the Japanese Forces who may be now temporarily in occupation.

He was given full authority to act upon his own initiative, and the powers to command 'all officers of His Majesty's naval or military forces, together with any of His Majesty's subjects' to afford him all assistance as may lie within their power. He was however ordered not to 'take any action with regard to any matters affecting the possessions south of the equator'.[90] Having made these preparations the Australian government telegraphed Harcourt on 13 November, informing him that the expedition was nearly ready to depart:

'[...] steamer Eastern with 200 troops [...] escorted by Komet will leave Sydney 26 November to relieve Japanese now occupying Yap and other islands north [of the] equator'.[91]

One of the islands that it was proposed to occupy was Anguar in the Palau (Pelew) Archipelago.[92] Patey had advised the Admiralty against taking this territory as far back as 5 September. He had contended that, whilst the wireless station there should be destroyed, occupying the island would involve responsibility for feeding the inhabitants. He argued that from experience and 'information received' he knew that the area was 'very short of food' and that the responsibility of 'feeding the inhabitants as well as the garrisons, will relieve the Germans of this responsibility, and become an anxiety to ourselves'.[93] He received no reply to this message, and the island was left undisturbed until 26 September when a party from HMAS *Sydney* landed and destroyed the wireless ancillary equipment, though leaving the antenna undamaged.[94]

When the possibility of taking Anguar was specifically mentioned to the British government on 21 November it brought forth a somewhat, to the Australian government, startling reply:

> [...] it would be discourteous and disadvantageous to the Japanese if we turned them out of Anguar when they are helping us in every way with their Fleet throughout [the] Pacific and in convoy[ing] Australian contingents. [The] Japanese are now erecting a wireless station on Anguar which they wish to use in connection with their Fleet movement. [...] [Australian ships are] not to call at Anguar or to interfere with its present occupation by Japan. This of course is without prejudice to permanent arrangements which will have to be made after the war when we come to settle terms of peace.[95]

Unbeknown to them Greene had informed Grey, also on 21 November, that the Japanese wished to retain Anguar, though would withdraw from Yap as previously agreed.[96] This message came as something of a surprise to the Australians, and, to his credit, the commander of the expedition, Pethebridge, sought clarification by having a direct interview with Japan's representative in the Commonwealth, Consul General Seizaburo Shimizu. During the course of this meeting Seizaburo referred to a statement he had seen in the press referring to the proposed occupation of the Marshall, Caroline and Mariana Islands by Australia, and, from his remarks, Pethebridge came to the conclusion that a 'misunderstanding' existed over the matter.[97] He therefore asked the Defence Department to clarify with the British government exactly what places were to be occupied by his force. The cable was sent on 24 November, a mere two days before Pethebridge was scheduled to embark: 'With reference to your telegram of 13 October regarding Yap please telegraph whether whole group of Caroline, [Mariana], Marshall, and [Palau] Islands except Anguar may be occupied by Australian expedition.'[98] This message crossed with one from Harcourt stating that the expedition 'should not proceed to any islands north of [the] equator'.[99] This volte-face on the part of the British government meant that Pethebridge's instructions issued on 14 November – 'proceed [...] to occupy the islands [...] north of the equator' – were now redundant, and he was accordingly ordered to postpone his departure.[100] The change of plan had also rendered the Australian position somewhat invidious politically, and indeed a full explanation was only vouchsafed to the Australian Premier, William Hughes, in 1916.[101] Naturally enough clarification was sought from London:

> [It had been] had arranged for expedition for occupation of German islands to sail 26 November and troops already embarked. Islands mentioned in my telegram, namely, [Palau], Mariana, Caroline, and Marshall Islands, form part of German New Guinea administrative area which was included in surrender by Governor of New Guinea. Would like early and definite information as to what is now desired. Expedition will not sail pending reply.[102]

The confusion over the issue, the 'misunderstanding' discerned during the meeting between Seizaburo and Pethebridge, was, from the Japanese standpoint, cleared up completely by Foreign Minister Kato on 1 December. On that date he met Greene and passed over a *note verbale* – a formal diplomatic communication.[103] This stated Japan's position clearly:

> All the islands of Germany [...] are in the occupation of forces of [the] Imperial Navy, and [the] Imperial Government desire that none of these

should be visited by Australian expeditions. The island of Yap, can, however, be excepted in view of a previous understanding respecting it, and if His Majesty's Government wish the Japanese forces will withdraw when the British forces reach [the] island.[104]

Although couched in impeccably diplomatic phraseology, this unmistakeably served notice that Japan would not be swiftly giving up any of the territory it had occupied (Yap excluded). That this occupation was to be permanent was made clear in a memorandum accompanying the note. This pointed out that whilst Japan accepted that its occupation of the German territory would be subject to 'final arrangements' arrived at 'when the allies come to settle terms of reference after [...] the war' it would expect the UK to support its claim for 'permanent' retention of the islands at that time. This support was in return for the 'very wide operations' that the Japanese Navy had been, and still was, engaging in, 'in cooperation with the British navy'.[105]

Faced with this stance on the part of Japan there was nothing that the British government could do, and accordingly the reply to the Australian query of 25 November was despatched on 3 December. It too was unequivocal, even if also couched in most diplomatic language:

> [Palau], [Mariana], Caroline, and Marshall Islands are at present in military occupation by Japanese who are at our request engaged in policing waters Northern Pacific, we consider it most convenient for strategic reasons to allow them to remain in occupation for the present, leaving whole question of future to be settled at the end of war. We should be glad therefore if the Australian expedition would confine itself to occupation of German islands south of the equator.[106]

The Japanese were clearly in the driving seat, as it were, in respect of terminating German possession of the various island territories, this being, as a later historian was to put it, 'a price the British Commonwealth had to pay for its inability to maintain a major fleet in the Pacific'.[107] The greatest prize however, and the one that the Japanese prepared for with the most diligence was Kiautschou, where, undoubtedly, 'Germany was engaged night and day in intensive war preparations.'[108]

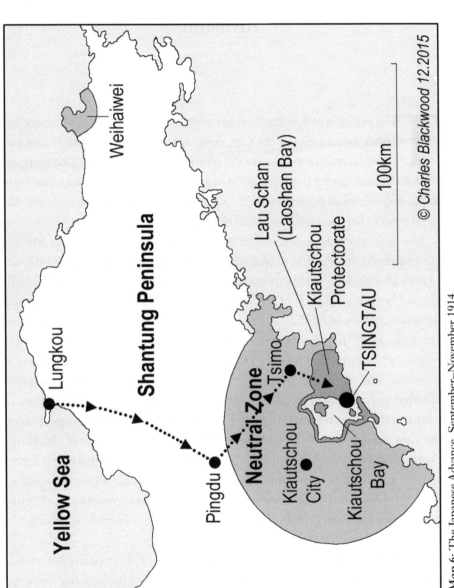

Map 6: The Japanese Advance, September–November 1914.

Chapter 5

Invasion

The position of Kiautschou, in military and naval terms, was hopeless once Japan entered the war; geography and force disparity ensured that German retention of the territory was impossible. The German administration, under the leadership of Governor Meyer-Waldeck had little in the way of resources with which to defend the area from the military and naval power that the Japanese could deploy.

The ultimatum delivered to Germany expired on 23 August, but Meyer-Waldeck had been making preparations for a potential outbreak of hostilities against an unknown enemy or enemy combination for some time previously. He had been kept abreast of the deteriorating situation in Europe following the assassination of Archduke Franz Ferdinand in Sarajevo on 28 June. For example, on 27 July he had been warned, by a message received from his superiors in Berlin, that Austria-Hungary and Serbia had severed diplomatic relations, and that the international situation was tense. He therefore initiated precautionary measures involving the recall of outlying forces in China to the Kiautschou Territory. The principal force in this respect being the East Asiatic Marine Detachment, which, under the terms of the Boxer Protocol of 1901, constituted the German component of the foreign forces stationed in the Chinese capital and at various key points along the route to Beijing.[1] This force, with a nominal strength of four companies of infantry and supporting arms, including artillery, was thus ordered to proceed to Kiautschou from Tientsin and Beijing.[2]

Information on the deteriorating condition of European peace was confirmed on 30 July with the stark news that Austria-Hungary had declared war on Serbia on 28 July. Such an action, it was well known, was likely to involve Russian intervention, which also meant French participation if Germany backed her ally. Clearly the peace of Europe, and perhaps the world, was at grave risk, a fact underlined by German mobilisation and declaration of war against Russia on 1 August. This was followed by a declaration against France two days later. German mobilisation meant that those German citizens in the Far East were now liable for military or naval duty, and so via the various German consuls in the region, Meyer-Waldeck ordered all those liable to bear arms to travel to Kiautschou.[3]

Also making the journey to the territory was an American citizen, Alfred McArthur Brace. Brace, who hailed from Green Bay, Wisconsin, graduated from the class of 1909 at Beloit College in the same state. He took up the post of Instructor in Rhetoric and English Literature at Pomona College, California, serving there during 1910–11; thereafter he seems to have moved to Shanghai, China and taken up journalism. Following the issue of the Japanese ultimatum to Germany, and engaged as 'a special correspondent for Reuters Agency', Brace related how he 'threw a few things into my suitcase [...] and caught the first train for the north to be on hand when the trouble began'.[4]

The defences of the territory were put in a state of readiness, though these, despite earlier reports of the area 'bristling with cannon', were, in reality, not formidable regardless of enduring popular belief to the contrary.[5] The most commanding position within the city limits of Tsingtau was Bismarck Hill, from the 128m summit of which there were wide views over the bay, the coast and surrounding territory.[6] An underground command post had been constructed there from 1899 onwards; a three-storey affair, with a further two storeys in parts, contributing a floor area totalling some 1600m². Constructed by excavation, concrete pouring and backfilling, the post was divided internally into command, storage and accommodation areas. Atop Bismarck Hill, positions were constructed for four 280mm howitzers, mounted in a line west–east, under armoured cupolas. Lower down the promontory to the north–north–west were situated two 210mm guns; the latter were for landward defence whilst the howitzers were designated as coastal defence weapons. The most potent coastal defence installation comprised the three 150mm Skoda and two 240mm Krupp guns that formed the Hui tsch'en Huk Battery, situated on the peninsula separating Iltis and August Viktoria Bays. Mounted in Gruson turrets, these weapons were proof against anything but a direct hit from an enemy heavy shell.[7] There were a total of five coastal defence batteries, with varying degrees of weaponry and types of installation (see Table 1, accompanying Map 7). Sources differ somewhat as to the number and armament of the batteries dedicated to land defence, particularly as these were augmented greatly by extemporised positions once war was declared (see Table 2, accompanying Map 7).

There was also a line of fortifications, known as the 'Boxer Line', which, as the name suggests, was constructed between 1909 and 1913 with the intention of being defensible against an irregular force at least.[8] The extent of the line, from the right flank on the Yellow Sea to the left flank on Kiautschou Bay, was about 6.5km in total. The main strongpoints consisted of five ferro-concrete redoubts, with trenches and dug-outs similarly constructed.

The pumping plant for the town water supply was located on the north bank of the Hai-po Creek, and covered the extreme left of the position. It was a strongpoint with the essential machinery and facilities of the pumping station (engines, pumps, fuel and other stores, as well as quarters for personnel) sited underground in a concrete emplacement. This was further protected by a bank of heaped earth and, being forward of the main ditch, surrounded by an outer ditch some 12m wide, 6m deep at the scarp and 2m at the counterscarp.[9] As with the main ditch, this was filled with barbed-wire entanglements and similar obstacles. The redoubts were garrisoned by 200 men, except 1 and 5, on the shores of the sea and the bay respectively, which had 250 men each. The garrison of the pumping plant was about 40 men and an officer.

The redoubts were for the protection and shelter of the infantry rather than being designed for fighting from within. In other words, the troops had to leave the redoubts and man a loopholed concrete parapet equipped with splinter proof shelters in order to fire on any advancing enemy. To prevent any such force moving easily on the infantry line there was a ditch, some 60m in width, constructed to an unusual 'saw-tooth' design. The sectional arrangement was uncommon inasmuch as there was no scarp as such; the bottom of the ditch sloped away for about half its width until it met what might best be termed an 'intermediate counterscarp' some 5m in height. Forward of this the ditch-bottom sloped away again until it reached the, stone-built, counterscarp proper, which was again about 5m tall. This was plastered and whitewashed so as to allow any infiltrators to be more easily seen by contrast. At the base of the counterscarp was a pathway, something like a Covered Way, some 80cm wide. Since it would not have been possible to utilise it in the traditional manner, then it was probably used by maintenance parties and the like, or conceivably as a Place of Arms.[10] Indeed the Japanese record that they found permanent iron ladders sited at various points. These would have allowed individuals to climb the counterscarp onto the glacis, which sloped away to allow a clear field of fire.[11] There were no arrangements for flanking fire within the ditch, though German heavy machine-gun doctrine of the time, with its emphasis on enfilade firing from concealment, provided a substitute for this. Each of the Infantry Works was equipped with up to ten machine guns of various types. In short, the line was undoubtedly proof against any attack by unsupported infantry and the like, but was vulnerable against an attacker equipped with artillery, particularly of the massed, heavy version.

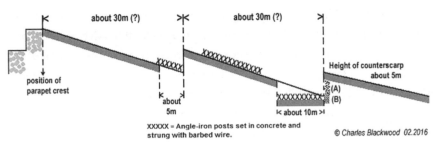

Drawing of a ditch.

Indeed the Boxer Line had severe limitations as regards the repulsing of a regularly constituted attack. Perhaps most evidently it was extremely close to the city of Tsingtau, with the Governor's residence only some 4km distant. This meant that an attacker with artillery could easily bombard, and thus render unusable, the city and port without the necessity of breaching the line.

Siting the main defences further forward to prevent any such situation was the obvious solution, and some 8–10km forward of the Boxer Line was a natural defensive line, the primary position of which, situated on the right flank, was Prinz-Heinrich-Berg. At around 275m, the summit of this dominating height gave a panoramic view of the surrounding terrain. This terrain was difficult to traverse and a number of other prominences provided obviously viable locations for the construction of defensive positions, as well as effectively canalising any advancing enemy. However advancing the main defensive position meant lengthening it as the peninsula broadened, and in order to defend effectively a frontage of some 16km a much larger force would have been required.

Approximately another 10km to the northwest was probably the best natural position for a defensive line given contemporary military technology. Running roughly northwesterly from Laoshan Bay to Litsun (Licun) the terrain was even more rugged, with peaks rising to some 400m in height. There were few decent passes through the range making it ideal defensive country given a sufficient force to defend it, and there was the rub. A force equivalent to corps strength, around 40,000 personnel together with the requisite equipment, would have, some authors have claimed, been required to properly defend this line, running as it did for some 20km, and this was beyond what was feasible both politically and economically.[12]

Maintaining such a force during peacetime would have absorbed vast resources, and the Imperial Navy, during the period of defensive construction around Tsingtau, was desperately short of all kinds of resources, particularly financial ones. Herwig has calculated that between 1897 and 1914 naval building had added 1,040,700,000 marks to the national debt.[13] He describes the financial state of the navy as 'horrendous' and notes that outlay had increased from 17.9 per cent of Imperial expenditure in 1901 to 23.7 per cent in 1908, occasioning the resignation of the State Secretary for the Treasury in the latter year.[14] It is true that the defences of the territory had been paid for by a *Reichstag* grant of 7 million marks made in 1907, only some 2.5 million of which went on the land defences.[15] However the running costs would have to be paid by the navy, and keeping the equivalent of a division, or even a corps strength unit, effectively on standby to defend a far-away territory would have been an unbearable drain on both finances and manpower. The Imperial Navy reconciled means and ends vis-à-vis the defences of Tsingtau with a system that was however difficult to explain logically. According to Burdick, there was an 'unwillingness to do much more than construct fortifications with the Chinese as the practical opponent and a hypothetical, unnamed, foe of little consequence as a possible attacker'.[16]

The 'unnamed foe' when it came to it was of massive consequence, and so it is somewhat ironic to note that on the very day the Japanese ultimatum expired, 23 August, Grand Admiral Tirpitz himself initiated the establishment of a naval unit, for use in the military context, of a size that could have provided an effective defence for Tsingtau. This was the Flanders Marine Division (*Marine Division Flandern*), the initial impetus that led to the creation of which was a telegram from Tirpitz. This arose following discussions between the army and navy over the path that the army was taking through Belgium. Put simply, Tirpitz wanted the capture of the Belgian and northern French ports, most importantly Ostend, before they could be destroyed or damaged by the retreating, and, as he perceived it, beaten enemy forces. Because the army refused to countenance any such diversion, as they saw it, Tirpitz pushed for the creation of a naval force that could protect naval interests, as he, in turn, saw them.

The creation of the Division, later expanded to become a Corps, caused endless friction with the army, who were determined that it should come under their strategic control and who had to find a quantity of personnel and equipment, drawn from the secondary reserve (*Landwehr*), to create, amongst other units, additional infantry, an artillery section and the cavalry component.[17] Tirpitz was successful in his quest for the creation of the force, which was officially formed on 29 August, and the strength of the division in September stood at nearly 17,000 personnel with an artillery component of 12 pieces.[18] In order to find enough manpower Tirpitz had to decommission the Sixth Battle Squadron and reduce the manning of the Fifth Battle Squadron.[19] Commanded by Admiral Ludwig von Schroeder, the unit was responsible for defending the naval bases on the Belgian coast, and to prepare for the implementation of a small-scale naval war (*Kleinkrieg*) against Great Britain using submarines and destroyers. This was of course the exact opposite of the strategy that Tirpitz had advocated for several years. In any event, because of the setbacks occasioned to the German plan to conquer France in six weeks, the division found itself used as a combat unit.[20]

Such retrospective judgements are however totally unfair, and the Imperial Navy had to meet, or not, future foes with the means available to it. That they were insufficient is clear with hindsight, but it was not necessarily so clear to those at the time. Local difficulties might have been expected, as related, with the Chinese, but there were few other powers that could have brought sufficient force to bear such that the Kiautschou defences were completely inadequate. The most obvious was the UK, which maintained relatively large naval forces in the region, and had access to the Indian Army in terms of military power, though this was in reality far distant. Russia too was a potential opponent, even if, since 1905, sorely deprived of naval assets. Russia was the only European power to maintain a substantial military force in East Asia, though again it was a long way from the Kiautschou Territory and would require a major logistical effort to travel to within attacking distance. France had few naval or military assets that could be brought to bear. Moreover when the First World War broke out in Europe none of the European powers could afford to divert substantial forces to a peripheral theatre.

The only potent potential opponents came down to the US or Japan. The US had a powerful, and growing navy, but only small military forces, which had been heavily engaged in the Philippines since 1899 and, according to some scholars, were still fighting there until 1913.[21] There had been occasions when the US and Germany had clashed to one degree or another. The German presence in Manila Bay in 1899, for example, had caused some friction, and, dependent upon which interpretation one chooses to accept, the Venezuelan Debt Crisis of 1902–3 was perhaps very close to resulting in conflict. The conditions for actual conflict never arose however, and the US and Imperial Germany, though mutual suspicion and occasional tension arose from time to time, maintained generally cordial relations throughout the Roosevelt Presidency.

Roosevelt did not stand for re-election in 1909 and his successor, William Howard Taft, was, as his nickname of 'Peaceful Bill' indicated, a less thrusting personality both personally and politically. Best known for 'Dollar Diplomacy', he has been described as sometimes lethargic and often unimaginative.[22] In any event, he exerted presidential power to a much lesser degree than his predecessor and was an avid proponent of arbitration as the most practicable method of settling international disputes. This approach stemmed no doubt from his legal credentials and training, a background that was to see him elevated to the Supreme Court as Chief Justice in 1921.[23]

Taft lost the 1913 election to Woodrow Wilson, thanks largely to Roosevelt splitting the anti-Wilson vote, who was the most highly educated US President with a doctorate gained at Johns Hopkins University.[24] On 19 August 1914 Wilson declared that the US would opt for a state of neutrality in respect of what was becoming a world war.

[…] Every man who really loves America will act and speak in the true spirit of neutrality, which is the spirit of impartiality and fairness and friendliness to all concerned. […] [O]ur duty as the one great nation at peace, the one people holding itself ready to play a part of impartial mediation and speak the counsels of peace and accommodation, not as a partisan, but as a friend. […] The United States must be neutral in fact, as well as in name, during these days that are to try men's souls. We must be impartial in thought, as well as action, must put a curb upon our sentiments, as well as upon every transaction that might be construed as a preference of one party to the struggle before another.[25]

Neither 'Peaceful Bill' nor the 'Scholar-President' were men to get involved in foreign adventures, though neither was backward in enforcing the 'Roosevelt Corollary' on a number of occasions. As with the latter portion of the Roosevelt term of office though, there were no occasions when the foreign policy aspirations of the US and Germany seriously collided. In any event, for the US to engage in operations to take Kiautschou from Germany would have meant an inevitable clash with Japan. The point being that whilst the US might well have had the means, it never had the motive.

The same can be said to apply to Japan, and being geographically closer the deployment of forces necessary to incommode Germany's occupation was that much easier. So whilst Japan always had the means it too lacked a motive, or at least the excuse to put into practice that motive, until the outbreak of war in 1914.[26] Once Japan had the necessary motivation to move on the German territories, the means were readily available. The Japanese maintained a standing army of some nineteen divisions in peacetime, and this was a force that could not be resisted by any level of German defence, for whatever the strength of the those defences, the Japanese could muster superior force.

The first step taken in dispossessing Germany of her 'place in the sun' was the assembling of a naval force, named the Second Squadron, under Vice Admiral Kato Sadakichi to enforce a maritime blockade. Kato had seen action during the Russo-Japanese War as commanding officer of the cruiser *Akitsushima* and his squadron was built around five obsolete vessels captured during the course of that conflict.[27] He flew his flag in *Suwo*, which had originally been the 'Peresviet' class battleship *Pobieda*. A veteran of the Battle of the Yellow Sea, *Pobieda* had been sunk by artillery fire at Port Arthur before being salvaged and re-commissioned into the Japanese Navy. Another combatant from the Yellow Sea battle was *Tango*, originally the 'Petropavlovsk' class battleship *Poltava*, and a vessel also salvaged from Port Arthur. Arguably his most powerful unit, and certainly the most modern, was *Iwami*, constructed as the 'Borodino' class battleship *Orel*. *Orel* had been part of the 1st Division of the 2nd Pacific Squadron and had surrendered on the orders of Rear Admiral Nikolai Nebogatov the day after the Battle of Tsushima, the only modern battleship to survive on the Russian side.[28] Two more survivors of Tsushima, members of the 3rd Pacific Squadron and unfit to fight in 1905, comprised the other heavy units of Kato's command. The *Mishima* and *Okinoshima* were 'Admiral Ushakov' Class coastal battleships commissioned in 1897 and 1899 as *Admiral Senyavin* and *General-Admiral Apraxin* respectively. One more unit of somewhat similar power and vintage, to Kato's better ships at least, was later added to the blockading force in the shape of the 'Swiftsure' class battleship *Triumph*. *Triumph* provided, along with the destroyer *Usk*, the British naval contingent.

Kato also had four armoured cruisers; the British constructed *Chiyoda*, *Tokiwa* and *Iwate*, and the, ironically, German built *Yakumo*.[29] In addition were several old lighter cruisers, including the American constructed protected cruiser *Chitose* and the protected cruiser *Akashi*. Other notable warships were *Takachiho*, constructed in Britain and originally designated a protected cruiser but re-classified as a second-class Coastal Defence Ship in 1912, and his former command, *Akitsushima*, originally considered a light cruiser but similarly re-designated in 1912. One of the few modern vessels in the squadron was the second-class protected cruiser *Tone*. If, apart from the last mentioned, the ships of the Second Squadron were firmly rooted in the past, then an additional vessel could be said to very much represent the future; the seaplane carrier *Wakamiya Maru*, a British-built freighter, captured from Russia in 1905 and commissioned into the Japanese Navy in 1913, carrying four seaplanes.[30]

Against this large, if largely outmoded, force Meyer-Waldeck had little in the way of assets. All the naval units scattered throughout East-Asian waters had been recalled to Tsingtau, but even though the majority successfully complied, the resultant force was very weak. There were four 'Iltis' class gunboats: *Iltis*, *Jaguar*, *Luchs* and *Tiger*. These vessels were not designed or equipped for fighting other ships; the heaviest weapon carried being the two 105mm guns of the latter two.

Of perhaps more utility was the minelayer *Lauting*, which had a capacity of 120 mines, and the Torpedo Boat *S-90*, it being the original of the design that had caused a step-change in the relationship between Torpedo Boats and Torpedo Boat Destroyers, known generally thereafter as just Destroyers. *S-90* was designed to accompany the battle-fleet to sea, and was thus larger and more substantially constructed than previous types. In reply to this danger the Royal Navy had introduced the 'River' class destroyers, which were able to keep the sea in much tougher conditions than their predecessors, the Torpedo Boat Destroyers, and displaced some 560 tonnes as against the *S-90*'s 315 tonnes.[31]

Augmenting this strength, if that is the correct term, was the Austro-Hungarian 'Kaiser Franz Josef I' class Ram-Cruiser *Kaiserin Elizabeth*. Austro-Hungarian Ram-Cruisers, also known as Torpedo-Rams, were envisaged as leading a division of warships, consisting of two light cruisers, two torpedo boat destroyers and twelve torpedo boats, in attacks on enemy battleships and heavy units. The philosophy of utilising torpedo-carrying craft to attack larger vessels came from the French *Jeune École* (Young School). Arising in the 1880s, this school of thought argued that equipping the French Navy with large numbers of torpedo-carrying vessels would nullify the overwhelming preponderance of heavy units in the British Navy. This 'strategy of the weak' was taken up by several lesser naval powers including Austria-Hungary. The British constructed one such vessel, *Polyphemus*, which was not followed up. The 'Kaiser Franz Josef I' class was quite heavily gunned as originally constructed, being armed with two 240mm guns, in turrets fore and aft, and six 150mm broadside guns in casemates, though the primary weapon was, at least initially, envisaged as the five torpedo tubes. The ramming function was, perhaps, a hangover from the Austrian victory over Italy in the 1866 Battle of Lissa. During the engagement the deliberate ramming of the Italian battleship *Re d'Italia* by the Austrian flagship, *Ferdinand Max*, caused the total loss of the former. In 1905–6, *Kaiserin Elisabeth* and her sister ship *Kaiser Franz Josef I* were refitted at Pola Navy Yard, and their 240mm guns, which had proved too heavy for their mountings, replaced with modern 150mm pieces. The casemate-mounted weapons, having proved difficult to work in anything but a calm sea, were moved up to main deck level.[32]

The *Kaiserin Elizabeth*, the only naval unit deployed by Austria-Hungary in East Asia, arrived at Tsingtau on 22 July following orders from the naval command; there being nowhere else friendly to go and, with war imminent, no prospect of making the long journey home.[33] Also present, though unserviceable, were the 'Bussard' class light cruiser *Cormoran*, which had been with Diederichs during the acquisition of the Kiautschou Territory, and the torpedo boat *Taku*, constructed by Germany for the Chinese Navy, but taken following the Boxer War. *Cormoran* had suffered engine failure, which was considered irreparable, and *Taku* had been severely damaged by a collision the previous year. There were three other German warships in the theatre that were unable to obey the order to make for Tsingtau, the purpose-built 'Vaterland' class river gunboats *Vaterland*, *Tsingtau* and *Otter*. Constructed in Germany specifically for service on the Chinese rivers, these vessels were then broken down before reassembly and commissioning in China. They were laid up at various Chinese ports in 1914, though the crews attempted to make the overland journey to Tsingtau and several succeeded.[34]

In order to maximise his defensive position from naval attack, Meyer-Waldeck had ordered mines be laid in the near approaches to the territory. The day before the Japanese ultimatum expired he decided to utilise the rest of the stock around some small groups of islands lying some 15–20km offshore to the southeast, during the course of which operation *Lautung* was covered by the *S-90*.

Unbeknownst to the Germans, units of the British China Squadron were at sea on that day engaged in setting up a patrol line in order to intercept ships attempting to leave Tsingtau before the expiry of the ultimatum. There were four destroyers engaged in this activity during the evening of 22 August, all, coincidentally, of the 'River' class built to counter the threat of the *S-90* Torpedo Boats; the *Colne*, *Jed*, *Kennet* and *Welland*. Seeing the smoke of the German torpedo boat the *Kennet*, which happened to be closest, increased to full speed and moved to engage. The *S-90* became aware of this vessel closing fast, and accordingly turned and made for Tsingtau at her full speed.

The design speed of the *S-90* was 27 knots as against the 25 knots of the *Kennet*. Both vessels were around a decade old however and it would appear that the *Kennet* was in better shape, inasmuch as she was able to close on her smaller opponent. *Kennet* was also the more heavily armed; carrying four 110mm (12-pounder) guns in comparison with the three 77.5mm (4-pounder) weapons of *S-90*, and with her heavier metal was able to open fire first.[35]

Here then, some ten years and 20000km from the arena that they were originally conceived as joining combat in, the torpedo boat and the (torpedo boat) destroyer finally came to blows, though in anything but the circumstances as originally envisaged. It was essentially a stern chase for the British vessel, and one that she would have won eventually given the maximum speed her opponent seemed capable of was just over 20 knots. During the course of the chase the British vessel fired some 300 rounds, and scored no hits, whilst *S-90* replied with 250, and hit *Kennet* several times. Notwithstanding this, what essentially saved *S-90* was some cunning on the part of her commander, who lengthened the distance by forcing *Kennet* to avoid shallow reef water, and, ultimately, the coastal artillery of Hui tsch'en Huk Battery. This began firing on *Kennet* whilst she was still out of range and thus gave warning of what the vessel could expect if she persisted. She did not, and turned away allowing *S-90* to escape; 'So vigorous had been the pursuit that the funnels of the *S-90* gleamed red-hot in the night.'[36] During the course of the engagement the torpedo boat suffered no casualties, whilst three men were killed and six wounded, including her commander, aboard *Kennet*.[37]

With these events in mind no doubt, the next sortie by *Lauting*, carried out the following day, was afforded a more powerful escort consisting of *S-90*, *Jaguar* and *Kaiserin Elizabeth*; the 150mm guns of the latter being seen as powerful enough to discourage the attentions of lighter units. The operation remained unmolested by surface units and passed off successfully, but when the minelayer turned to return to port she was almost overwhelmed by a massive explosion some distance astern. The ship had clearly not hit a mine, weighing only some 580 tonnes she would have been totally destroyed by such an event, and, despite reports that a shard of steel marked with the word 'Portsmouth' was found on her deck after the explosion, indicating the presence of British ordnance, the most likely explanation is that one of her recently laid mines had malfunctioned and exploded.[38] The damaged ship was able to return to port under her own steam, but required two days of repairs in the floating dock before she was fit for service again, though this was somewhat academic as, early in the morning of 27 August, Kato's squadron appeared off the coast.[39]

The Japanese came no closer than about 25km, and requested, by radio, permission for an emissary to approach Tsingtau and land. This was refused; Kato's next action was to proclaim, by radio and in English, a blockade:

> I hereby declare that on the [27 August 1914] the blockade of the whole coastline [...] of the leased territory of Kiautschou is established and will be maintained with the naval force under my command [...] the ships of friendly and neutral powers are given twenty-four hours grace to leave the blockaded area and that all measures authorised by international law [...] will be enforced [...] against all vessels which may attempt to violate the blockade.[40]

The Japanese also landed on and proceeded to occupy two small islands lying offshore, Taikungtao and Tschu tscha tau, upon which they constructed signals posts and navigation lights, and commenced minesweeping operations.

With the announcement of a naval blockade, and the cutting of the undersea cables to Shanghai and Chefoo (Yantai) on 14 and 24 August respectively by the Singapore-based Eastern Extension Australasia & China Telegraph Company (EEA&CTC) Cable Ship *Patrol*, the territory was cut off from maritime and cable communication with the outside world. Radio communication was also interdicted with the network of radio stations constructed in the Pacific territories, Anguar, New Guinea, Nauru, Samoa and Yap, having been, or in imminent danger of being, captured. Communication was possible with the Telefunken station in Shanghai, but either directly or indirectly with Nauen, the powerful station near Berlin that was the core of the network, much more problematical. There was of course still the inland telegraph and the Shantung Railway, though these would come under threat if the Japanese landed military forces.

Despite their inferiority the Germans were able to strike a blow, albeit minor, against the Second Squadron on 31 August with the assistance of the unseasonable weather. A severe storm had blown up the previous day and raged overnight; when the skies cleared somewhat they revealed a Japanese destroyer aground on Lien Tau Island some 10km to the south. The unfortunate vessel was the 'Asakaze' class *Shirotaye*, which had gone, or been driven, onto the island during the night. Other ships were undertaking a salvage attempt, but these were dispersed by the fire of Hui tsch'en Huk Battery thus allowing a foray by *Jaguar*, which was able to destroy the beached warship by gunfire before fleeing back to safety.[41]

The improvement in the weather was temporary, which precluded any further naval action. It also did massive damage to the territory's infrastructure with the swollen watercourses demolishing roads, bridges and several sections of the Shantung Railway. In respect of the latter, nature performed the work that German engineers were preparing to carry out, inasmuch as Meyer-Waldeck had ordered that preparations be made for demolishing several railway bridges. This was in order to prevent the Japanese capturing the railway intact, and, if they landed in the north, using it to facilitate their operations. The weather also benefited the Japanese, in the sense that along with the railway went the telegraph running alongside it. From the beginning of September then Kiautschou was effectively cut off in almost every sense of the word.[42]

Despite the adverse weather, a Japanese military force landed at Lungkou in the north of Shandong Province on 2 September; the vanguard of the augmented Japanese 18th Division commanded by Lieutenant General Kamio Mitsuomi. Kamio was widely experienced, seeing action during the Sino–Japanese War as a staff-officer to 2nd Army. He also served against Russia as a member of Marshal Oyama's staff and then as commander of the 22nd Infantry Brigade during the siege of Port Arthur. He was held to have distinguished himself in the latter position, and awarded the 2nd Class of the Rising Sun and Golden Kite.[43]

He had also been involved in training the Chinese Army during the 1890s, and so had extensive staff and administrative knowledge.[44] The plan followed by Kamio involved the distant landing at Lungkou, which was some 150km away from the objective in a straight line and probably nearer twice that taking into account the terrain. This force would then advance in a roughly west–south–west direction across the Shandong peninsula towards Pingdu, before moving east–south–east to Tsimo (Jimo). From there, only some 8km outside the boundary of the German territory, they would proceed through the natural defence line of the territory, as related above, via the pass that carried the Shantung Railway. This force would thus create a diversion, and provide cover, that would allow for further landings in Laoshan Bay some 30–40km to the east of Tsingtau, scheduled for 18 September. An initial landing at Laoshan was ruled out because it would have been relatively easy for the Germans to interrupt it and it was believed that mines were sown in the bay. This cautious, one might even characterise it as ultra–cautious, approach was to typify the entire course of the Japanese operation.[45]

One complication inherent in landing so far north, in relation to contemporary politics and diplomacy, was that it involved decisively breaching Chinese neutrality. China had 'in accordance with the law of nations' issued a declaration of neutrality on 6 August. The Chinese government of President Yuan Shikai desired two things; that the war be limited to Europe, and, that if any conflict arose in China between the warring nations, the neutrality of China might be respected.[46] In both desiderata China was to be disappointed, inasmuch as the conflict had indeed spread and Japan carried out the invasion against the will of the Chinese government, which found itself too weak to resist. That this deepened the suspicion of Japan and Japanese motives in respect of the US counted for little or nothing.[47]

The landing, carried out in weather that swiftly turned atrocious, was undertaken by components, amounting to some 8,000 personnel, of the 24th Infantry Brigade commanded by Major General Yamada Ryuosi over an open beach. The initial party comprising an infantry battalion, with two machine guns, plus a troop of cavalry from 22nd Cavalry Regiment, landed safely and moved off to establish a defensive perimeter. A company of engineers then landed, and began the task of constructing piers to avoid the need for the following soldiery to wade through waist-deep water when disembarking from the light craft that ferried them from the ships. The worsening weather forced several postponements to the operation so that it was not until 7 September that the full complement of men and horses was landed, as was the Commander in Chief. Yamada had gone ashore on 3 September and urged the necessity of pushing ahead regardless of conditions. He ordered the cavalry to advance well ahead of the infantry and set them the object of entering and securing the town of Pingdu, some 110km distant, by 7 September, living off the country if necessary. The schedule could not be met, and it was on 10 September that the exhausted horsemen, and their equally spent mounts, which had suffered losses of around 30 per cent, finally entered Pingdu. It was, by any standards, no mean feat. Fortunately there were no German forces there to meet them.

Yamada ordered a general advance on 4 September, and the infantry set off in the wake of the cavalry. However, upon coming ashore again on 7 September, Kamio perceived that a pause in operations was necessary in order to try and sort out the several problems, in particular the movement of food supplies to the advancing troops. Not only was there a shortage of transport carts, but the dreadful road conditions engendered by the continuing torrential rain made the roads virtually impassable and the living conditions of the advancing units intolerable. Two days, 9–10 September, were spent on consolidation and repair, and, by coincidence, the weather cleared somewhat on 11 September. It would now be possible to effect repairs to roads without the attempt being washed away, and the various watercourses should became fordable again, though a reduction in levels was not evident in some cases for another two days.

The cavalry at Pingdu had meanwhile pushed forward patrol units to the town of Tsimo, an advance of some 40km, where a small German detachment had been encountered. This unit had swiftly withdrawn leaving the Japanese in tenuous occupation, and a call, which reached cavalry advancing from Pingdu on 13 September, was sent for reinforcements. A further detachment was rapidly despatched followed by the entire regiment, which departed Pingdu the next day on the orders of Yamada. Tsimo was an important goal in the Japanese plan as there were, relatively, good roads from there into the German territory and then on to Tsingtau. Elements of the cavalry force reached Tsimo at noon on 14 September and took measures to secure it against a German counter move. These included sending a detachment to the town of Kiautschou, some 40km to the west and on the route of the Shantung Railway. With the Japanese at Kiautschou on 17 September the railway, and adjacent telegraph, was effectively in their control. Tsingtau was now absolutely cut off by sea and land, and almost so through the ether.[48]

There remained only the air, and both sides had elements of an air component; the Japanese Navy had the *Wakamiya Maru* with its complement of four Maurice Farman floatplanes, whilst the army detachment, initially consisting of three machines, deployed from an improvised airstrip near Tsimo on 21 September.[49] Japanese aviation was, as was the case in every other nation, a recent phenomenon in terms of powered aircraft. Previous interest in aeronautics had centred on the use of balloons for reconnaissance, the first Japanese military balloons were sent aloft in May 1877, and an advanced kite type was designed and constructed in 1900 and successfully used during the Russo–Japanese War. A joint committee, with army, navy and civil input, was created on 30 July 1909 to investigate and research the techniques and equipment associated with ballooning; the Provisional Military Balloon Research Association or PMBRA.

Nominated by the Japanese Army to serve on the PMBRA were two officers with the rank of captain, Tokugawa Yoshitoshi and Hino Kumazo. Both had some experience with aviation. Hino designed and constructed a pusher type monoplane with an 8hp engine that he unsuccessfully, the engine was underpowered, attempted to get off the ground on 18 March 1910. Tokugawa was a member of the balloon establishment during the Russo–Japanese War. Both were sent to Europe in April 1910 to learn to fly at the Blériot Flying School at Étampes, France. Having passed the rudimentary course, they purchased two aeroplanes each and had them shipped to Japan; Tokugawa obtained a Farman III and a Blériot XI-2bis in France whilst Hino purchased one of Hans Grade's machines and a Wright aircraft in Germany.[50]

The first flights of powered aeroplanes in Japan occurred on 19 December 1910 at Yoyogi Park in Tokyo. Tokugawa flew the Farman III, powered by a 50hp Gnome engine, for 3 minutes over a distance of some 3000m at a height of 70m. Hino followed him immediately afterwards in the Grade machine, powered by a 24hp Grade engine, which flew for just over a minute and covered a distance of 1000m at a height of 20m.

A naval member of the PMBRA, Narahara Sanji, started on designing and constructing an aeroplane, with a bamboo airframe and a 25hp engine,

Japanese: Order of Battle, November 1914[1]

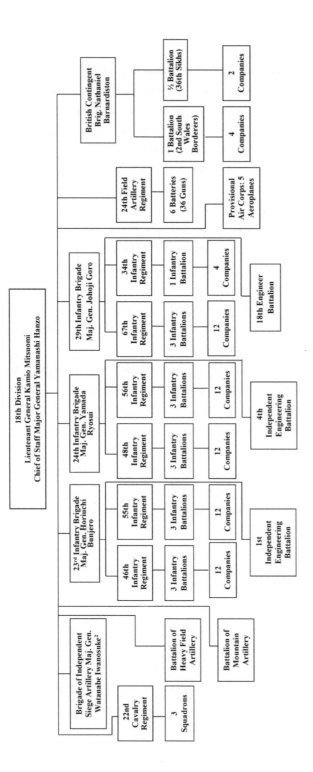

1. Not including non-combat units such as Pioneers, Medical Services etc., or the 'Independent First battalion of Infantry' under Major Kanazawa, which occupied the Shantung Railroad from 25 September 1914.

2. Incorporating: 1st Independent Battalion of Heavy Siege Artillery; 2nd Independent Battalion of Heavy Siege Artillery; 3rd Independent Battalion of Heavy Siege Artillery; 4th Independent Battalion of Heavy Siege Artillery; the Naval Heavy Artillery Corps. Included in this complement were detachments from the Heavy Artillery Regiments that formed the coastal defences around strategic points on the Japanese main islands. These included elements from the Yokosuka Regiment, usually found protecting Tokyo Bay, and the Tadanoumi Regiment from Hiroshima, as well as units that, as a rule, defended Yura and Shimonoseki. Watanabe thus disposed of an immensely powerful unit with over 100 tubes ranging in calibre from 120mm to the 280mm of the coastal artillery pieces.

during March 1910. Because of the low powered engine the machine failed to lift off when this was attempted on 24 October 1910, but with a second machine, the 'Narahara Type 2' powered by a Gnome engine similar to that used in the Farman III, he managed a 60m flight at an altitude of 4m on 5 May 1911. This flight, at Tokorozawa, in Saitama near Tokyo, the site of Japan's first airfield, is considered to be the first Japanese civilian flight as Narahara had left the navy when he made it. It was also the first flight by a Japanese-manufactured aeroplane.[51]

The first military flight by a Japanese-manufactured machine took place on 13 October 1911, when Tokugawa flew in a 'PMBRA Type (Kaisiki) 1' of his own design, based on the Farman III at Tokorozawa. These pioneers, whilst they had made astonishing progress, did not however possess the necessary research and technological resources to take Japanese aviation further.[52] Because of this the Japanese decided to import aviation technology from Europe, though the navy established the Naval Aeronautical Research Committee in 1912 to provide facilities to test and copy foreign aircraft and train Japanese engineers in the necessary skills.[53] Via this system, the foundations of a Japanese aviation industry were being laid; in July 1913 a naval Lieutenant, Nakajima Chikuhei, produced an improved version of the Farman floatplane for naval use. Nakajima Aircraft Industries, founded in 1917 after Nakajima resigned from the navy, went on to massive success.[54]

The French were the world leaders in military aviation, with 260 aircraft in service by 1913, whilst the Russians had 100, Germany 48, the UK 29, Italy 26 and Japan 14. The US deployed 6.[55] It comes as no surprise then to note that during the campaign against Tsingtau all the aeroplanes deployed by both Japanese services were French. Four Maurice-Farman MF7 bi-planes and one Nieuport 6M monoplane formed the Army's Provisional Air Corps, flying eighty-six sorties between them, whilst the navy deployed one Maurice-Farman MF7 floatplane and three Henri-Farman HF7 floatplanes. The navy planes flew 49 sorties and dropped 199 bombs.[56]

A floatplane from the *Wakamiya Maru* flew over Tsingtau on 5 September, causing something of a surprise to the defenders, on a reconnaissance and bombing mission, releasing three bombs that caused no harm. It wasn't the first aerial bombing ever – that had taken place during the 1911–12 Italo-Ottoman War – but it was a total surprise to the defenders. The reconnaissance element of the mission was more useful, being able to ascertain that *Emden* was not in harbour but that there were several other warships present. It was to be the first of several visits by both army and navy aeroplanes, against which the Germans could offer little defence, though the fact that the defenders had their own air 'component' was to result in what was probably (there are other contenders) the first air-to-air combat in history. Indeed, despite the remoteness of the campaign from the main theatre, this was only one of a number of such 'firsts'.

Aviation on the German side was represented by one man and one machine; *Kapitänleutnant* Gunther Plüschow and his Rumpler Taube. Plüschow had served in the East Asiatic Cruiser Squadron, at the time under the command of Vice Admiral Carl Coerper, as a junior officer aboard SMS *Fürst Bismarck* in 1908. Assigned to the Naval Flying Service in autumn 1913, he arrived on 2 January 1914 at Johannisthal Air Field near Berlin to commence pilot training, and, having first taken to the air only two days previously, acquired his licence on 3 February 1914.[57] The Naval Air Service, which had been created in 1912 and divided between aeroplane and airship sections the following year, was, in 1914, something of a misnomer; naval aviation was in a greatly underdeveloped state with sole assets consisting of two Zeppelin airships, four floatplanes and two landplanes.[58] This was largely due to Tirpitz, who, despite his later assertions that, prior to 1914, he saw the aeroplane as the weapon of the future as against the airship, was not prepared to, as he saw it, divert funds from the battle-fleet in order to develop the technologies and techniques required.[59]

Having not seen it for some six years Plüschow arrived in Tsingtau by train on 13 June – an extremely long and undoubtedly tedious journey across the Siberian steppe – whilst two Rumpler Taube aeroplanes with 100hp engines, especially constructed for service in China, travelled by sea arriving in mid-July 1914.[60] The second machine was to be piloted by an army officer assigned to the III Naval Battalion, Lieutenant Friedrich Müllerskowski, and the arrival of the two aviators and their machines took the total 'air force' available in the territory to three men and aircraft. The third aviator was Franz Oster, a former naval officer who had settled in Tsingtau in 1899, but returned to Germany in 1911 and learned to fly. He returned to the territory in 1912, via Ceylon (Sri Lanka) complete with a Rumpler Taube equipped with a 60hp engine. During his sojourn in Ceylon he attempted a flight at Colombo Racecourse in a Blériot Monoplane on 30 December 1911 that ended in near disaster; the machine was wrecked and Oster was hurt. He nevertheless, after having returned to the territory and replaced the engine in his Taube with a 70hp Mercedes unit, made a series of flights from the Tsingtau racecourse, the first being on 9 July 1913.[61]

Plüschow and Müllerskowski took charge of reassembling the two aeroplanes delivered by sea and the former successfully made several flights from the extremely small and dangerous landing ground at the racecourse on 29 July 1914. A further two days were needed to get the second aeroplane constructed, and on the afternoon of 31 July Müllerskowski set off on his first flight. It ended in disaster; after only a few seconds in flight, and from an altitude estimated to be 50m, the machine lost control and plunged over a cliff onto the rocks below. Müllerskowski was seriously, though not mortally, wounded and the Taube completely wrecked.[62]

Whether it was just bad luck or whether there were atmospheric conditions pertaining at the time that made flying problematical we cannot know, but it would seem to have been a combination of the two that afflicted Plüschow on 3 August. Having taken off successfully and flown a reconnaissance mission over the territory, his first 'important' sortie, he was experiencing difficulty in attempting to land when his engine failed and he crash-landed into a small wood. He was unhurt but the Taube was badly damaged and, upon accessing the spare wings and propellers sent out with the aeroplanes, he discovered that the replacement parts had rotted away or suffered moisture-induced damage during the voyage. He was fortunate that the engine, for which replacement parts could only have been extemporised with difficulty, was still serviceable and that there were skilled Chinese craftsmen available; the latter fashioned him a new composite propeller from oak. Despite this device having to be repaired after every flight, having been assembled with ordinary carpenter's glue it exhibited a disconcerting tendency to revert to its component parts under the strain of operational usage, it remained serviceable throughout the rest of the campaign.[63]

Plüschow's machine was out of action until 12 August, but on the 22 August an attempt was made to augment it with Oster's aeroplane; he attempted to lift off from the racecourse in his older craft but stalled and crashed, occasioning damage necessitating several days of repair though remaining unhurt personally. Another attempt was made on 27 August with the same result, though this time the damage was more severe with the aeroplane 'completely destroyed' to such an extent that 'reconstruction was no longer viable'.[64] It seems however that Oster did not concur as the diary entry for 13 October 1914 made by the missionary Carl Joseph Voskamp, records Oster once again, and apparently finally, attempting and failing to take off, and notes that this might be due to unfavourable atmospheric conditions.[65]

Plüschow and his Taube, by default the sole representatives of German aviation, could not of course provide anything much in the way of air defence against the Japanese. Nor could they achieve a great deal in the way of keeping open communications with the world outside the Kiautschou Territory. What was possible though, within the operational capabilities of man and machine, was reconnaissance, and the clearing up somewhat of the weather on 11 September allowed an aerial sortie to take place two days later. Plüschow flew northwestwards to investigate rumours of the Japanese landing and advance, and discovered their forces in some strength at Pingdu; the marching elements of the Japanese force reached Pingdu between 11 and 14 September.[66] He also received his 'baptism of fire' from the infantry, returning with around ten bullet holes in his plane and resolving not to fly below 2000m in future in order to preserve his engine and propeller.[67]

The news that Japanese forces had advanced to Pingdu in strength, despite the difficulties of terrain and weather, was disturbing to Meyer-Waldeck and the garrison; it indicated to them that the advance was progressing assuredly. In actuality it was not, and the difficulties encountered by the advance forced a reappraisal. Elements of the Japanese 23rd Infantry Brigade under Major General Horiuchi Bunjero had followed their compatriots of the 24th Brigade ashore at Lungkou, and these were now toiling along the road towards Pingdu. Because of the difficulties of following this route, and the more men and transport pushed along it then the more impassable it became, utilising it as originally envisaged threatened dislocation to timing as did the weather. The Japanese Plan specified a concentration around Tsimo by 20 September, but the difficulties encountered rendered this problematical. Kamio communicated this to his superiors on 14 September and was instructed next day to halt the landing, re-embark those elements of the 23rd Brigade already ashore onto the troopships and send them around the peninsula so as to effect a landing at Laoshan Bay on 18 September. By dint of prodigious efforts of extemporisation the re-embarkation was achieved in sufficient time for the landing to take place.[68]

Thus far there had been no serious fighting and infantry units of the 24th Brigade had begun reinforcing the cavalry that had reached Tsimo on 14 September; the Japanese Army was only some 8km from the boundary of German territory.

On the morning of 18 September the 3rd Squadron of the 22nd Regiment led by Captain Suida Sakama, nominally comprising 167 personnel, moved out from the town towards Liu Ting (Liuting), a village situated on the Pai-sha River, which delineated the border and was only about 32km from Tsingtau. Some days previously, on 15 September, a mounted German patrol reconnoitring the area had come into contact with Japanese advance parties, resulting in an inconclusive firefight following which the Japanese had withdrawn.[69] The squadron split up into troops as it approached the river, one of which, as it moved towards the village, encountered a forward patrol from V Company of the III Naval Battalion deployed between the village and the riverbank. General firing quickly broke out and continued for some twenty minutes whilst the Japanese attempted to flank the German position.[70] They failed in this because the Germans withdrew in good order, and, despite the length of the engagement and the number of shots fired, there was only one fatality on either side – the Japanese squadron commander and 2nd Lieutenant Gottfried von Riedesel zu Eisenbach, formerly Second Secretary at the German Embassy in Beijing. Though honours were more or less even, it had been the Germans that retreated this time.[71]

Meyer-Waldeck had correctly predicted that one of the routes that the Japanese might profitably advance along was via Tsimo and Liu Ting and had ordered units thrown forward to screen the area. This position was though well in advance of the potential defensive line Laoshan Bay to Licun (Litsun). To attempt a defence of this line, or at least the several passes through the mountains the Governor had some eight companies of infantry; the four companies of the III Naval Battalion as well as the mounted company, and two further companies, VI and VII, formed from reservists and other Germans that had managed to make their way to Kiautschou after mobilisation on 1–2 August. VI Company was formed mainly from the civilians whilst VII Company contained men with greater military experience. There was also the East Asiatic Marine Detachment, which was ordered to the territory at the end of July, and complements of engineers and support troops. In command of the land front was Lieutenant Colonel Friedrich von Kessinger, commander of the III Naval Battalion.[72]

The initial disposition of these forces, prior to the Japanese ultimatum, had been focused on manning and strengthening the Boxer Line. The five infantry works were manned and blockhouses built in the intervals between them, and communication trenches were dug and barbed wire defences laid out from coast to coast. Additional artillery batteries were constructed utilising weapons removed from the warships, and a mobile railway battery of two 88mm guns was fabricated. Some 500 mines were also manufactured from dynamite and planted at various points ahead of the main line.[73] Following the expiration of the ultimatum it was decided to advance elements of the defence further into the territory.[74]

Before the brief action of 18 September had indicated that the route of the Japanese forces advancing from the north would almost certainly be along the line of the Shantung Railway, the possibilities of another landing had exercised the defenders. Given the nature of the terrain along the route from Liu Ting, there would be potential to mount an effective defence able to give them pause at least. However reports of Japanese shipping off Lau Schan (Laoshan) Bay to the west of Kiautschou, and the attendant prospect of a landing there, required a change of emphasis. This was put into effect on 12–13 September when units of the East Asiatic Marine Detachment, together with an artillery battery and supporting components, were shifted to positions in the Lau Schan Mountains.[75]

The Japanese landing, preceded by a bombardment of the area behind the beach, which was unnecessary as it happened, took place at Wang-ko-chuang (Wanggezhuang, Jiaonan) Bay located at the northern end of Lau Schan Bay on 18 September as scheduled. First ashore, after the preliminary parties had secured the beach, were elements of the 23rd Infantry Brigade that had re-embarked at Lungkou some three days previously. There was no resistance and by noon the beachhead had been secured and spearheads thrust out to occupy strategic points. Amongst these was the village of

Wang ko Chuang and the eastern entrance to the Duchess Elizabeth Valley (*Herzogin Elisabeth Tal*) through which the Hotung Pass (*Hotungpaß*) and March Pass (*Marschpaß*) allowed passage through the Laoshan Mountains.[76] The pass – the names were for the eastern and western ends of the same route – traversed extremely rugged terrain and the road, really a glorified footpath, was only wide enough at certain points for two men to stand side by side; it was thus territory eminently suited for defence.[77]

Despite the difficulties of creating strong defensive works in the short period since being deployed there, a platoon of German troops were installed in loopholed trenches awaiting any Japanese attempt to move through the pass.[78] Accordingly when a Japanese infantry company sized unit approached their position, located some 7km from the beachhead, they commenced firing. Using 'fire and movement' techniques the Japanese began to outflank the position and pin down the defenders in turn. This process lasted some three hours, from, approximately, 15:00–18:00hr, before, fearing that total darkness would prevent their pressing on with the attack, the Japanese stormed the position without regard to caution. They captured the strongpoint with no loss; the Germans had taken advantage of the deterioration in visibility to abandon their position. It was a significant victory in that it secured the pass for the Japanese, meaning that the beachhead was not now liable to a counterstroke. There was further good news for the Japanese when another company sent in the direction of Tsimo, in order to establish communication with the forces there, swiftly came into contact with a Japanese cavalry squadron sent in the opposite direction for a similar purpose. With the link up of the two portions of the invading forces, albeit tenuous at first, the Kiautschou Territory was surrounded by sea and land.[79]

During the night of 18–19 September the German platoon retraced their steps back up the pass and harassed the Japanese with rifle fire, but made no serious attempt to retake the positions that they had abandoned, before retiring to the *Mecklenburghaus*, a spa and sanatorium some 7km along the pass.[80] Determined that there should be no repetition of this annoyance, the Japanese company advanced, reaching the *Mecklenburghaus* at about 17:30hr on 19 September, and began attacking the establishment, which comprised a number of buildings. As in the engagement the previous day the Germans withdrew before the enemy could come to close quarters with them, but not before firing the complex. As they retreated along the pass a 12m bridge crossing a ravine was blown behind them in an attempt to impede Japanese exploitation. This action, resulting in only two wounded on the Japanese side, was the only significant exploit of the day, as, having successfully landed all the planned units, a period of consolidation was specified by Kamio, who had reached Tsimo the same day.[81] This consolidation involved the construction of landing piers at Wang-ko-chuang Bay to facilitate the landing of further personnel and equipment, and the construction of an airfield near Tsimo for the, eventual, five-aircraft complement of the Provisional Air Corps, which became operational on 21 September.[82]

The German response to the invasion was necessarily muted; they established a lookout position on Prinz-Heinrich-Berg on 22 September and next day mounted a spoiling attack on a Japanese position in the Kletter Pass (*Kletterpaß*) that dislodged the defenders but was not pursued.[83] Otherwise they largely drew back from the borders of the territory to the line flanked on the right by Prinz-Heinrich-Berg. This meant abandoning attempts to defend the eastern passes through the Laoshan Mountains; a decision of little consequence as Kamio did not intend to use them as the primary routes for his concentration.

Indeed the Japanese had established divisional headquarters at Liu Ting and were building up men and supplies around that position ready for a forward move towards Litsun. In order to reach this point the troops and equipment had to travel some 21km from the landing area to Tsimo and then a further 14km to Liu Ting. In order to facilitate this movement, particularly in relation to materiel, the construction of a Decauville Railway was undertaken.[84] The line was not used with locomotives; rather Chinese labourers manhandled the railway cars along the track. The track sections hooked together as they were laid, requiring only a relatively smooth track-bed that needed the minimum of preparation. A round trip from the beachhead to the main supply depot, soon to be located in a dry creek of the Litsun River, took four days.[85]

The Japanese were also joined by an Allied contingent despatched by the British. This unit, the 2nd Battalion, South Wales Borderers under Lieutenant Colonel Hugh Gilbert Casson, was the direct counterpart of the German East Asiatic Marine Detachment, having comprised the British contingent at Tientsin under the terms of the Boxer Protocol of 1901.[86] They travelled by sea, in order to avoid disputes with the Chinese government over neutrality, embarking at Tientsin on 19 September and proceeding via Weihaiwei where they took on stores. Escorted by *Triumph* and *Usk*, they arrived at the landing ground on 22 September and made arrangements to debark the following day. In command of the British contingent, which was due to be reinforced by half of the 36th Sikh Battalion under Lieutenant Colonel Edward Langford Sullivan, was Brigadier Nathaniel Barnardiston. Barnardiston, who had graduated from Staff College in 1888, had extensive experience in military diplomatic matters; he had occupied the post of Military Attaché at various European capitals and so was suited for conducting coalition warfare in a subordinate position.[87] That the British force was subsidiary to the Japanese, and not an independent command, had been made clear in August when the inclusion of a British military component had been decided; 'British troops are only engaged to show that England [*sic*] is cooperating with Japan in this enterprise.'[88] Accordingly Barnardiston became the first British military officer to serve under an Asian in a field command.

Upon landing, Barnardiston, obviously not cognisant with Kamio's planning and perhaps still retaining some thoughts of independence, sent an officer to reconnoitre the passes through the Laoshan Mountains. His rationale being that the British would operate on the left of the Japanese with their line of communication through the mountains to the beachhead. He was swiftly apprised of the difficulties: 'One of these roads was found to be quite unsuitable and the other only possible with a complete re-organisation of the transport, using pack mules or coolies over the worst parts of the Pass, and man-handling such carts as were necessary for use on the further side.'[89] His difficulties in this regard were alleviated when he learned on 25 September that his force was required to march, via Tsimo and Liu Ting, towards Litsun and take up a position in the centre of the line. He also learned that Kamio planned to advance on 26–7 September with a view to attacking and taking the German advanced line on 29–30 September. This would enable the Japanese siege train to be brought up in order to reduce the Boxer Line fortifications.[90] The South Wales Borderers thus joined the rest of the debarked Japanese force in footslogging the *c.* 35km from the beachhead to Liu Ting along the only available, and extremely poor, track; it took two days to make the journey on foot.[91]

By the time the British arrived at Liu Ting on 27 September, Kamio had departed on his move to Litsun. The movement had begun on 26 September with the 18th Division crossing the Pai-sha River in force, deploying four infantry regiments, the 46th and 55th (23rd Infantry Brigade) and the 56th and 48th (24th Infantry Brigade), arranged from east to west respectively. The 22nd Cavalry Regiment was on the right flank operating with 24th Infantry Brigade, whilst 24th Field Artillery Regiment provided fire support to the movement.[92]

The German forces could do little to stop them, though as they advanced two naval vessels, *S-90* and *Jaguar*, moved into Kiautschou Bay and steamed northwards in order to project enfilade fire onto the advance with their three 77.5mm and two 105mm guns respectively. To this was added that of the few field weapons possessed by the defenders, who were constantly worried that if they stood and fought the Japanese would fix them and then outflank them, particularly during the night. The Japanese progressed cautiously though steadily and by nightfall had covered some 8–10km, bringing the centre within 2–3km of Litsun. Several confused, but inconsequential, actions occurred through the night, leaving the 18th Division ready to resume its manoeuvres on the morning of 27 September. Meanwhile the defenders had begun destroying installations prior to pulling back, the main item in this regard being the Litsun pumping station, which, utilising the nearby river, provided Tsingtau with its primary water supply.[93]

When the advance resumed properly at first light on 27 September – some Japanese elements had started during darkness only to have to halt after becoming entangled with other units – the attackers discovered that the naval gunfire on their right flank had been significantly augmented. The Austro-Hungarian *Kaiserin Elisabeth*, despite having had several of her 150mm guns removed for land use on 24 August, had joined the two German vessels.[94] Her six remaining 150mm guns made a powerful reinforcement, and the Japanese took steps to mitigate the menace that these floating batteries presented. The first attempts were revolutionary; three aircraft of the Provisional Air Corps went after them with bombs extemporised from artillery shells, thus carrying out the first ever air–sea attacks. Revolutionary they may have been, and persistent they certainly were, but they were also unsuccessful. Kamio thus directed one of the field batteries to target the ships but they had no more success.[95] Ominously for the defenders the first elements of the Japanese siege train, under Major General Watanabe, began to appear on the battlefield following its initial landing on 23 September.

In a similar manner to their previous day's endeavours, the Japanese advance was unspectacular though certain, and likewise the defenders were only able to make limited counters through their fear of being overwhelmed by superior numbers. One advantage accruing to the defenders was that as the fighting moved closer to Tsingtau they would come within range of the fortress artillery mounted there. They also, in the observation post atop Prinz-Heinrich-Berg, had a superlative view of the battlefield. This meant they would be able to punish any large formations of Japanese, and, given that the attackers were advancing down a narrowing peninsula, then it might be reckoned that a degree of bunching was unavoidable. The Japanese answer to this potential difficulty was to take the observation post, which, in their hands, would also provide an outstanding view of Tsingtau and the defences. Accordingly Kamio made its capture a priority and a reinforced company from the unit on the left of the German line, the 46th Infantry Brigade, together with a section from the 18th Engineer Battalion, was tasked with accomplishing this.[96]

The peak, which could only be reached after a 'long, arduous climb', was accessible by at least two paths, and, astonishingly, these do not appear to have been guarded judging by the surprise occasioned to the observers by the appearance of the attackers on the morning of 28 September.[97] The struggle for control of the post lasted several hours, the matter being settled by the appearance of attackers using the second path and appearing in the rear of the defenders. By noon, and at a cost of twenty-four men, the Japanese had taken the position and captured most of the German personnel manning it.[98]

Japanese operations throughout 28 September involved consolidation and preparation as well as forward movement, which the Germans attempted to disrupt with artillery fire from their field ordnance. It might have been the presence of the first elements of 24th Artillery Brigade, which would eventually total more than 100 tubes varying in calibre from 120mm to

280mm, that made itself felt with withering counter battery fire that quickly silenced the German guns. In any event, this fire was greatly aided by the newly captured observation post on Prinz-Heinrich-Berg, which superseded to some extent the aircraft of the Provisional Air Corps in carrying out the necessary reconnaissance. The anti-ship artillery had also been reinforced, and this proceeded to direct heavy fire at *S-90*, *Jaguar* and *Kaiserin Elisabeth* when they made their appearances, at around 07:30hr. In this instance however the ships got the better of the engagement, silencing the Japanese batteries by about 09:30hr. Despite this small victory the advance continued as previously, slowly but remorselessly, with the infantry making full use of the cover provided by the terrain. As they progressed the fortress artillery started to come into play, and both the Upper Iltis Hill and Bismarck Hill batteries fired their first shots at around 09:00–09:30hr.[99]

The Japanese were now encroaching upon the line dominated by Prinz-Heinrich-Berg, some 8–10km forward of the Boxer Line, and for the first time called in naval gunfire in support. Offshore four battleships, *Suwo*, *Tango*, *Iwami* and *Triumph*, ran in at about 09:00hr and, with the cruiser *Tone* spotting, fired on the defences. These vessels between them deployed 8 × 305mm (*Tango* and *Iwami*) and 8 × 254mm guns (*Suwo* and *Triumph*) in respect of their main armament; a significant addition to the artillery already deployed ashore. The bombarding division made 2 runs, firing in total some 148 heavy shells. Opposed by the coastal artillery battery at Hui tsch'en Huk, which fired with increasing accuracy as the engagement progressed, the vessels withdrew at around 10:00hr.[100] Plüschow records that the bombardment, though impressive, did not cause much damage and that he saw to it that his aeroplane was moved into a less exposed position on the racecourse.[101]

A more significant naval operation took place at Schatsykou (Shazikou) Bay when a landing force from the armoured cruisers *Tokiwa* and *Yakumo*, took possession of the area – it had been evacuated the day previously after the German detachment there had become isolated by the advancing Japanese.[102] The bay was significant in that it offered a more direct line of communication than the Wang-ko-chuang–Litsun route.[103]

The German response to the advancing Japanese was as on previous days; they fought briefly then retreated. Indeed this was the day when they moved back within the Boxer Line – the order to do so being issued at 11:00hr and the movement completed by mid-afternoon.[104] This then was their final position – they could not retreat any further and would have to fight or surrender. That they would engage in the former was certain, but that the latter was just as certain was acknowledged that evening by the scuttling of three of the disarmed gunboats – their weaponry had gone to the land defences – blockaded in the harbour; *Cormoran*, *Iltis* and *Luchs*.[105]

Since the first serious firefight on 18 September the Japanese had advanced in force some 32km whilst the attempts to impede them had been, of necessity, somewhat feeble. The Japanese operations had gone exactly to plan in terms of time, though had necessitated some logistical modification, as per the recall of the troops landed at Lungkou and their amphibious redeployment to Wang-ko-chuang. The Japanese rear had been secured by the seizure of the Shantung Railway by the 'Independent First battalion of Infantry' on 25 September, and the observation post atop Prinz-Heinrich-Berg was in their hands. On the same day a squadron of 22nd Cavalry Regiment took occupation of Kiautschou town, some 10km north of the northern shore of Kiautschou Bay and 40km west of Tsimo. This effectively prevented any communication with Tsingtau across the bay, and, in any event, the cavalry were now of less utility than previously. Having eschewed any attempt at storming the defences, the next operation undertaken by Kamio and the 18th Division involved conducting a formal investment, an undertaking the Japanese Army had recent, and salutary, experience in. Indeed the Japanese had planned on conducting formal, Port Arthur style siege operations from the start, and had accordingly formed a specialised bombardment unit under the command of Major General Watanabe Iwanosuke. Watanabe, an artillery expert, had formulated his requirements in Tokyo between 24 August and 10 September, and these were substantial. As well as two regiments of heavy artillery (the 2nd and 3rd Regiments), there were four 'Independent Battalions of Heavy Siege Artillery' and an 'Independent Battery of Heavy Siege Artillery', as well as a 'Naval Heavy Artillery Corps' to augment Kamio's force. In addition, the C-in-C had two independent battalions of engineers under his hand as well. He would now utilise these assets in a formal investment of his target.

Chapter 6

The East Asiatic Cruiser Squadron: 'A Secret Departure into the Pacific'

Because they were unsure of the whereabouts of Spee and his squadron, Kato's command initially included three modern heavy units: the battleships *Settsu* (1912) and *Kawachi* (1912) and the 'Semi-Dreadnought' *Satsuma* (1910). These were detached when it was ascertained that the East Asiatic Cruiser Squadron was not in the vicinity. It was impossible to tell, unless and until further information was forthcoming, where it might have gone. What it might try to accomplish was understood with more certainty.

The role of the Cruiser Squadron in the event of Germany becoming involved in a conflict with another power was, primarily, to conduct a *guerre de course* (a sea-war that was directed against an enemy's commerce) as well as to effect the possible destruction of the depots and bases. Operations against various enemies had of course been contemplated, which included the UK; in which case Asian and Australasian merchant trade would be the target. Indeed in 1905 the guidelines for operations in the Pacific had focused particularly on British trade, stressing the following:

Damaging of British trade was the main goal of all operations. A secret departure into the Pacific would require the enemy to search and thereby divide his forces, creating an opportunity for success against the parts.

By creating uncertainty on the main trading routes, a temporary cessation of British shipping in Asia could be achieved.

If conditions were favourable, an immediate attack on enemy warships could be considered, in order to cripple British trade and to achieve superiority at sea.[1]

There was a secondary, though equally important, objective. For even if the particular strategy of forcing the British to negotiate through the creation of economic disruption, and concomitant social unrest, proved a failure, then the campaign might still have the effect of weakening the Royal Navy in home waters. This would be achieved by necessitating the despatch of considerable forces to protect shipping from, and hunt down, the German raiders.[2]

How that might have worked out is unknowable, but it is certainly the case that German strength in the Far East was significant. The original East Asiatic Cruiser Division had been augmented over time as newer and more powerful vessels were constructed. These included vessels of the 'Victoria Luise' class such as the protected cruiser SMS *Hertha* – armed with 2 × 210mm and 8 × 150mm guns, and with a top speed of 19 knots – that were intended for colonial service from their inception. The vessel relieved *Kaiser* in June 1899 and became the flagship of Vice Admiral Felix von Bendemann, who replaced Prince Heinrich of Prussia in February the following year. Bendemann and *Hertha* took part in operations against the Taku Forts during the Boxer War, for which he received the Order of the Rising Sun from the Mikado.[3] An even more powerful vessel became squadron flagship in 1903 in the shape of Germany's first Armoured Cruiser *Fürst Bismarck* – name ship and sole example of her class, with 4 × 240mm and 12 × 150mm weapons this vessel constituted a great leap in capability. Combined with two 'Victoria Luise' class ships, *Hertha* and *Hansa* and the older *Kaiserin Augusta*, the strength of what was now dubbed the East Asiatic Cruiser Squadron was thus steadily increased.

The potency of the squadron, as well as the need to concentrate heavy units in North European waters, were recognised by Sir John Fisher. Upon his assumption of the position of First Sea Lord in October 1904 he reorganised the way the Royal Navy was deployed by recalling from overseas stations those vessels he designated as being too old to fight and too slow to run away. His argument was cogent: 'The known intentions of our possible enemies quite preclude the hope that the ill armed unprotected second and third class cruisers, which have recently been removed from the fighting fleet, would have been of any real service as commerce protectors.'[4] The replacements for these vessels, and for the battleships of the China Station, which he also recalled – following the conclusion of the Anglo-Japanese Alliance there was little justification for keeping battleships in the area – were to consist of armoured cruisers, though following Japan's defeat of Russia this programme slipped somewhat.[5]

That the East Asiatic Cruiser Squadron was a force capable of carrying out effective commerce warfare and raiding was obvious to any observer, though how it might approach this task and what its contingency plans were was less so. All military and naval planners in every state conceive of plans to be carried out in various eventualities. The naval planners of Imperial Germany were no different in this regard and accordingly drew up plans for carrying out naval operations against several powers in the region, which were updated as circumstances dictated. German naval planning also took into account the holistic nature of maritime warfare, inasmuch as the squadron in the Pacific could have an effect on operations in the Atlantic simply by remaining in being and thus threatening. Such matters had been exemplified, though in reverse as it were, on 7 July 1898 when, during the Spanish-American War, Rear Admiral Manuel de la Cámara y Libermoore's Philippine Relief Expedition had been recalled from its voyage to the Pacific because of the dangers of US naval operations against Spain in the Atlantic.[6] As has been argued previously though, such a strategy was largely ineffective against the Royal Navy because of its superiority in ship numbers, which of course was not the case with the Spanish Navy in 1898.

There were however echoes of certain aspects of the Spanish-American conflict in a 1903 plan to be put into practice in the event of war with the US. This was War Case A, which was not, contemporaneously, as ludicrous, in at least some of its proposals, as it might appear to later generations. Bentemann's successor Curt von Prittwitz und Gaffron, who had taken over command in 1902, envisaged his squadron engaging in attacks on not only US merchant shipping, but also naval bases and population centres on the US west coast. Given the panic and political furore caused on the east coast by the possible depredations of a Spanish squadron under Pascual Cervera y Topete, which sailed from the Cape Verde Islands across the Atlantic to defend Cuba against US attack in 1898, whereby a 'deafening clamour' had forced the US Navy to divide its fleet, such strategy apparently had much to commend it.[7]

However attacks on the American western seaboard were not envisaged as an end in themselves, but rather auxiliary to a larger operation whereby the main body of the German fleet would cross the Atlantic and engage in decisive battle with the US Navy in the Caribbean. This would be followed by a landing on, and occupation of, Long Island with a resulting threat to New York from the west end of this island. The attitude of the British was ignored in this appreciation, which seems a strange omission given that any German expedition could not travel anywhere without the acquiescence of the Royal Navy. This lacuna was acknowledged some three years later when it was stated that such an operation could only be mounted if the UK was an allied state; a somewhat remote contingency at the time. This fact was recognised when Vice Admiral Wilhelm Buchsel of the German Admiralty Staff had the plan downgraded to the level of a theoretical exercise.[8]

In purely naval terms German strength in East Asia and the Pacific underwent another accretion in strength in 1909 when the 'Scharnhorst' class Armoured Cruiser *Scharnhorst* replaced *Fürst Bismarck* as squadron flagship. The new flagship set out on 1 April flying the flag of Vice Admiral Freidrich von Ingenohl, the new commander, and crossed paths with the outgoing commander, Vice Admiral Carl Coerper, and his flagship at Colombo. Ingenohl, later to be a commander of the High Seas Fleet, arrived at Tsingtau on 29 April and remained in command until June the following year when Vice Admiral Erich Gühler relieved him. Gühler, having been a Marine Attaché at Tokyo, had some familiarity with the region, however he had only been some six months in the position when he contracted typhus, perishing from the disease on 21 January 1911.[9] Vice Admiral Günther von Krosigk took over and remained in the position until being in turn relieved by the most famous, and last, of the holders of the post, Vice Admiral Maximilian Graf von Spee, in December 1912.

During Krosigk's tenure there had been another significant increment in the power of the squadron when the sister ship to *Scharnhorst*, SMS *Gneisenau*, had been assigned, joining the force in March 1911. On 21 June 1911 Krosigk had reported to his superiors in Berlin that, in order to maximise the effectiveness of the force under his command, it should show itself on the most frequented Australasian trade routes. Thereafter, and in the event of a conflict, the knowledge of its general presence combined with ignorance as to its exact whereabouts would maximise its disruptive power in respect of commerce.[10] This concept was in accordance with Mahan's notion of the sea as '[…] a wide common, over which men may pass in all directions, but on which some well-worn paths show that controlling reasons have led them to choose certain lines of travel rather than others […]'.[11] The strategy was essentially sound, but would be in danger of being undermined if naval units equal or superior to the attacking force were to be encountered along those 'well-worn paths'.

Such undermining took place in 1913 however upon the arrival of HMAS *Australia*, which formed a formidable focal point for the Australian fleet. Indeed the presence of this single vessel completely altered the strategic options of the German Squadron, which would now have to make avoidance of an encounter with it a primary consideration.[12] The vessel was, as Spee put it, 'in itself an adversary so much stronger than our squadron that we should be bound to avoid it'.[13] Had the original intention of keeping the battlecruiser *New Zealand* in East Asian waters not been departed from in 1912–13, then the difficulties facing the German Squadron would have been greatly increased. In any event, and even without this adversary, Australia and New Zealand, and their trade routes, were no longer the easy targets that had previously been envisaged.

This would have been particularly so had the mercantile convoy system been introduced, though the difficulties and delays the British, in particular, had with respect to introducing convoys for merchant shipping during the First World War are well known. This was despite historical precedent; in 1798 an Act, the Compulsory Convoy Act, was passed that gave the Admiralty the power to enforce convoy on all ocean-going ships. According to Mahan's analysis of the system in the Indian Ocean, 'under this systematic care the losses by capture amounted to […] less than those by the dangers of the sea'. He went on to point out that those who neglected to adopt the system faced 'disaster' and that the convoy system 'warrants the inference that, when properly systemised and applied, it will have more success as a defensive measure than hunting for individual marauders'.[14] Perhaps the British Admiralty had not read Mahan. Nor it seems had they read the work of one of their own, for in 1907 Admiral Sir Cyprian Bridge published a short work, in which he stated: 'the strategy of commerce defence will be found in practice to be necessarily based on the convoy method, or the cruising method, or a combination of the two'. The cruising method being 'the keeping of so many cruisers on or about the trade-routes that an intending assailant is more likely to be encountered by one or more of them than to pick up prizes'. If the 'cruising method' was impractical due to the volume of warships required, then the lesson of the trooping convoys was surely to hand as these were never despatched except with a powerful escort and usually in convoy.[15]

Nevertheless despite the new factor of the RAN, the East Asiatic Cruiser Squadron constituted a force far too large and powerful to be treated lightly by any enemy if a conflict arose, though it would be immeasurably weakened if it were to lose the use of its 'solid outpost' of national territory, Tsingtau. Given that this was the only base proper in the entire Pacific that the squadron possessed, there being only minimally equipped anchorages and depots scattered throughout the rest of Germany's Pacific territories, it was indispensable for the pursuance of an effective *guerre de course* in the region. Without this base, the only first-class base outside of Germany, or alternatives, the squadron was, to use Churchill's later phrase, 'a cut flower in a vase, fair to see and yet bound to die'.[16] This was acknowledged in a post-war German assessment of the naval situation: 'keeping warships abroad has proved to be a mistake in the absence of secure bases. They are bound to be inferior in number and power at all times.'[17]

When warnings of a possible outbreak of hostilities between Germany and Austria-Hungary on the one hand, and Russia, France and, possibly, the UK on the other were broadcast to the region during July 1914, Spee's command was not concentrated. The commander, together with his most powerful units, the armoured cruisers *Scharnhorst* (Flag) and *Gneisenau*, had been visiting the Japanese port city of Nagasaki, and on 28 June, in company with their collier *Titania*, they departed on a pre-arranged cruise through the German Islands. It was intended that this voyage would last some four months, by which time they should have returned to Tsingtau, where, in the meantime, Captain Karl von Müller of the *Emden* had become the senior naval officer. Spee was at Truk (Chuuk) in the Carolines on 7 July when he received news of the tense political situation pertaining in Europe following the assassination, on 28 June, of Franz Ferdinand and his wife. On 11 July he was advised that the UK would 'probably' be an opponent if it should lead to a general war.[18]

He sailed for Ponape (Pohnpei) in the Caroline Islands on 15 July and reached there two days later, whereupon he sent orders for the various small, weak and obsolescent vessels in the Far East (the Gunboats *Iltis*, *Jaguar*, *Tiger* and *Luchs*; the River Gunboats *Vaterland* and *Otter* (at Nanking) and *Tsingtau* (at Canton); and the Torpedo Boat *S-90*) to concentrate at Tsingtau. The more powerful, modern units, the *Nürnberg*, a 'Königsberg' class light cruiser, and *Leipzig*, of the 'Bremen' class, were to join him where he was, as was the *Emden*. Whilst awaiting developments at Pohnpei he received news of the rupture in relations between Serbia and Austria-Hungary, and eventually, on 1 August, the official 'Warning of War' in respect of the UK, France and Russia. This message was passed on via radio to the German Islands, and those German vessels at large; various merchantmen and the *Geier*, *Planet* and *Komet*, which were in southern waters. Over the next five days the squadron was to learn of the outbreak of war with Russia, France and, last and most fatefully of all, the UK.

Meanwhile, *Emden* had sailed from Tsingtau on 31 July to join Spee, and, having been informed of war with France and Russia on 2 August, promptly captured the Russian merchant vessel *Ryazan* on 4 August.[19] On 6 August, following the arrival of *Nürnberg*, the squadron left for Pagan Island in the Northern Marianas, arriving 11 August, where it was joined the next day by *Emden* and the auxiliary cruisers *Yorck* and *Prinz Eitel Friedrich*. A number of supply vessels and colliers also reached the rendezvous over the next few days.

Spee had been pondering his options, as his War Diary, which survived, demonstrates:

In case of war [...] against France, Russia, and England, without complication with Japan, war upon commerce *is* possible so long as the coal supply holds out. But – in view of the fact that it is probably intended to bring up the Australian warships – it is only possible for a short time.

If Japan imposes conditions in order to avoid the moral obligation of translating into action her alliance with England, this would render impossible the plan of carrying on a cruiser-war in the waters of East Asia. For this event, therefore, I propose to follow a similar course of action to that in a war in which Japan is a direct opponent; for which [...] a withdrawal from East Asia is already intended.

In the case of war [...] against England, if Japan imposes conditions, the cruiser squadron had best go with the main body to the west coast of America, because the coal supply is surest in that region, and the squadron can probably hold out longest there. To stay in the Indian Ocean, with coal supply from the Dutch Indies, is on the other hand much too uncertain.[20]

Spee's analysis demonstrates that the creation of the RAN, and particularly the commissioning of HMAS *Australia*, meant that Germany's strategic options in the Far East, as expressed in the various plans for waging a *guerre de course*, were now severely circumscribed. This lends weight to Billy Hughes' later justification of the navy: 'But for the Navy, the great cities of Australia would have been reduced to ruins, coastwise shipping sunk, and communications with the outside world cut off.'[21] Though Hughes was no doubt indulging in hyperbole, his remarks nevertheless encompass a great truth.

The entry of Japan into the conflict, even if only conditionally, was adjudged by Spee to completely negate any chance of carrying out a cruiser campaign, and, from the tone of his analysis, it was an eventuality he deemed likely. This was made explicit during a conference held by Spee with his captains on 13 August, an account of which was later set down by Karl von Müller:

The Commander in Chief drew attention to the threatening attitude of Japan, and to the advantage of maintaining the squadron together and concealing its whereabouts as long as possible, thereby holding a large number of enemy ships. He had decided to take the squadron to the west coast of America. When we commanding officers were asked for our opinion, I said I was afraid that the squadron would be able to do practically nothing during a long cruise in the Pacific, and questioned whether so much value should be attached to the 'fleet in being' theory.

Alfred Meyer-Waldeck. As governor of the Kiautschou Protectorate from 1911, he commanded the German forces until forced to capitulate on 7 November 1914. (*Author's Collection*)

German and Chinese personnel posing at the stern of a torpedo boat in the floating dock. (*Author's Collection*)

Members of SMS *Scharnhorst*'s crew pose for a group photograph. (*Author's Collection*)

A Scharnhorst class armoured cruiser, the 150-ton crane and an Iltis class gunboat. (*Author's Collection*)

S.M.S. "ILTIS"

SMS *Iltis*. The lead ship of the six Iltis class gunboats built for the German Imperial Navy in the late 1890s and early 1900s.

Pre-war manoeuvres. Members of the 3rd Naval Battalion move a heavy machine gun through the rough terrain around Tsingtau. (*Author's Collection*)

Prince Heinrich of Prussia at the head of the 3rd Naval Battalion complete with band. (*Author's Collection*)

An unknown seaman from the gunboat
SMS *Tiger*. (*Author's Collection*)

Arkona Island and lighthouse with Tsingtau in the background. To the Chinese the isle had been
Green Island (Tsing Tau), which the Germans took for the name of the town. (*Author's Collection*)

SMS *Fürst Bismarck*, Germany's first armoured cruiser, was flagship of the East Asiatic Cruiser Squadron from 1900–9. She was replaced by the more powerful *Scharnhorst*. (*Author's Collection*)

A Scharnhorst class armoured cruiser. Built for overseas service, *Scharnhorst* and *Gneisenau* were assigned to the East Asia Squadron in 1909 and 1910 respectively.

German sailors posing with some of the local inhabitants. (*Author's Collection*)

A birds-eye view of Tsingtau from the signal station. (*Author's Collection*)

A view of the floating dock with three vessels inside. The two outer ones appear to be the *Taku* (left) and *S-90*. (*Author's Collection*)

SMS *Taku* alongside *Scharnhorst* or *Gneisenau*. (*Author's Collection*)

Kapitanleutnant Gunther Pluschow and his Rumpler Taube aeroplane represented the only viable source of airpower available to the defenders. Accordingly the besiegers devoted great efforts to downing both man and machine. They were unsuccessful, and Pluschow managed both to escape from Tsingtau before the capitulation and make his way back to Germany. (*Author's Collection*)

A modern view of the complex armoured observation cupola of the Bismarck Hill complex. The smaller cupola atop the device rotated 360 degrees. (*Courtesy of Dennis and Adrienne Quarmby*)

'We Will Never Forget'. A graphic rendering of German sentiments concerning the fall of Tsingtau. The Kaiser is supposed to have remarked that it would be more shameful to surrender the city to the Japanese than to surrender Berlin to the Russians. (*Author's Collection*)

A member of the 5th (Mounted) Company of the 3rd Naval Battalion. The company were mounted infantry rather than cavalry, the horses conveying mobility. (*Author's Collection*)

The railway battery (Intermediate Battery No. 4) extemporised by mounting two 88mm guns on railway trucks. (*Author's Collection*)

One of the obsolete guns that formed a significant proportion of the German defences. This particular piece was probably part of the Hsiauniwa Battery, which was largely destroyed by the defenders prior to the capitulation. (*Author's Collection*)

Captured *Maschinengewehr*. Based on the water-cooled Maxim machine gun, and widely adopted by the forces of several states, these particular examples appear to have had their breeches severely damaged. (*Author's Collection*)

A photograph showing the wire entanglements at the northern end of the Boxer Line's ditch where the Haipo River entered Kiautschou Bay. (*Author's Collection*)

The effects of the bombardment on the Bismarck Hill fortification, as photographed by the Japanese following the surrender. (*Author's Collection*)

A Japanese soldier beside a smashed gun mounted on a siege carriage. Such carriages allowed the weapon to fire over a tall parapet as shown. (*Author's Collection*)

The Japanese landing equipment at Lungkou. The sheer scale of the operation is evidenced by the number of ships in the shot. (*Author's Collection*)

Members of 3rd Naval Battalion deploying a machine gun in the field. (*Author's Collection*)

A Japanese artillery piece in the siege lines. (*Author's Collection*)

The *S-90* torpedo boat at speed. This vessel caused a major upset to the attackers by torpedoing and sinking IJN *Takachiho* on 17 October 1914. (*Author's Collection*)

A clearly posed photograph of an infantryman of the 3rd Naval Battalion. (*Author's Collection*)

Lieutenant General Kamio Mitsuomi and Brigadier General Nathaniel Barnardiston pose for a photograph after the victory. (*Author's Collection*)

Major General Yamanashi Hanzo. As well as being Kamio's Chief of Staff, Yamanashi performed the function of siege engineering commander. (*Author's Collection*)

One of the pair of 240mm guns mounted in Gruson turrets that formed part of the Hui tsch'en Huk coastal artillery battery. (*Author's Collection*)

One of the 280mm coastal artillery howitzers the Japanese emplaced as part of their siege train. (*Author's Collection*)

The German version of the 280mm howitzer atop Bismarck Hill. The emplacement was destroyed by the crew prior to surrendering. (*Author's Collection*)

Damage to civilian property in Tsingtau caused by the bombardment. (*Author's Collection*)

Below: Damaged rolling stock hit by splinters or similar. (*Author's Collection*)

SMS *Kaiserin Elisabeth* of the Austro–Hungarian Navy. A Kaiser Franz Joseph I-class protected cruiser, her guns were removed and mounted ashore. She was scuttled on 2 November 1914 to prevent capture.

> If coaling the whole squadron in East Asian, Australian and Indian waters presented too great difficulties, we might consider detaching one light cruiser to the Indian Ocean.[22]

Müller's idea met with Spee's approval and the following morning, while the Admiral led the squadron east from Pagan Island, the *Emden* and collier *Markomania* headed west to the Indian Ocean, and into naval legend.[23]

It is worth giving a brief account of the cruiser war waged by Müller; during September and October *Emden* stopped and took captive sixteen British vessels, which were then sunk by gunfire or by demolition charges.[24] He also captured eight more, of varying nationalities, which he did not sink. This activity caused chaos on the trade routes and caused a huge amount of disruption to the commerce of the region. Müller seemed to have a natural aptitude for this kind of activity, resorting to ruses from days gone by in disguising his vessel.

He did not restrict himself to activities far out at sea; on 22 September the city of Madras (Chennai) was shelled. The attack began shortly after 021:30hr and lasted for something over twenty minutes, during which around 120–30 shells fell on and around the harbour. The most visible damage was caused to the storage tanks of the Burmah Oil Company; two were hit and set alight, burning throughout the next day, with a loss amounting to some 365,000 gallons of oil. The merchantman *Chupra*, anchored in the harbour, was also hit, but once fire began to be returned the *Emden* swiftly left the scene.[25] The psychological effects of the bombardment were greater than the physical, it being a severe blow to British prestige and the cause of several thousand of the inhabitants fleeing the city. Rumours of the ship in the vicinity of Ceylon (Sri Lanka) caused panic, but possibly the greatest single coup scored during the cruise was the raid on George Town, on the northeast corner of Penang Island, on 28 October.[26]

Müller rigged a dummy fourth stack on his vessel, so that it resembled a British cruiser, and steamed into the roads at high speed flying false colours. Once in a tactically advantageous position he, literally, showed his true colours by running up the German naval ensign. There were a number of Allied ships in the harbour, the most important probably being the Russian light cruiser *Zhemchug*. The Russian warship was torpedoed from close range and subjected to a short bombardment, which broke her in two. As *Emden* made her escape back to the open sea the French destroyer *Mosquet* attempted to engage her off Muka Head, but was swiftly despatched by the heavier metal of her opponent.[27] Once again Müller demonstrated his humanity by stopping and lowering boats in order to rescue the distressed French seamen, earning the approbation of parts of the American press:

> It was here that the chivalrous bravery of the Emden's Captain, which has been many times in evidence throughout her meteoric career, was again shown. If the French boats were coming out, every moment was of priceless value to him. Nevertheless, utterly disregarding this, he stopped, lowered boats, and picked up the survivors from the Mosquet before steaming on his way. The English here now say of him, admiringly, 'He played the game.'[28]

In terms of resources expended as against results achieved, the exploits of the *Emden* can only be viewed as a highly efficient operation of war. This of course begs the question as to what might have been achieved had Spee dispersed his entire squadron in the same way. It must not however be forgotten that one of the first targets of the British and Japanese naval forces was the German wireless system, with stations based on several of the Pacific islands. Once these had been captured or destroyed, and all of them had been within two months of the outbreak of war, then the squadron, whether taken collectively or as individual units, was effectively incommunicado. It had to rely on whatever information it might glean from various sources, or rely on guesswork.[29] It is also the case that the armoured cruisers were, because of their fuel consumption, not well suited for commerce warfare, but they might have had a role to play in terms of support as, for example, was evidenced on the mission to sever the British trans-Pacific cable at Fanning (Tabuaeran) Island on 7 September.[30]

The *Nürnberg*, despite having boiler problems, accompanied by the collier *Titania*, carried out this operation; flying the French ensign the vessels gained the anchorage without exciting suspicion and landed an armed party.[31] These swiftly captured the cable-station personnel and, over a period of about twelve hours, effectively put the station out of action by destroying the equipment. Meanwhile the *Titania* dredged up the cable and severed it.[32] When news of this exploit reached the outside world it prompted some fevered speculation. *The Times* of London, for example, published a short piece based on information obtained from Canadian naval sources. This reported that 'the object of the German cruiser *Nürnberg* in cutting the cable and taking Fanning Island is to establish a new Pacific base since the enemy has lost Samoa'.[33] Spee however, who covered this operation with the rest of the squadron whilst remaining out of sight of land, had no intention of fixing himself geographically. Indeed after ascertaining that no enemy vessels were in evidence in the area he moved on to Christmas Island and waited for the two raiders to join him.

It was during an essentially similar raid that the *Emden* came to grief. On 9 November Müller decided to raid the cable and radio station on Direction Island, one of the Cocos (Keeling) Islands. A fifty-strong landing party went ashore at about 06:30hr and began destroying the facilities, unaware that the presence of the *Emden* had been betrayed by a radio signal she had sent to a collier. Not only had the station at Direction Island heard this, but so had several of the transports and escorting vessels making up the first ANZAC convoy from Australia and New Zealand. Shortly afterwards the station reported by radio that there was a 'strange warship approaching' and repeated this some ten minutes later, prefixing it with the distress signal SOS. At the same time a message was sent by cable to Australia stating that a three-funnelled warship was sitting off the island and landing a party by boat.[34]

The ANZAC convoy also received this message when it was, by chance, only some 80km away from the island. There were three warships on escort duty, the Japanese battlecruiser *Ibuki* and the Australian light cruisers *Melbourne* (Flag) and *Sydney*. Upon receiving the signals HMAS *Melbourne* made to respond, but then delegated the duty to *Sydney* so as to remain protecting the convoy, the primary responsibility. It took about two hours for *Sydney* to reach visible distance of Direction Island, when she was spotted by lookouts on *Emden*. Müller immediately raised anchor and set out to engage the approaching vessel, abandoning the landing party.[35] It was not a contest *Emden* could win against the bigger, faster and more heavily armed *Sydney*.[36] Müller was eventually, after receiving more than 100 hits that reduced *Emden* to near impotence, forced to run his ship aground on North Keeling Island (now Pulu Keeling National Park). German losses were 131 dead and 65 wounded whilst Müller and the remaining crew were taken prisoner. Müller's exploits had earned him the admiration of even his enemy; he was lauded as a gallant and chivalrous opponent in *The Times*: 'If all the Germans had fought as well as the Captain of the *Emden*, the German people would not today be reviled by the world.'[37]

It is somewhat ironic that Müller became undone through the agency of a vessel that had been deployed because of fear of his depredations. The ANZAC force was only transported as an escorted convoy because of fear of German cruisers, and the Allies had known with some degree of certainty that these would not include Spee's main squadron; he had bombarded Papeete, Tahiti, on 22 September, placing himself some 2000 miles east of New Zealand. Therefore the danger devolved around *Emden* alone, though the *Konigsberg*, which was thought to be off the coast of Africa, was a slighter worry.

It is fruitless to investigate 'might have beens' to any degree, but given the relative success of *Emden* one cannot avoid pondering what could have been achieved had Müller been supported. Certainly if one of the armoured cruisers had been in the vicinity it would have been the *Sydney* that came off worst, though of course even more powerful assistance was relatively near at hand in the shape of *Ibuki*. Had the whereabouts of Spee not been ascertained with some certainty, the original flagship of the convoy escort, *Minotaur*, would also have been in attendance. Against such a powerful escort the East Asiatic Cruiser Squadron would have been unlikely to prevail, so it is fanciful to suggest that the ANZAC convoy would have been threatened.

Nevertheless it is still arguable that whilst Müller achieved something, his erstwhile superior's voyage was a failure, as he had foreseen at the meeting of 13 August at Pagan Island. Having ventured to the west coast of South America, it is true that Spee inflicted a major defeat on the Royal Navy at the Battle of Coronel on 1 November 1914, when a weaker force commanded by Rear Admiral Sir Christopher Cradock chose to offer battle rather than, as discretion might have demanded, seek to avoid it.[38] However despite crushing his opponents in short order sinking Cradock's flagship, the 'Drake' class armoured cruiser *Good Hope*, and the weaker 'County' class *Monmouth*, with all hands (1,654 officers and men), it was essentially a pyrrhic victory. All it gained was the assurance that overwhelming force would be deployed in an attempt to crush him.

With over half his ammunition expended at Coronel, Spee decided to attempt a return to Germany. We shall never know if he would have succeeded, because on 8 December, having rounded Cape Horn, he decided for reasons that are somewhat obscure to launch an attack on Port Stanley in the Falkland Islands; as Surgeon Thomas Benjamin Dixon aboard HMS *Kent* wrote: 'very kind of them to come here and save us the trouble of going round the Horn to find them'.[39] Dixon's ship was a sister of the recently sunk *Monmouth*, and was part of a 'task force' sent to the South Atlantic with the specific object of catching and destroying Spee's squadron.

Indeed it might be argued that German maritime strategy had succeeded to some degree when no less than three battlecruisers and associated support were detached from northern waters and sent to seek out Spee and avenge Cradock.[40] This however still left the Grand Fleet with a marginal superiority in battleships and parity, if the hybrid SMS *Blücher* be included, in battlecruisers vis-à-vis the High Seas Fleet.

The heart of the South Atlantic force, under Vice Admiral Sir Frederick Doveton Sturdee, consisted of two 'Invincible' class battle cruisers, *Invincible* (Flag) and *Inflexible*.[41] Spee of course did not know this overwhelmingly superior force was coaling at Port Stanley, and he took no precautions to establish just what might be there before approaching with his entire squadron on the morning of 8 December 1914.[42] The result was inevitable; after a general chase lasting several hours the British force caught and destroyed four of Spee's ships, only the *Dresden* escaping to survive for another three months.

We can only surmise what impulses led Spee to attempt a raid on Port Stanley, and why he failed to effectively reconnoitre before approaching. Had he sent *Dresden*, the fastest of his light cruisers, to ascertain what enemy presence was in the vicinity, whilst staying beyond visual range with the rest of his ships, he might well have avoided destruction, particularly if Sturdee had then moved his force into the Pacific. It is then possible, though improbable, that he might have succeeded in getting his squadron home to Germany, which would have been a great propaganda coup if little more. As it was his decision to maintain his squadron as a 'fleet in being' forfeited any chance of a large-scale and effective *guerre de course* being conducted in the Pacific, short-lived though this might have been, whilst his actions at the Falkland Isles led to his destruction.

Strategically it is difficult to find fault with Spee's decisions. Following Japan's decision to enter the war against Germany he was pitted against insuperable odds and the problems of fuel and ammunition precluded any prospects, beyond the short term, of waging cruiser warfare against trade. It is, in any event, difficult to conceive any acceptable, realistic, alternatives. Tactically Spee made a huge error in approaching an unreconnoitred Port Stanley and paid for it dearly. Whatever the 'might have beens' though, it was the case that within five months of the outbreak of war, the German Navy had been swept from the Pacific.

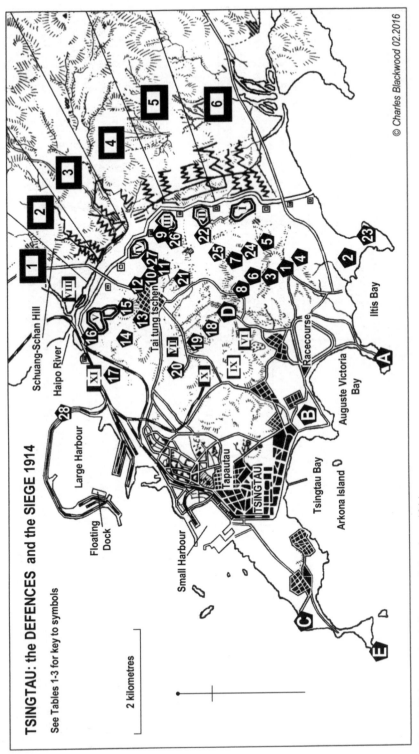

TSINGTAU: the DEFENCES and the SIEGE 1914

See Tables 1-3 for key to symbols

2 kilometres

Schuang-Schan Hill

Haipo River

Large Harbour

Floating Dock

Small Harbour

Tai tung Tschen

Tsingtau

Tapautau

TSINGTAU

Racecourse

Tsingtau Bay

Arkona Island

Auguste Victoria Bay

Iltis Bay

Map 7: Tsingtau: the defences and the siege, 1914.

Table 1: Tsingtau 1914: Coastal Artillery Batteries

	Battery	Armament	Type of Mounting	Remarks
A	Hui tsch'en Huk	2 × 240mm	Mounted under shields in concrete emplacements	Ex-Chinese weapons – obsolete. Manned by I Company Marine Artillery Detachment
		3 × 150mm	Mounted in Gruson turrets in concrete emplacements	Modern weapons mounted in turrets. Manned by I Company Marine Artillery Detachment
B	Tsingtau	4 × 150mm	Open pits	Constructed by China pre-1897 – obsolete. Manned by IV Company Marine Artillery Detachment
C	Hsiauniwa	4 × 210mm	Under shields	Krupp weapons removed from the Taku Forts after the Boxer War. Obsolete. Capable of land or sea service. Manned by II Company Marine Artillery Detachment
D	Bismarck Hill	4 × 280mm howitzers	Under shield in concrete emplacements with 360 degrees traverse	Modern. Capable of land or sea service. Manned by III Company Marine Artillery Detachment. Situated atop the Bismarck Hill Command Complex
E	Yunuisan	4 × 88mm Rapid Fire	Open pits	Obsolete weapons. Manned by II Company Marine Artillery Detachment

Source: Information taken from: TNA, MPI 1/546/3 'China: Tsingtao. A 'Point of Aim' chart, showing part of the coast and defences.' Charles B. Burdick, *The Japanese Siege of Tsingtau* (Hamden CT: Archon, 1976), pp. 21, 22, 24, 43. Kurt Aßmann, *Die Kämpfe der Kaiserlichen Marine in den deutschen Kolonien (The Struggle of the Imperial Navy in the German Colonies)* (Berlin: Mittler, 1935), pp. 108–9. 'Map of Tsingtau showing the Defences During the Siege' located at TNA, MPI 1/546/16. Information from Dennis and Adrienne Quarmby. Captain Bernard Smith, 'The Siege of Tsingtau', *The Coast Artillery Journal*, November–December 1934, pp. 405–19. Commander Charles B. Robbins, 'German Seacoast Defences at Tsingtau, 1914', *The Coast Defence Journal*, May 2007, pp. 85–90. Philip Sims, 'German Tsingtao Mounts Photographs', *The Coast Defence Journal*, November 2006. For an overview of the territory and the defences see, Jork Artelt, *Tsingtau: Deutsche Stadt und Festung 1897–1914 (Tsingtau: German city and fortress 1897–1914)* (Duesseldorf: Droste, 1984).

Table 2: Tsingtau, 1914: Land Artillery Batteries

	Battery	Armament	Remarks
1	Battery No. 1	6 × 90mm	
2	Battery No. 1a	2 × 50mm	
3	Battery No. 1b	2 × 88mm	
4	Battery No. 2	7 × 37mm	Maxim-Nordenfeldt 'pom-poms'
5	Battery No. 2a	4 × 37mm	Maxim-Nordenfeldt 'pom-poms'
6	Punktkuppe	4 × 60mm	Removed from gunboats
7	Lower Iltis Hill	6 × 120mm	
8	Upper Iltis Hill	2 × 105mm	On fixed mountings with shields
9	Battery No. 5[1]	4 × 37mm	Maxim-Nordenfeldt 'pom-poms'
10	Battery No. 6	6 × 120mm	Field guns
11	Battery No. 6a	2 × 47mm	Removed from *Kaiserin Elizabeth*
12	Battery No. 7[2]	6 × 90mm	Field guns
13	Battery No. 8	2 × 47mm	Removed from *Kaiserin Elizabeth*
14	Battery No. 8a	2 × 47mm	Removed from *Kaiserin Elizabeth*
15	Battery No. 9	4 × 37mm	Maxim-Nordenfeldt 'pom-poms'
16	Battery No. 10	4 × 37mm	Maxim-Nordenfeldt 'pom-poms'
17	Battery No. 11[3]	6 × 90mm	Field guns
18	Battery No. 12 (Lower Bismarck Hill)	2 × 210mm	Fixed mountings; unshielded
19	Battery No. 13	4 × 88mm	
20	Battery No. 14 (Moltke Hill)	4 × 88mm	
21	Battery No. 15	2 × 150mm	Removed from *Kaiserin Elizabeth*
22	Howitzer Battery	3 × 150mm	Field howitzers
23	Intermediate Battery No. 1	2 × 88mm	Field guns
24	Intermediate Battery No. 1a	2 × 77mm	Field guns
25	Intermediate Battery No. 2	2 × 77mm	Field guns
26	Intermediate Battery No. 3	2 × 77mm	Field guns
27	Intermediate Battery No. 3a	2 × 77mm	Field guns
28	Intermediate Battery No. 4	2 × 88mm	Mounted on railway truck

Source: This table is a synthesis of the details that appeared in Kurt Aβmann, *Die Kämpfe der Kaiserlichen Marine in den deutschen Kolonien* (*The Struggle of the Imperial Navy in the German Colonies*) (Berlin: Mittler, 1935), pp. 108–9, and, a 'Map of Tsingtau showing the Defences During the Siege' located at TNA, MPI 1/546/16. According to an added inscription, 'The original of this map was taken from a German artillery officer, now a prisoner of war in Hong Kong.' The shaded portions indicate batteries that were in existence prior to the outbreak of hostilities.

1. Aβmann states that there was also a Battery No. 4 equipped with 2 × 37mm machine guns.
2. Aβmann divides these weapons between Batteries 7 and 7a.
3. Aβmann divides these weapons between Batteries 11 and 11a.

Table 3: Tsingtau, 1914: Defence and Other Works

I	Infantry Work 1 (Hsiao-chan-shan Fort)
II	Infantry Work 2 (Hsiao-chan-shan North Fort)
III	Infantry Work 3 (Central Fort)
IV	Infantry Work 4 (Tai-tung-chen East Fort)
V	Infantry Work 5 (Seacoast Fort)
▭	Blockhouses
VI	Bismarck Barracks
VII	Moltke Barracks
VIII	Water Works and Pumping Station.
IX	Diederichs Hill Signal Station
X	Artillery Depot
XI	Oil Tanks

The Besiegers

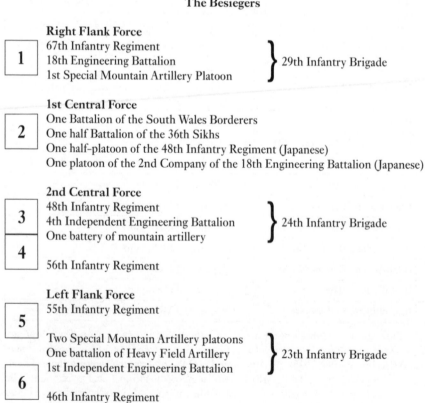

Right Flank Force
1
67th Infantry Regiment
18th Engineering Battalion
1st Special Mountain Artillery Platoon
} 29th Infantry Brigade

1st Central Force
2
One Battalion of the South Wales Borderers
One half Battalion of the 36th Sikhs
One half-platoon of the 48th Infantry Regiment (Japanese)
One platoon of the 2nd Company of the 18th Engineering Battalion (Japanese)

2nd Central Force
3
48th Infantry Regiment
4th Independent Engineering Battalion
One battery of mountain artillery
} 24th Infantry Brigade
4
56th Infantry Regiment

Left Flank Force
5
55th Infantry Regiment

Two Special Mountain Artillery platoons
One battalion of Heavy Field Artillery
1st Independent Engineering Battalion
} 23th Infantry Brigade
6
46th Infantry Regiment

Chapter 7

The Siege of Tsingtau

The Japanese Army that fought the Russians in 1904–5 had been modelled on its Prussian counterpart, and consequently its doctrine had been largely derived from lessons taught by a Prussian officer, Major Jacob Meckel. Meckel had gained significant combat experience during the Franco-Prussian War of 1870–1 and passed this on during his tenure (1885–8) as a professor at the Army Staff College and as an advisor to the General Staff. It was his influence that is often credited with the victory at Port Arthur in 1894 and over China's military forces in general.

The methods taught by Meckel, and subsequently adopted, were grounded in the 1888 version of the German Field Service Regulations. They found their formal expression in Japan's 1891 Infantry Field Manual which laid out the tactical doctrine to be utilised. The core of this manual was based around the execution of the attack, and this differed in few essentials from the methodologies preached in Europe.[1]

In an attack the artillery would open the way for the infantry, the main body of which would be preceded by a skirmishing line; this should reveal the outlines of the enemy defences. When these had been determined then the assault would be delivered by a dense formation, with the soldiers closely ordered to be no more than a metre apart, in four ranks on a narrow front. The defenders would be overwhelmed by the superior organic firepower of this formation as it closed. Frontal assaults were to be avoided except in cases where the enemy positions were only lightly held.

The doctrine outlined in the 1891 manual was put into effect against China in the 1894–5 war, and proved effective. However the Chinese forces, badly trained, equipped and led, were weak opponents, which allowed the massed Japanese formations to successfully accomplish their objectives with light casualties.

Tsingtau Garrison: Order of Battle November 1914

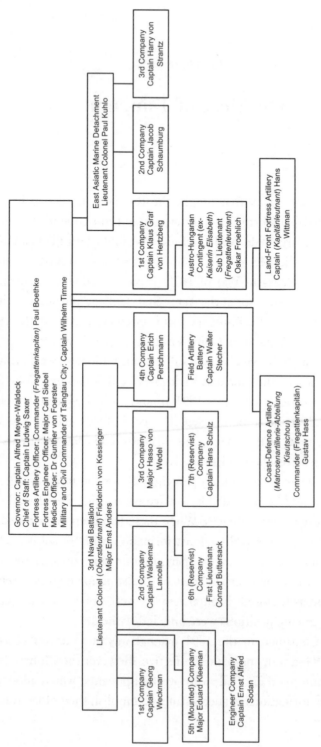

Governor: Captain Alfred Meyer-Waldeck
Chief of Staff: Captain Ludwig Saxer
Fortress Artillery Officer: Commander (*Fregattenkapitan*) Paul Boethke
Fortress Engineer Officer: Major Carl Siebel
Medical Officer: Dr Gunther von Foerster
Military and Civil Commander of Tsingtau City: Captain Wilhelm Timme

3rd Naval Battalion
Lieutenant Colonel (*Oberstleutnant*) Friederich von Kessinger
Major Ernst Anders

- 1st Company Captain Georg Weckman
- 2nd Company Captain Waldemar Lancelle
- 3rd Company Major Hasso von Wedel
- 4th Company Captain Erich Perschmann
- 5th (Mounted) Company Major Eduard Kleeman
- 6th (Reservist) Company First Lieutenant Conrad Buttersack
- 7th (Reservist) Company Captain Hans Schulz
- Engineer Company Captain Ernst Alfred Sodan
- Field Artillery Battery Captain Walter Stecher

Coast-Defence Artillery (*Matrosenartillerie-Abteilung Kiautschou*)
Commander (*Fregattenkapitän*) Gustav Hass

East Asiatic Marine Detachment
Lieutenant Colonel Paul Kuhlo

- 1st Company Captain Klaus Graf von Hertzberg
- 2nd Company Captain Jacob Schaumburg
- 3rd Company Captain Harry von Strantz

Austro-Hungarian Contingent (ex-*Kaiserin Elisabeth*)
Sub Lieutenant (*Fregattenleutnant*) Oskar Froehlich

Land-Front Fortress Artillery
Captain (*Kapitänleutnant*) Hans Wittman

Following withdrawal behind the Boxer Line the initial deployment was as follows: Infantry Work I: 1st Company. Infantry Work II: Half 7th Company. Infantry Work III: Half 7th Company (*Oberleutnant* Paul Otto Ramin in command). Infantry Work IV: 2nd Company. Infantry Work V: 3rd Company.
Forces deployed between and behind the permanent works: Left Wing (Kuhlo): East Asian Marine Detachment; Austro-Hungarian Contingent; Austro-Hungarian Contingent (part); Centre (Kleeman): 5th Company; Austro-Hungarian Contingent (part); Engineer Company. Right Wing (Anders): 4th Company; 6th Company.
Source: Hans Klehmet, *Tsingtau: Rückblick auf die Geschichte, besonders der Belagerung und des Falles der Festung, mit kritischen Betrachtungen* (Berlin: Georg Bath, 1931), pp. 24–8.

Despite this success several shortcomings were identified. It was judged that the troops were insufficiently motivated, inasmuch as instances where they had hesitated to press the advance under fire were recorded. At the next level, individual units tended to be insular and reluctant to support their neighbours, which necessarily led to a lack of overall coordination and thus effectiveness. In order to accommodate these, and other, lessons the Field Manual was revised and reissued in 1898.

The new manual laid great stress on inculcating fighting spirit amongst the soldiery. It also modified the assault technique by abolishing the fourth rank, which slowed the pace of the advance and allowed the tightening of formations, and stressed that company commanders must retain tight control of their units and mass them for bayonet attacks.

However, the Russo-Japanese War of 1904–5 demonstrated beyond doubt that these tactics were deficient when facing an enemy armed with modern weaponry and of broadly similar capabilities. Though Japan prevailed, the casualties were horrendous; some 60,000 at Port Arthur (1 August 1904–2 January 1905) and about 75,000 at Mukden (20 February–10 March 1905) for example. Losses on that scale exhausted Japan's strategic manpower reserve, and post-war analysis revealed that over 93 per cent of them had been suffered by the infantry. There was similar attrition of officers, who could not quickly or easily be replaced. [2]

Problems in respect of the artillery, and their supposed combination with the infantry in delivering attacks, also came to the fore. A shortage of shells and poor handling of the guns, leading to ineffective coordination with the infantry, meant that the latter were often left unsupported because the function of the artillery, as the gunners saw it, was to silence enemy batteries.

So whilst the artillerists duelled each other, the attackers were subject to unsuppressed small arms fire from the defenders' positions. To avoid this the attackers were forced to seek cover, which had the effect of slowing the momentum of the advance. Thus it was that, contrary to expectations, the majority of casualties (on both sides) were caused by infantry weapons and not artillery.[3] Experience, bitterly gained, demonstrated that frontal attacks launched from 500m or more were doomed to fail, and that any attacks in daylight against strongly held defensive positions only rarely succeeded.

There were also problems with the munitions fired by the artillery, many of which turned out to be duds. [4]

As the war went on tactics changed to meet the conditions encountered, and massed infantry formations gave way to more open versions. For example, lessons taken from the inconclusive Battle of Sandepu (25–9 January 1905) indicated that dispersed infantry tactics nullified the effects of artillery fire. [5]

Lessons derived from the experience of the Russo-Japanese War as a whole were embodied in a revised Infantry Field Manual published in 1909. There were major departures from the previous version; the infantry was now the primary arm. Their offensive spirit was the foundation of victory, and was accorded more importance than materiel superiority. Firepower was relegated to secondary importance. Tactically the infantry would advance in open formations and seek to manoeuvre to turn the enemy flank. Casualties would be minimised by skilful use of natural features or by the construction of trenches and the like. Night fighting and manoeuvring was also emphasised. The artillery would attempt to reduce the defender's resistance, but even without fire support the infantry were expected to advance and press home the attack with the bayonet. This applied even when outnumbered, and ground taken had to be held regardless. [6] This insistence on aggressive mobility, of turning enemy flanks and encircling opponents' positions, was to be an enduring feature of Japanese tactics for several decades.

Perhaps more importantly in the current context however, was the fact that Japan's army was, in 1914, the only modern force that had direct experience of conducting formal siege operations. This experience had been hard-won during the investment of Port Arthur by Japan's 3rd Army under General Nogi Maresuke. Ironically perhaps, the operation had been accomplished once before by Nogi, in 1894, during the Sino-Japanese War. On that occasion, the 1st Infantry Brigade, with Nogi in command as a major general, had successfully stormed the defences and taken occupation in only one day with the loss of sixteen men. His second attempt was not to be so easy, and the 3rd Army, initially comprising some 90,000 personnel, was engaged from 1 August 1904 to 2 January 1905, incurring massive casualties of around 60,000 in the process. Initially Nogi had attempted to emulate his earlier feat with attempts to penetrate the defences by infantry assault; these were only called off on 24 August after some 16,000 men had been lost.

Kamio and the Japanese Army did not intend to re-learn the lesson, and, even if the defences of Tsingtau in 1914 in no way compared with those of Port Arthur in 1904, they were nevertheless treated with respect.[7]

Not only the lessons learned during the 1904–5 siege were used at Tsingtau in 1914; so were some of the key offensive weapons. In order to reduce the Port Arthur defences the Japanese had dismantled, shipped across the Yellow Sea, re-assembled, and emplaced six of their coast defence howitzers. These weapons, based on the Krupp 1892 280mm howitzer, had proved devastating and decisive; their use in the field had not previously been considered feasible. The deployment of such heavy ordnance, each piece weighed in at some 36 tonnes, could not though be accomplished quickly; therefore there was a lull in the advance whilst the Japanese made their preparations.

The defenders were now little more than passive observers of their impending defeat, and the only realistic counter-measures they could take involved using their artillery to disrupt Japanese arrangements. One unrealistic measure was however attempted on the night of 2–3 October, when a force equal to three companies, mainly composed of personnel from the East Asiatic Marine Detachment, set out at 21:00hr on a foray against a Japanese position on Schuang-Schan Hill on the far left of the German front. This was pursuant to intelligence received from a reconnaissance carried out on the night of 29 September, when some twenty men had advanced from Infantry Work 5, past the pumping station and across the Haipo River, 'a small stream running over a broad bed of sand', and scouted the hill.[8] They discovered that a platoon strength unit was deployed there, about a kilometre in advance of the Boxer Line. The manoeuvre was coordinated with artillery fire, from both land batteries and *Jaguar* and *Kaiserin Elisabeth*, which started an hour before the troops advanced. The barrage was intended to isolate the hill from the Japanese main force preventing any interference from that quarter. With one company held in reserve the force moved into the darkness and divided, intending to approach the target from left and right. Within twenty minutes the operation was a shambles; the members of the right-hand column lost their bearings and, in talking and using flashlights, betrayed their presence. Enemy fire from rifles and machine guns was directed at them, and misdirected friendly fire, from the 37mm Maxim-Nordenfeldt 'pom-poms' in the Infantry Work, also took a toll.

The left-hand column was more careful, or had more luck, and reached the objective unobserved; there were no enemy there as they had been drawn away by the firefight to their left. However, when the force drew attention to its presence, fire began to be directed towards it indicating that the position was not free of Japanese. Schuang-Schan Hill was by this time well illuminated by flares and the glare of searchlights (*scheinwerfer*) directed from within the German lines, which did not help the infiltrators who perceived themselves to be in difficulties. Accordingly the order was given to withdraw and all those that could had returned to the German lines by 01:00hr on 3 October. Stragglers continued to appear for the next day or so, but the final account reckoned that thirty-five failed to return – a loss rate of some 10 per cent for no gain.[9] Even if one attempts to discount the inestimable benefit of hindsight, the rationale behind the foray remains elusive. It was, in all likelihood, similar to that which lay behind the 'trench-raid' attitude that developed on the Western Front in France; it maintained the 'illusion of an offensive posture'.[10] When not pursued for a specific purpose, such ventures were carried out to foster 'soldierly spirit' and 'maintain morale'.[11] Just whose morale was maintained is a difficult question to answer, but it probably wasn't that of those who had to carry out the activity.

The aftermath of the raid convinced the defenders that their artillery was indeed the only means of carrying the war to the Japanese.[12] Spotting for this was however problematical, particularly since the loss of Prinz-Heinrich-Berg. One less than perfect option was to use the naval vessels in Kiautschou Bay, which could at least get behind the Japanese line and perhaps spot, though only from the left flank, targets of opportunity. Not only could the vessels fire upon such targets themselves, but also they could coordinate the fire of the fortress guns. *Kaiserin Elisabeth* and *S-90*, with *Jaguar* coordinating, had undertaken just such a mission on 30 September, and it was deemed a success as the ships were able to silence several batteries that shelled them by counter-battery fire. Some intelligence was also gained, that the British contingent had joined the Japanese being an example. Similar missions, including support for the 2 October raid, continued until 4 October, when, on that day, the Japanese made a concerted effort to destroy

Jaguar. The attacks started at dawn with four aeroplanes unsuccessfully bombarding the vessel, followed up by a concerted artillery effort as she made her way to the Japanese flank, causing the ship, though undamaged, to retire briefly from the action and request support from the land artillery. As the German guns shelled the reported positions, *Jaguar* once again forayed into the bay, only to be once again targeted and forced to retire. Returning for the third time proved to be an error; once again a considerable effort was made to hit the ship – this time with success. A shell hit the bow, fortunately above the waterline, creating a large hole in the ship's side and forcing an immediate withdrawal – venturing into Kiautschou Bay could clearly no longer be considered a feasible proposition.[13]

Reconnaissance duties devolved then on to the air component, represented by Plüschow and his Taube. There was also a balloon detachment consisting of two observation-balloon envelopes and the necessary ground infrastructure.[14] The German observation balloons of 1914 were known as *Drachen*, a name commonly adopted for all sausage-shaped kite-balloons, and had been developed by Parseval-Sigsfeld.[15] Adopted for use in 1893, they represented a significant investment in terms of equipment and manpower for the Tsingtau garrison, the standardised balloon section in 1914 consisting of 1 balloon (plus 1 spare envelope), 4 observers, 177 enlisted ranks, 123 horses, 12 gas wagons, 2 equipment wagons, a winch wagon and a telephone wagon.[16] The balloon had made several ascents from Tsingtau during the course of the conflict, but the observer had been unable to see anything of value. In order to attempt to remedy this the device was moved closer to the front and another ascent made on 5 October. It was to be the last such, as the Japanese artillery immediately found its range with shrapnel shell and holed it in several places.[17] A ruse involving the spare balloon was then tried; it was sent up to draw the attackers' fire and so reveal the position of their guns. According to Alfred Brace:

> It contained a dummy looking fixedly at the landscape below through a pair of paste-board glasses. But there happened to arise a strong wind which set the balloon revolving and finally broke it loose and sent it pirouetting off over the Yellow Sea, the whole exploit, I learned afterwards, being a great puzzle to the British and Japanese observers outside.[18]

Plüschow flew reconnaissance flights every day that the weather, and his propeller, permitted, sketching the enemy positions and making detailed notes. He achieved this by setting the engine so as to maintain a safe altitude of over 2000m, and then steering with his feet, the Taube had no rudder and horizontal control was achieved by warping the wings, whilst peering over the side of his cockpit. The Japanese had extemporised a contingent of anti-aircraft-artillery – the 'Field-Gun Platoon for High Angle Fire', with the necessary angle achieved by dropping the gun-trail into a pit behind the weapon – and although the shrapnel barrage thus discharged proved ineffective it was deemed by Plüschow to be troublesome nevertheless.[19] Where he was at his most vulnerable was on landing, and a battery of Japanese artillery was tasked specifically with destroying the Taube as it descended to the racecourse, which of course was a fixed point at a known range. Little more than good luck, and what he called 'ruses' such as shutting off the engine and swooping sharply to earth, saw him through these experiences, but remarkably both man and machine came through without serious injury.[20]

Whatever inconveniences Plüschow and the fortress artillery might inflict upon the force massing to their front, they could do nothing to prevent the landing of men and materiel at Wang-ko-chuang and Schatsykou, nor could they prevent the deployment of these once landed. The previous efforts by the navy in terms of minelaying did though still pay dividends, as when the Japanese 'aircraft carrier' was badly damaged. As the report from the British Naval Attaché to Japan put it in his report of 30 November:

[...] a few minutes after 8 a.m. [on 30 September] the 'Wakamiya Maru' struck a mine in the entrance of Lo Shan Harbour, and had to be beached to prevent her sinking; her engines were disabled owing to breaking of steam pipes, No. 3 hold full, and one man killed – fortunately no damage done to aeroplanes though it is feared that a spare engine may be injured. [...] As the Aeroplane establishment is all being moved ashore at this place this accident will not affect the efficiency of the Aeroplane Corps.[21]

Though the ship was saved, and the efficiency of the flying component was not affected, two more Japanese vessels were sunk on the same day – albeit they were only trawlers used for minesweeping and the like. The Japanese suspected that Chinese vessels in the vicinity were laying mines; accordingly they sank them.[22]

There was however nothing in the past, the present or the immediate future that either the Germans or the Chinese could do, or have done, about another aspect of the Japanese presence – their seizure of the Shantung Railway. Control of the line had been effectively in Japanese hands since 17 September when a detachment of cavalry had entered Kiautschou town, and on 23 September Kamio had assigned a larger unit, the Independent First Battalion of Infantry, to ensure greater control. The impetus behind this manoeuvre was not military, but rather political, and to ensure that the line remained in Japanese hands further reinforcements were despatched from Japan in the shape of the 29th Infantry Brigade under Major General Johoji Goro. The brigade, which landed on 10 October, was somewhat under strength (whilst its 67th Infantry Regiment comprised three battalions the 34th Infantry Regiment had only one). Kamio directed the 67th Regiment to take up position on the right of his line, whilst the single battalion of 34th Regiment went to the railway.[23] The political aim behind the increased presence on the railway was, via military occupation, to utilise this primary means of communication, which was economically vital, in order to dominate the whole of Shantung province.[24]

Kamio sought to avoid casualties amongst his force and, despite the defenders' belief to the contrary, was largely successful in this. The Japanese had adopted what was in certain quarters termed 'mole warfare' in front of Port Arthur, and similar techniques, albeit on a greatly reduced scale, were to be put into practice before Tsingtau just as they were beginning to be, though entirely unplanned, in Northern France.[25]

Kamio's Chief of Staff, Major General Yamanashi Hanzo, former Chief of the General Affairs Section of the General Staff, performed the function of siege engineering commander.[26] Thus it was he that drew up and, on 7 October, issued the outline plan for the operation. The methodology to be employed harked back to 1904–5, and indeed to Vauban.[27]

Some 1–2km in front of the Boxer Line the Japanese would establish an advanced investment line, digging in securely and ensuring that it was proof against any German foray. Behind this line the artillery, including the siege train under Major General Watanabe, would deploy, and when this had been positioned, and sufficient munitions brought up, the bombardment would commence.

This bombardment would be coordinated with a similar effort from the naval forces, thus Tsingtau would be caught between two fires. The object of the combined bombardment would be the destruction of the enemy artillery, including that mounted on naval vessels, and the reduction of the Boxer Line.

Watanabe's command was impressive. He had two regiments of Heavy Siege Artillery, the 2nd (120mm howitzers) and 3rd (100mm and 150mm guns), as well as a number of separate independent units. These included four Independent Battalions of Heavy Siege Artillery: the 1st (Major Nomura) 150mm howitzers; 2nd (Lieutenant Colonel Ogata) 200mm and 240mm howitzers; 3rd (Major Asakawa) 100mm guns; 4th (Major Motokawa) six 280mm (former coast defence) howitzers. In addition there was an Independent Battery (Captain J. Komori) of 150mm guns and the Naval Heavy Artillery Detachment (Lieutenant Commander Masaka) deploying 6in (1st and 2nd Batteries) and 4.7in (3rd Battery) naval guns mounted on land-service carriages.

Some 2,500 Chinese labourers, and 800 locally owned waggons, were needed to help move this vast amount of heavy metal from the beachhead and into position, and keeping it supplied with the necessary ammunition was another logistical hurdle. To that end a Siege Artillery Park, commanded by Lieutenant Colonel Yamagata, was established and light railways laid out to transport shell directly to the batteries. Construction of these railways was entrusted to the Special 3rd Railroad Battalion.

Chinese labourers also provided porterage for the less heavy supplies and their one-wheeled barrows, simultaneously pushed and pulled by a two-man team, proved, as might be expected from an indigenously developed device, highly efficient at moving loads weighing up to 150kg along the rudimentary roads. It is impossible to calculate how many Chinese were involved in the operations at Tsingtau, how they were recruited and paid, and their casualty rate. It is though fair to conclude that without their participation the campaign could not have progressed as expeditiously as it did.[28]

Only when the artillery had begun suppressing the defences would the engineers and infantry advance, digging saps as they went, in order to construct the first parallel. From there, and still under the protection of the bombardment, further saps would be advanced towards the enemy and a second parallel constructed. These trenches would be constructed so as to be at least 2m wide, well protected against enfilade fire and shell burst by following a zigzag pattern, and have overhead cover. A third parallel would then be constructed, at which time the infantry would be hard up against the enemy main positions and at a point where a breach of their line could take place and an assault launched.[29]

In order to achieve the enormous amount of digging that the plan required, the organic engineering component of the 18th Division, the 18th Battalion of Engineers, was augmented by two more battalions; the 1st Battalion of Independent Engineers (Lieutenant Colonel Koga) and the 4th Battalion of Independent Engineers (Lieutenant Colonel Sugiyama). The infantry that would man the siege works were also provided with weaponry specifically suited to trench warfare; two light platoons and one heavy detachment of bomb–guns (mortars).

In order to gain detailed knowledge of the defences the naval and army air components were tasked with flying reconnaissance missions over the German positions. They also flew bombing missions, which caused little damage, and attempted to discourage their single opponent (though they were initially uncertain how many German aircraft they faced) from emulating them; the latter with some degree of success. Plüschow records that he was provided with extemporised 'bombs' made of tin boxes filled with dynamite and improvised shrapnel, but that these devices were largely ineffectual. He claimed to have hit a Japanese vessel with one, which failed to explode, and to have succeeded in killing thirty soldiers with another one that did.[30] It was during this period that he became engaged in air-to-air combat, of a type, with the enemy aeroplanes.[31] Indeed, if Plüschow is to be believed, he succeeded in shooting down one of the Japanese aeroplanes with his pistol, having fired thirty shots.[32] It would appear however that even if he did engage in aerial jousting of the kind he mentions the result was not as he claimed; no aircraft were lost during the campaign. The Japanese did however do their utmost to prevent him reconnoitring their positions, as they were in the process of emplacing the siege batteries and, if the positions became known, they could expect intense efforts from the defenders to disrupt this process. Experience showed the Japanese that the time delay between aerial reconnaissance being carried out and artillery fire being concentrated on the area so reconnoitred was around two hours.

Indeed Watanabe insisted that his batteries were emplaced during the hours of darkness, despite the inconvenience this caused, and carefully camouflaged to prevent discovery.[33] That the threat from Plüschow, albeit indirect, was very real had been illustrated on 29 September; he had overflown an area where the British were camped and noted their tents, which were of a different pattern to the Japanese versions. This had resulted in heavy shelling, causing the camp to be moved the next day to the reverse slopes of a hill about 1.5km east of the former position.[34] He also posed a direct threat though perhaps of lesser import; on 10 October he dropped one of his homemade bombs on the British. It failed to explode, but the unit concerned moved position immediately – such an option was not available to 36-tonne howitzers that required semi-permanent emplacement.[35]

The ability of the German artillery to disrupt his preparations, and the relative inability to reply – the Japanese did not wish to give away the positions of their siege batteries by using them prematurely – caused Kamio to ask for naval support. Kato however proved reluctant to hazard his vessels by moving into waters that might contain mines, and where they could come under the fire of the coastal artillery at Hui tsch'en Huk. On 6 October, under prodding from his military counterpart, he did detail two vessels, *Suwo* and *Triumph*, to shell the Iltis Battery but, in an effort to stay out of danger, the ships remained beyond effective range and their bombardment fell short. The *Suwo* was sent in alone to try again on 10 October, but again did not press the matter and withdrew in the face of the perceived danger. A more powerful effort was mounted on 14 October, with *Suwo*, *Tango* and *Triumph* deployed. On this occasion the *Suwo* was detailed to engage Hui tsch'en Huk, and listed so as to improve the elevation of her guns and thus increase range. The German battery was engaged at 09:00hr from 15750m and was unable to effectively reply with *Suwo* out of range. Whilst Hui tsch'en Huk was engaged with *Suwo* the other vessels moved in closer to bombard the Iltis Battery, but the coastal artillery shifted fire onto *Tango*, which was within range. No hits were made, but the vessel withdrew, whilst *Triumph* moved into a position to attack the battery and slightly before 10:00hr fired some thirty shells. Shortly after 10:00hr the vessel prepared to move off, and as it did so a shot from Hui tsch'en Huk hit the mainmast. Little major damage was caused, the ship was ready for action again in two days, and the casualties amounted to one killed and two wounded, but it ensured that Kato would be cautious in hazarding his heavy ships again. In a like manner the bombardment caused only minor damage to the defences. The Iltis battery was not put out of action, nor was Hui tsch'en Huk, and the shells that landed on the main defence line did no major harm.[36]

On 13 October meanwhile a truce that the two sides had agreed, in order that non-combatants might be evacuated from Tsingtau, came into force. Kamio had proposed this on 4 October, but Barnardiston, who felt that he should have been consulted on the proposal, had initiated a bout of political wrangling over the matter. The answer, though not swift was thorough; Barnardiston was informed on 12 October that he was subordinate to Kamio. Thereafter the matter progressed smoothly and the mail steamer *Tsimo*, formerly *Rauenthaler*, conveyed various civilians, neutrals and other non-combatants, to Taputou, the port of Kiautschou town, across the bay.[37]

Perhaps Barnardiston was concerned more with form than substance, because the British contingent, following orders issued by Kamio on 10 October, had taken their place in the line of investment by 15 October. This ran, more or less parallel with the Boxer Line, from Kiautschou Bay on the right to Prinz-Heinrich-Berg on the left. Barnardiston's command was augmented with a half-platoon of the 4th Company from the 48th Infantry Regiment and a platoon of the 2nd Company of the 18th Engineering Battalion; the latter to assist with the engineering work. The whole had been assigned a frontage of around half a kilometre and were designated the 1st Central Force.

Immediately to their right, and between them and Kiautschou Bay, was the recently arrived 67th Infantry Regiment and the rest of the 18th Engineering Battalion. Designated the Right Flank Force, and under Major General Johoji, extra resources in the shape of the 1st Special Mountain Artillery Platoon were attached.

To the left of the British was the 2nd Central Force, consisting of the 24th Infantry Brigade (Major General Yamada), the 4th Independent Engineering Battalion and a battery of mountain artillery.

Lastly, the 23rd Infantry Brigade, reinforced by a battalion from the 3rd Regiment of Heavy Field Artillery, two Special Mountain Artillery platoons and the 1st Independent Engineering Battalion, formed the Left Flank Force under the command of Major General Horiuchi.

It requires no great analytical effort to see that the British contribution, both in terms of manpower and equipment (or the lack thereof), was small.

The terrain along the line was eminently suitable for an attacking force, being intersected by numerous deep ravines of clay 'excellent for protection and accommodation in dry weather'.[38] Unfortunately for the attackers though, 15 October was the date on which the heavy rain resumed, and this caused havoc in the line. The sides of the ravines collapsed, carrying away the troops' shelter, and their floors became rivers, making it impossible for the besiegers to find cover from either enemy fire or the weather. The roads and tracks turned into a morass of liquefied mud often knee-deep, preventing supplies and reinforcements from moving forward, and much equipment already in position was buried by falling earth or corroded by the waterlogged state of the ground. The troops simply had to sit it out, remaining soaked through until the downpour abated. The situation was, if anything, even more serious in the rear areas; the main supply depot and siege park had been located in a dry creek of the Litsun River, which was suddenly dry no more. Almost the entire contents, or at least all that would float, was washed into Kiautschou Bay whilst that which remained was submerged in mud and water. The light railway also failed, with large sections of track undermined or washed away completely. This unexpected downfall lasted two days, during which all preparations for an attack were halted.[39]

The weather moderated on 17 September and allowed the besiegers to begin sorting out their positions and equipment, a tedious and time-consuming business particularly as the German artillery continued with its harassing fire. The defenders had hatched a plan for discomfiting the enemy even further though, and as darkness descended on the evening of 17 September they put it into effect. The *S-90*, under Lieutenant Helmut Brunner, slipped out of her berth and headed for the mouth of Kiautschou

Bay. Once out of the bay the vessel would prowl around and tackle any targets of opportunity that might reveal themselves. It was, apparently, a fruitless exercise until midnight when Brunner began heading back towards home and noticed a blacked out vessel on an opposite course. It could only be an enemy ship, so he turned to the attack and launched three torpedoes at the target from some 500m. Two of the weapons struck home, the second causing a massive explosion that completely destroyed the vessel. His target had been the British built 'Naniwa' class protected cruiser *Takachiho* (1885); re-designated a 2nd class Coastal Defence Ship in 1912, the vessel had then been converted to a minelayer. On the night of 17 October she was carrying a large quantity of munitions and it was this ordnance that caused the massive explosion, completely destroying the ship and, aside from three survivors, all of her crew – the biggest single loss of life suffered by Japan during the course of the First World War.[40]

It was, in the grand scheme of things, a relatively minor blow, but to Kato and his command it was stunning, and further compounded by a lack of knowledge regarding the whereabouts of *S-90*. Until this could be ascertained with certainty all shipping movements were suspended and sweeps conducted in search of the predator, as reconnaissance flights over Tsingtau and Kiautschou Bay were unable to ascertain the presence or otherwise of the torpedo boat with any degree of certitude. In fact, Brunner had opted not to return to his base after making the attack, reasoning that the enemy would be out in force and he would be unable to avoid detection. Plüschow records a radio message being received at 01:30hr on 18 September: 'Am hunted by Torpedo Boat Destroyers, return Kiautschou cut off, trying escape south and shall destroy boat if necessary.'[41]

Whether Plüschow's recollection is entirely accurate, he was writing with the benefit of hindsight, is arguable, but in any event Brunner did indeed steer a course south along the Chinese coast and beached *S-90* before setting off on foot. The vessel was discovered two days later and a cavalry unit sent to investigate. The craft had been destroyed, but of the crew there was no sign, and it seems the Japanese found some useful paperwork in the wreck. The most useful information though was of course that *S-90* was no longer in play and naval operations could resume. They were though conducted under a much stricter regime henceforth.[42]

For the defenders the exploits of *S-90* proved morale boosting, though irrelevant to the situation in general. Indeed, though they were probably unaware of the fact, the reinforcement for the British contingent, the men of the 36th Sikhs, arrived at the beachhead on 22 October and proceeded, with difficulty given the poor state of the roads following the recent rain, to their place with Barnardiston's command; they arrived on 28 October.[43] By then the Japanese were nearly ready to begin the final stages of their investment. Watanabe reckoned that he was ready to proceed with issuing his fire plan to his siege batteries on 27 October, even though the communications system was not complete, nor were all his artillery pieces emplaced. The primary artillery observation post was situated on Price-Heinrich-Berg and telephone lines, five in number for inbuilt redundancy, had to be relayed to each of the batteries and positions. This post also had radio communication with Kato's command at sea. The plan contained few surprises; the first priority was the German artillery, both that on land and at sea. When these had been dealt with the barrage would shift to the installations in the Boxer Line, and following that to the German rear areas. There would be enough ammunition for a ten-day bombardment, but it was anticipated that the process would only take seven days before the defenders were forced to capitulate. There would be no artillery registration before the main barrage commenced, and ranges would only be adjusted then. By 29 October most of the siege artillery was emplaced satisfactorily (the 4th Independent Battalion wasn't operational until 4 November) and all supporting services were functioning; Watanabe was ready to deliver an overwhelming weight of ordnance onto the Tsingtau defences.[44]

The Japanese Navy began sending in vessels to shell the city and defences again. On 25 October the *Iwami* approached, though staying outside the range of Hui tsch'en Huk. By listing the ship to increase the range of her main armament, *Iwami* was able to fire some thirty 305mm shells at Hui tsch'en Huk, Iltis Battery and Infantry Work I. The next day the vessel returned in company with *Suwo* and the two vessels bombarded the same targets. On 27 October *Tango* and *Okinoshima* replaced them, and the same ships returned the next day to continue the assault. Because of the distance involved, some 14.5km, this fire was inaccurate in terms of damaging the specific installations in question, but nevertheless was destructive of the nerves of the trapped garrison. It was particularly frustrating in terms of the gunners at Hui tsch'en Huk who were unable to effectively reply.[45]

In addition to this display of naval force, Japanese air power had been much in evidence over the period, their operational activity increasing with sorties over the German lines and rear areas.

Almost every day these craft, announcing their approach by a distant humming, came overhead, glinting and shining in the sun as they sailed above the forts and city. At first they were greeted by a fusillade of shots from all parts of the garrison. Machine guns pumped bullets a hundred a minute at them and every man with a rifle handy let fire. As these bullets came raining back upon the city without any effect but to send Chinese coolies scampering under cover, it was soon realised that rifle and machine-gun fire was altogether ineffective. Then special guns were rigged and the aeroplanes were subjected to shrapnel, which seemed to come nearer to its sailing mark each day but which never brought one of the daring bird-men down. One day I saw a biplane drop down a notch after a shell had exploded directly in front of it. I looked for a volplane [glide with engine off] to earth, but the aviator's loss of control was only momentary, evidently caused by the disturbance of the air. During the bombardment these craft circled over the forts like birds of prey. They were constantly dropping bombs, trying to hit the ammunition depots, the signal station, the Austrian cruiser *Kaiserin Elizabeth*, the electric light plant, and the forts. But […] these bombs were not accurate or powerful enough to do much damage. A few Chinese were killed, a German soldier wounded, tops of houses knocked in, and holes gouged in the streets, but that was all. The bombs fell with an ominous swish as of escaping steam, and it was decidedly uncomfortable to be in the open with a Japanese aeroplane overhead. We are more or less like the ostrich who finds peace and comfort with his head in the sand: In the streets of Tsingtau I have seen a man pull the top of a jinrickisha over his head on the approach of a hostile aeroplane and have noticed Chinese clustering under the top of a tree.[46]

They also managed an aviation first on the night of 28–9 October when they bombed the defenders' positions during the hours of darkness. Attempts to keep Plüschow from effectively reconnoitring were largely successful, even though the efforts to dispose of him or his machine permanently were ineffective. However, because problems with the Taube's homemade propeller kept him grounded on occasion, and because the Japanese positions were worked on tirelessly, when he did take to the air he found the changes in the enemy arrangements – 'this tangle of trenches, zigzags and new positions' – somewhat bewildering and difficult to record accurately.[47] Precision in this regard was not assisted by the Japanese attempts to shoot him down or otherwise obstruct him.

The artillery coordinating position on Prinz-Heinrich-Berg reported itself ready for action on 29 October and Kato sent four warships in to continue the naval bombardment whilst acting under its direction. Between 09:30hr and 16:30hr *Suwo*, *Tango*, *Okinoshima* and *Triumph* bombarded the Tsingtau defences, adjusting their aim according to the feedback received from the position via radio. They withdrew after discharging some 197 projectiles from their main guns, following which SMS *Tiger* was scuttled during the hours of darkness.[48]

Plüschow managed to get airborne on the morning of 30 October and was able to over-fly the Japanese positions before the enemy air force could rise to deter him. This might have been lucky for him as one of the aeroplanes sent up had been fitted with a machine gun. He was able to report the large-scale and advanced preparations of the besieging force, information that the defence used to direct its artillery fire. This was repaid when Kato's bombarding division returned at 09:00hr to recommence their previous day's work. Despite the communication channel working perfectly, and the absence of effective return fire from Hui tsch'en Huk – they had established the maximum range of this battery was 14.13km and accordingly stayed just beyond its reach – the firing of 240 heavy shells again did little damage.[49]

The 31 October was, as the defenders knew well, the birthday of the Japanese Emperor and by way of celebration Kamio's command undertook a brief ceremony before, at about 06:00hr, Watanabe gave the order for the siege train to commence firing, or, as one of the correspondents of *The Times* put it: 'daylight saw the royal salute being fired with live shell at Tsingtau'.[50] The Japanese fire plan was relatively simple.

On the first and second days, in addition to bombardment of the enemy warships, all efforts would be made to silence the enemy's artillery so as to assist the construction and occupation of the first parallel.

From the third day up until the occupation of the second parallel (about the fifth day) the enemy artillery would be suppressed, his works destroyed and the Boxer Line swept with fire in order to assist in the construction of the second parallel.

Following the occupation of the second parallel, the majority of the artillery fire would be employed in destroying the enemy's works, whilst the remainder kept down hostile infantry and artillery that attempted to obstruct offensive movement in preparing, and then assaulting from, the third parallel.

After the Boxer Line had been captured, the artillery would support the friendly troops in securing it from counter-attack and then bombard his second line; Iltiss, Moltke and Bismarck Hills.

There were, roughly, twenty-three Japanese artillery tubes per kilometre of front, a density that was comparable to that attained during the initial stages of the war on the Western Front, though soon to be dwarfed as artillery assumed the dominant role in positional warfare.[51] The land-based artillery was augmented, from about 09:00hr, by the naval contribution as Kato once again sent his heavy ships into action.

The combined barrage soon silenced any German return fire because, even though they had refrained from pre-registering their siege batteries, the Japanese knew where the fixed defensive positions were and shortly found their range; fire was also brought to bear on any targets of opportunity. The German batteries were suppressed less by direct hits than by their positions being submerged in debris from near misses. This was to prove of some importance for the defenders were able in several cases to return their weapons to service, largely due to the relative antiquity and thus lack of sophistication of much of the ordnance, without the need for extensive repairs.[52] Indeed, despite the crushing superiority enjoyed by the attackers, the defensive fire was to continue to some degree throughout the day and into the night. The most obvious sign of the effects of the bombardment, at least to those observing from a distance, were the huge plumes of smoke caused by hits on the oil storage tanks adjacent to the Large Harbour. Two of these, owned by the Asiatic Petroleum Company – the first Royal Dutch/ Shell joint venture – and Standard Oil respectively, had been set afire early on and their contents in turn caused other fires as they flowed around the installations, these proving beyond the capacity of the local fire brigade to control.[53] In fact the destruction of the Standard Oil installations was accidental. The General Staff History records that a note had been received via the Japanese Foreign Office from the US government asking that they be spared. Accordingly the objective was struck out of the plan but to apparently no effect, perhaps demonstrating the relative inaccuracy of the fire.

There were a number of independent observers of the operations at this stage; correspondents from various journals and foreign military observers had arrived in the theatre in late October. Though the Japanese were intensely secretive they could not conceal the fact of their bombardment or the plainly visible results.

> The thunder of the great guns broke suddenly upon that stillness which only dawn knows, and their discharges flashed readily on the darkling slopes. The Japanese shooting, it is related, displayed remarkable accuracy, some of the first projectiles bursting upon the enormous oil tanks of the Standard Oil Company and the Asiatic Petroleum Company. A blaze roared skywards, and for many hours the heavens were darkened by an immense cloud of black petroleum smoke which hung like a pall over the town. Shells passing over these fires drew up columns of flame to a great height. Chinese coolies could be seen running before the spreading and burning oil. Fires broke out also on the wharves of the outer harbour.[54]

Many of the Japanese shells, no doubt due to the lack of pre-registration, were over-range and landed in Tapatau and Tsingtau, though the former received the worst of it. It has been estimated that at least 100 Chinese were killed during this period and a deliberate targeting exercise carried out later in the day on the urban areas.[55] The bombardment continued with varying levels of frequency throughout the daylight hours of 31 October, and at nightfall the Japanese gunners switched to shrapnel – by bursting shrapnel shell over the defenders' positions they made it difficult, if not impossible, for repairs to be carried out. Such fire also covered the forward movement of the Japanese engineers as they extended their saps towards the Boxer Line and began constructing the parallel works some 300m ahead of the advanced investment line.[56]

At daylight on 1 November the high-explosive barrage resumed, again concentrating primarily on the German artillery positions though many of these were now out of action. The secondary targets were the defences in the Boxer Line, particularly the infantry works and the extemporised defences between them. The ferro-concrete redoubts withstood the bombardment without any serious damage, and, though they were scarred and badly battered externally, none of the projectiles penetrated any vital interior position. The communication trenches and other intermediate field works were however obliterated and this, together with the destruction of much of the telephone system, isolated the personnel manning the works, both from each other and from the command further back. The targeting of the signal station further hindered communication of every kind, and with the bringing down of the radio antenna even one-way communication from the outside world was terminated.[57] Shutting this down was probably a secondary objective; the primary reason for targeting the signal station was to prevent it jamming and otherwise interfering with Japanese wireless communications which had become a problem.

After nightfall the sappers returned to their task of advancing the siege works whilst infantry patrols went forward to reconnoitre and probe the defences. One such probe crossed the Haipo and a four-man party entered the ditch near Infantry Work 4, which was under the command of Captain von Stranz, and began cutting the wire.[58] They remained undetected for some time, indicating the lack of awareness of the defenders who stayed under cover, but were eventually heard and forced to retire with the loss of one man after machine-gun fire was directed at them. A second patrol took their place a little later and, under the very noses of the defence, completed the wire-cutting task before they too were detected.

The defenders conceived that an assault in strength was under way and called down artillery fire in support from Iltis Battery and moved a reserve formation made up of naval personnel, whose ships had been scuttled, towards the front. The Japanese patrol withdrew, leaving the defenders under the erroneous impression that they had defeated a serious attempt at breaching the line, rather than, as was the case, an opportunistic foray. However, what the probe had revealed to the attackers was that the defenders were remaining largely inside the concrete works, leaving the gaps between them vulnerable to infiltration. This was confirmed by the experiences of a separate patrol that reconnoitred near Infantry Work 3, also known as the 'Central Fort' to the Japanese; the knowledge gained being of some potential worth.[59] Also of value was an understanding of the nature of the barbed-wire obstacles. These were permanent fixtures, with extra heavy wire holding barbs 'so closely together that it would be difficult to get a pair of pliers in a position to cut it'.[60] It did prove possible to cut the wire, but the stakes it was strung on, made from heavy duty angle-iron secured to a square base-plate some 300mm per side and sunk into the ground to a depth of about half a metre, proved almost impossible to dislodge. Initial intelligence had indicated that the wire was charged with 30,000 volts, but direct examination showed this not to be the case.

Apart from repelling the Japanese attack, as they thought, the defenders spent the night of 1–2 November destroying further equipment that might be of use to the besiegers. Chief amongst this was *Kaiserin Elisabeth*; shortly after midnight, having fired off her remaining ammunition in the general direction of the Japanese, the vessel was moved into deep water in Kiautschou Bay and scuttled. Explosive charges extemporised from torpedo warheads ensured that the ship was beyond salvage even if the wreck was located. The Austro-Hungarian cruiser was only one of several vessels scuttled that night, including the floating dock, which was seen to have disappeared the next morning. Only the *Jaguar* remained afloat at sunrise at which point the rapid rate of advance of the attackers, up to the edge of the Haipo River between Kiautschou Bay and the area in front of Infantry Work 3, was revealed to the Germans.[61]

Revealed to the Japanese, by their action during the hours of darkness, was the precise position of the Iltis Battery and this was promptly targeted and put out of action by counter-battery fire. The remorseless battering by the siege train also resumed, and the German inability to respond effectively due to the accuracy of Japanese return fire began to be exacerbated by a shortage of ammunition.[62] The Japanese bombardment, though intense, was perhaps not as destructive as it could have been. What seems to have mitigated the effect to some extent was the high rate of dud shells. One press correspondent that entered Tsingtau after the conclusion of operations noted the proliferation of 'giant shells, some three feet long and a foot in diameter, [that] were lying about on side-walk and street still unexploded'.[63] Burdick, working from contemporary German estimates, calculates that between 10 and 25 per cent of the Japanese ordnance failed to explode. This shortcoming, being attributable to faulty manufacture, played a major role in sparing the defenders a worse ordeal than they had to endure anyway.[64]

Also sparing the defenders to some extent on 2 November was the onset of rain, which affected the assailants more than the defence inasmuch as the attackers' diggings became waterlogged and collapsed in some cases. Further alleviation was attributable to the reduction of the rate of fire of the 280mm howitzers. Their temporary emplacements suffered from the immense recoil and had the potential to render firing both dangerous and inaccurate.[65] The remainder of the siege train concentrated its fire on the Boxer Line, particularly in an attempt to destroy the wire and obstacles in the trench and thus mitigate the need to resort to manual methods with their inevitable human cost. The power station was also targeted, with the result that the chimney was brought down in the evening, thus rendering the city dependent on primitive forms of lighting.[66]

The 3 and 4 November saw further progress in the advancement of the siege works and continuing bombardment, though useful targets for this were now at a premium as little of the defences remained other than the concrete Infantry Works. The defenders had begun destroying their batteries on 2 November as they ran out of ammunition, and in any event returning the Japanese fire was a hazardous business due to the rapidity and accuracy of the response. The lack of defensive fire allowed some reorganisation of the siege artillery and several of the batteries were moved forward and swiftly re-emplaced with the minimum of disruption. On the far right of the Japanese line the sappers attached to 67th Infantry Regiment had advanced their works to within a short distance of the Haipo River, and thus close to the city's water pumping station situated on the eastern bank. The decision was taken by 29th Infantry Brigade to attempt to take the station on the evening of 4 November and a company sized unit, comprising infantry and engineers, was assembled. It had not been bombarded by the siege artillery; the idea seemingly being to preserve it for future use by the occupying force. So the engineers cut through the defensive wire with Bangalore Torpedoes, thus allowing the infantry to surround the place, whilst a box artillery barrage insulated it from any attempted relief.[67]

Despite its relative isolation the pumping station was actually a well-fortified strongpoint. The machinery rooms, stores and personnel quarters were located underground and well protected by ferro-concrete. The whole was surrounded by a bank of earth some 6m in height, itself protected by a ditch, about 12m wide and 2m deep at the counterscarp, that was filled with barbed-wire obstacles. The leader of the platoon investigating the area, 2nd Lieutenant Yokokura, later reported that the personnel manning the station had locked themselves inside behind 'iron doors' and were still working the pumps, but when they realised that the enemy were upon them they opened the doors and surrendered. The haul amounted to one sergeant major, twenty rank and file, two water works engineers and five Chinese, together with twenty-five rifles. The station was immediately fortified against any counter-attack and with its loss Tsingtau was without a mains water supply and thus dependent on the several, somewhat brackish, wells within the city.

Elsewhere along the line the nocturnal 'mole warfare' techniques advanced the saps and trenches ever nearer to the ditch in order to construct the third parallel – the final assault line. This progressed everywhere apart from the British sector of front, where enemy fire prevented the final approach being made. As Barnardison reported:

On 5 November I was ordered to prepare a Third Position of attack on the left bank of the river. This line was to a great extent enfiladed on both flanks by No. 1 and 2 Redoubts, especially the latter, from which annoying machine-gun fire was experienced. The bed of the river [...] had also to be crossed, and in doing so the working parties of the 2nd Battalion South Wales Borderers suffered somewhat severely, losing 8 non-commissioned officers and men killed and 24 wounded. The 36th Sikhs had only slight losses. Notwithstanding this a good deal of work was done, especially on the right flank. I considered it my duty to represent to the Japanese Commander-in-Chief the untenable nature, for permanent occupation, of the portion of the Third Position in my front, but received a reply that it was necessary for it to be held in order to fit in with the general scheme of assault.[68]

Though most diplomatically phrased, it is possible to distinguish in the final sentence of this quotation a hint of asperity in the relations between the Allies. Indeed, though suppressed for political reasons at the time, the British military contribution did not impress the Japanese in any way, shape or form. Reports from the front revealed the perception that the British were reluctant to get involved in the fighting and 'hard to trust'. More brutal opinions had it that they were no more than 'baggage' and 'decoration' on the battlefield. The nature of these observations filtered through to the Japanese press, one report stating that: 'Only when nothing happened were British soldiers wonderful and it was like taking a lady on a trip. However, such a lady can be a burden and lead to total disaster for a force when the enemy appears.'[69]

Daylight on 5 November saw three Japanese aeroplanes overfly the German positions dropping not explosive devices, as might have been expected, but rather bundles of leaflets carrying a message from the besiegers:

To the Respected Officers and Men of the Fortress.
    It would act against the will of God as well as humanity if one were to destroy the still useful weapons, ships, and other structures without tactical justification and only because of the envious view that they might fall into the hands of the enemy.
    Although we are certain in the belief that, in the case of the chivalrous officers and men, they would not put into effect such thoughtlessness, we nevertheless would like to emphasise the above as our point of view.[70]

On the face of it this message seemed to clearly indicate that the besiegers, perceiving that they would shortly be in occupation of the city, desired that as much of it be preserved as was possible. If so they adopted a rather contradictory attitude inasmuch as shortly after dispensing it a naval barrage, delivered by *Mishima*, *Tango*, *Okinoshina* and *Iwami* from Hai hsi Bay to the west of Cape Jaeschke, was directed onto the urban area of Tsingtau. Backed by the land batteries, this bombardment caused great damage to the city, though one shot, apparently misaimed, struck one of the 240mm gun positions at Hui tsch'en Huk, destroying the gun and killing seven of the crew. Without a mains water supply the possibility of fire-fighting in Tsingtau was greatly reduced and several buildings were burned down, though because of the relative spaciousness of the city fires did not jump easily from building to building and so there was no major conflagration. Tapatau, the Chinese quarter, was not constructed on such generous proportions, though the relatively smaller size of the dwellings and their less robust structural strength meant they collapsed rather than burned, and it too was spared an inferno.[71] Because the German artillery was now virtually silent the sapping work continued during daylight hours without fear of interruption, and the third parallel was completed during the day close up to the defensive ditch. Unable to effectively counter these moves the defenders, also ignoring the Japanese plea as contained in their airdropped leaflet, began putting their coastal artillery batteries out of action, which in any event, other than Hui tsch'en Huk, had proved mostly ineffective. It was clear to all that the end was not far off, and only the ferro-concrete infantry works remained as anything like effective defensive positions, though a report from one to Meyer-Waldeck 'reflected the universal condition':

The entire work is shot to pieces, a hill of fragments, without any defences. The entire trench system is knocked out; the redoubt still holds together, but everything else, including the explosives storage room, is destroyed. Only a single observation post is in use. I shall hold the redoubt as long as possible.[72]

Given the impossibility of offering effective resistance to the besiegers, Meyer-Waldeck was under no illusions as to the length of time left to the defence force. Evidence for this may be adduced from his ordering Plüschow to make a getaway attempt the following day. He was to carry away papers relating to the course of the siege and several symbolic items such as the fastenings from the flagpole, as well as private letters from members of the garrison.[73]

The attackers saw the elusive Taube take to the air the next morning, and, according to Plüschow himself, make a last circuit of Tsingtau before setting off southwards; 'never,' as the Japanese General Staff history put it, 'to come back'. Though the Japanese artillery made what was to turn out to be their final efforts to shoot him down, hostile aircraft did not attempt to follow and he made good his escape towards neutral China, eventually reaching Tientsin where he was reunited with the crew of *S-90*. As he left his ground crew destroyed any remaining equipment, but his place over the city was soon taken by the Japanese aeroplanes who sortied in force, dropping numerous bombs onto the defenders' positions, as a less than effective adjunct to the efforts of the artillery. As the bombardment from land and air went on the Japanese infantry began to move into their final assault positions in the third parallel. The British however, still troubled by the fire from the German machine guns, only occupied their sector with a thin outpost line. The Governor, noting the proximity of the attackers and expecting an imminent assault, ordered a general alert for the afternoon.[74]

Kamio now had all his infantry where he wanted them, with the exception of the British contingent, and all his equipment in place. His orders for the night of 6–7 November did not however call for a general assault, but rather stipulated small scale, though aggressive, probing of the Boxer Line to test for weak spots, together with the usual artillery barrage. He emphasised flexibility and the exploitation of success. As darkness fell the sappers dug forward from the third parallel and, using mining techniques, burrowed through the counterscarp before blowing several breaches in it. This allowed the infantry direct access to the ditch without the need to leave the entrenchments. It was also discovered that the ditch in front of Infantry Works 1 and 2 differed somewhat from the saw-tooth version already noted, being a conventional channel in section. It was also found to be subject to flanking fire from the Central Fort (Infantry Work 3).

Wire that had remained intact following the previous attention of the artillery was cut or covered, allowing more or less unrestricted access within the ditch, and patrols moved across it and out onto the German side as darkness fell. At around 23:00hr a firefight broke out around Infantry Work 2 as a patrol from the 56th Infantry Regiment attempted to infiltrate and bypass it. The defenders were more alert than they had been on

1 November and sallied out to meet them. Eventually, after about an hour of fighting, the Japanese retreated and called down an artillery barrage onto the defenders for their pains.[75]

More or less concurrently Infantry Work 3 (Central Fort) under the command of Captain Lancelle was the object of similar tactics. The results were however rather different. Engineers from the 4th Independent Battalion, preceding units from the 56th Infantry Regiment, discovered that they met with no resistance whatsoever when they began cutting two 'roads' through the entanglements in both the inner and outer ditches in front of the fortification. Accordingly this work was completed expeditiously, and the information on the apparent passivity of the defenders in that sector passed up the chain of command. Major General Yamada, commander of the 2nd Central Force, immediately decided to attempt an assault to take the work, but sought the sanction of Kamio before so doing. The division commander concurred, so a company sized unit under Lieutenant Nakamura Jekizo of the 56th Infantry Regiment crossed the ditch at about 01:00hr.

The plan required some courage on the part of the participants, who were all volunteers. They comprised twenty engineers and six infantry NCOs who were armed with hand grenades, whilst further infantry units, complete with mortars, stood ready in immediate support. The whole regiment was also awaiting developments and was ready to advance at a few minutes' notice. Formed into two detachments, the raiders used ladders to climb into the ditch away from the breach and, unseen, safely reached the German parapet which they scaled before moving to reform. The plan called for a stealthy advance until the occupants of the redoubt opened up on them, and then a charge forward throwing the grenades in an attempt to disable the defenders and damage the machine guns. This procedure was modified when it became apparent that the fortification was, effectively, unguarded and Nakamura instead sent his men left and right around it to the rear (or 'gorge' in fortification terms) where they occupied the shelter trenches.

Detailing ten grenadiers and an NCO to resist any German potential counter-attack, he used the rest of his men to block the redoubt's exits and then sent for reinforcements. Before these could arrive however the Japanese were detected by defence posts on the flanks of the fortification, whereby a hot fire with machine guns was opened. Several volleys of grenades stemmed that, and in the meantime the redoubt's telephone wires were cut and access was forced into the signal room where, after the occupants were overcome, the power was cut. This plunged the whole work into darkness and prevented any further telephoning or signalling.

By this time two platoons of reinforcements had begun to arrive; half of them formed a defensive line behind the redoubt whilst the rest broke into it. It was claimed that they found the occupants in bed, but whatever the truth of the matter Lancelle immediately surrendered the work complete with its complement of about 200 men to Nakamura. It had taken forty minutes and been, to quote Burdick's words, 'ridiculously easy'.[76] It was undoubtedly a famous and daring victory, and Nakamura was awarded the Order of the Golden Kite (4th class) which he undoubtedly deserved.[77]

In practical terms however, there was now a large and growing gap in the very centre of the Boxer Line, and word quickly got to Meyer-Waldeck who ordered his reserves to counter-attack under cover of a German barrage. Whilst such a move was theoretically sound, it was, practically, almost impossible. There was simply not enough artillery left to provide an effective bombardment, and precious little manpower, particularly in comparison with that available to the attackers, to seal the breach. The effort was made, but the counter-attackers, including a contingent of Austro-Hungarian sailors landed from *Kaiserin Elisabeth*, were simply too weak to throw back the rapidly reinforcing Japanese.

The Boxer Line, being a linear defence, was vulnerable to being 'rolled up' from the flanks once breached at a given point. The Japanese having made the breach now proceeded to widen it by moving against Infantry Works 2 and 4 on either side. Both works held out for some hours, assisted by the *Jaguar*, the last German warship afloat, which fired away her remaining ordnance in support. The outcome however could be in no doubt and both works surrendered after about three hours of resistance. The Boxer Line was now useless, for with no defence in depth the penetration meant the route to Tsingtau was now as good as wide open. The Japanese infantry surged through the gap and began a general advance on Tsingtau and various strategic points, such as Iltis and Bismarck Hills. The batteries on the former fought the attackers for a time before surrendering, whereas the artillerymen on the latter, having fired away the last of their ammunition, set charges to destroy their guns and vacated the position at about 05:00hr. This final destruction of land-based artillery had its counterpart on the water; *Jaguar*, after attempting to repulse the infantry attack, had been scuttled in Kiautschou Bay.[78]

At 06:00hr Meyer-Waldeck held a meeting at his headquarters in the Bismarck Hill Command Post where the latest information was assimilated. It had long been an unwritten rule of siege warfare that a garrison could honourably surrender following a 'practical breach' being made in their defences. The Japanese, using classic siege warfare methodology, had now achieved just such a breach. Whether the Governor was aware of the 'rule' is unknown, but he had now only two options; surrender or a fanatical 'fight to the last man and last bullet' scenario. Meyer-Waldeck was no fanatic. Brace put it thus:

> If the governor had permitted the unequal struggle to go on his men would have lasted only a few hours longer. It would be an Alamo, and the name of the German garrison would be heralded throughout history as the heroic band of whites who stood against the yellow invasion until the last man. On the other hand the governor had with him a large part of the German commercial community of the Far East which Germany had built up with such painstaking care.[79]

The Governor ordered the white flag hoisted on the signal station and over the German positions and composed a message to Kamio: 'Since my defensive measures are exhausted I am now ready to enter into surrender negotiations for the now open city. [...] I request you to appoint plenipotentiaries to the discussions, as well as to set time and place for the meeting of the respective plenipotentiaries. [...]'[80] The carrier of this message was Major Georg von Kayser, adjutant to Meyer-Waldeck's Chief-of-Staff, naval Captain Ludwig Saxer – the latter being the Governor's appointee as German plenipotentiary. Despite Barnardiston's contention that all firing ceased at 07:00hr Kayser had difficulty getting through the lines in safety, but he was eventually allowed to proceed under his flag of truce to the village of Tungwutschiatsun, some 4km behind the Japanese front line, more or less opposite the celebrated Central Fort (Infantry Work 3).[81] It was agreed that a general armistice would come into play immediately, and that formal negotiations for the capitulation would commence that afternoon at 16:00hr in Moltke Barracks.[82]

The Japanese had meanwhile advanced into the area between the Boxer Line and the city, as had their ally – though the latter had seen no fighting.[83] As Barnardiston was to state it: '[At] about [07:30hr] I received orders to advance, and, the enemy along the whole of our front having then retired, I marched into Tsingtau'.[84] It is then ironic to note that probably the last casualties of the campaign, at least caused by direct enemy action, were two British soldiers who thought that all fighting had ceased and left cover. They were hit by an artillery shell; fighting went on for some time in areas difficult to communicate with, particularly Infantry Works 1 and 5, which, being largely peripheral to the advance, were not seriously assaulted and did not capitulate until reached by German staff officers.[85]

The meeting of the plenipotentiaries, Kamio being represented by his Chief-of-Staff, Major General Yamanashi Hanzo, was largely a formality, inasmuch as the Japanese were in a position to dictate terms as they pleased. The terms were presented to the Germans, led by Saxer, at the 16:00hr meeting and an adjournment then took place for him to consider the document setting them out. It was, in all essentials, very simple; the Kiautschou Protectorate would formally transfer to Japan on 10 November. German military and naval personnel would become prisoners of war, whilst all equipment, of which there was to be no further destruction, would become Japanese property. The plenipotentiaries reconvened at 19:00hr. Yamanashi had largely taken up the somewhat lengthy interval with a visit to the city at Saxer's request, the latter being concerned about the possible depredations of the Japanese soldiery. The Chief-of-Staff promptly ordered all the troops out of the urban area and set up a demarcation line some 2–3km outside, which they were forbidden to pass. The only qualification of the terms proposed by Saxer was that the German officers be allowed to retain their swords, which was refused on the grounds that Yamanashi did not possess the authority to accede to the request.[86] The parties then signed; Yamanashi for the Japanese Army, Commander Takakashi for the navy and Saxer for the German administration. Brigadier Barnardiston was neither consulted as to the terms nor asked to attend the meetings, and the sole British officer present, Lieutenant Colonel Everard Calthrop, was there by virtue of his being the liaison officer attached to the 18th Division.[87]

General Kamio's conquest marked the end of the German territorial presence in East Asia and the Pacific. The naval presence was also drawing to a close as has already been related; *Emden* was destroyed on 9 November and Spee, having revealed himself to be at the very periphery of the theatre with his defeat of Cradock on 1 November, was to meet superior force on 8 December in another ocean.

Kamio had shown himself to be a prudent and professional commander of an effective and well-trained force. The campaign against Germany's Kiautschou Territory had been conducted throughout with competence. There had never been any doubt as to the outcome, and the numbers finally involved, some 50,000 on the Japanese side as against something over 4,000 on the German, clearly demonstrate the scale of the disparity in forces.[88] The losses to casualties on both sides were small; Japanese losses amounted to 415 dead and 1,451 wounded, a rate of about 3 per cent, whilst Barnardiston's command of some 950 lost 13 dead and 61 wounded (a number of whom later died from their wounds), nearly 8 per cent. German losses were 100 per cent inasmuch as they were all taken prisoner, but the battlefield casualties amounted to 199 dead and 294 wounded, which equates roughly to 10 per cent of the total.[89] The capture of Tsingtau left the Japanese with 4,689 German and Austro-Hungarian prisoners ultimately, many of them reservists and somewhat advanced in years.[90] These were shipped to Japan and incarcerated in various prisoner of war 'camps' throughout Japan; these places of imprisonment, comprising temples, former barracks and other non–purpose built structures, were ill adapted for the purpose and unsuited to Europeans unused to the cold winter weather. Though the conditions under which the prisoners were held were undoubtedly unpleasant, there appears to have been little or none of the brutality that was associated with those in Japanese captivity later in the century. Indeed the Japanese authorities allowed the power representing German interest, the US, to send officials on an inspection tour of the camps in 1916 following a barrage of complaints from the Germans.[91]

The official that conducted this tour of inspection was a young diplomat of impeccable breeding and background who was to later go on to somewhat greater fame; Benjamin Sumner Welles.[92] Welles, accompanied by a Japanese-speaking companion, Joseph W. Ballantine, set out on 29 February 1916 for a two–week tour of ten of the camps. He found that the conditions varied from camp to camp, and in his final report of some 120 pages, dated 21 March 1916, he detailed his findings at each of the 10 sites visited. Four, he adjudged, had sub-standard regimes including, for example, the commandant at the camp, an ex-army barracks, located outside the town of Kurume, on the island of Kyushu, who allowed his men to strike the prisoners for minor offences. Welles was pleased to note, whilst on a return visit to the sites at the end of 1916, that the commandants of the four camps in question had been replaced.[93]

The campaign threw up few novel elements, perhaps the most original being the use made of air power on the Japanese side. It was the most intensive use of aircraft up to that time, with several firsts as has been related, and predated the beginnings of the integration of aircraft into battle for reconnaissance purposes.[94] Indeed Kamio had gone further, and used aeroplanes for what would later be termed strike missions, though with little success, and in attempts to shoot down enemy aircraft, as represented by the sole example on the German side.

With the fall of the territory the various outside observers began to depart. Brace's description of his leave-taking is somewhat poignant:

> When I left Tsingtau it was on the back of a hardy Mongol pony, for the Germans had put their railway out of commission by blowing up the bridges. The cutting north wind was chasing the dry leaves around the Moltke Barracks where the Japanese had established staff headquarters [...] Everywhere the country was gouged with the great holes and gashes of shells [...] Then we went through the maze of Japanese trenches. One last glance at the little city [...] With its roofs of red tile and many gables Tsingtau was still, in appearance, at least, the Little Germany Across the Sea. But already the Japanese had begun to rename the streets and hills.[95]

As one Japanese writer put it (in translation): 'Sei-To has fallen under the gallant leadership of Lieutenant-General Kamio Mitsuomi.'[96] This demonstrates that the change of sovereignty begat a change of name for Tsingtau itself, becoming, in its Romanised English version, Sei-To.[97] Actions such as this were not of the kind that suggested a quick restoration to China was in the offing.

Chapter 8

Into the Future

There can be little doubt that Japan's entry into the war in 1914 was of immense benefit to her ally the UK, and by extension to the *Entente* or Allied cause generally. In naval terms, and as Spee himself had noted, Japanese involvement meant a forced withdrawal from East Asia for his East Asiatic squadron. Without that involvement he might not have been forced to evacuate the Pacific completely, or at least as early as he did. What could have been done had he remained is open to question, or at least with respect to the heavy ships of his command, as has already been discussed.

On the other hand it is legitimate to argue that, even without Japanese intervention, British and Australian naval forces could have circumscribed his operations to some degree. This is particularly so given that they would undoubtedly have blockaded Tsingtau, German's only base in the area. It would though have been a long-winded and bothersome business requiring significant, and no doubt grudgingly granted, reinforcements from the European theatre.[1]

Where Japanese intervention was of importance was in relation to Kiautschou generally and Tsingtau specifically. It would have been extremely difficult, though not impossible, for the British and Australians to have blockaded the port *and* conducted the various other operations needed to contain the East Asiatic Cruiser Squadron simultaneously. It would have been even more difficult, and probably impossible, for British, French or Russian forces (or some ad hoc combination thereof) to have invaded Kiautschou and taken Tsingtau. The formation of an expeditionary force of something around corps strength and its transport to, and maintenance in, China would have involved a major effort that would have been difficult to justify. It would also have constituted a logistical nightmare. The Japanese, unencumbered elsewhere, were able and willing to commit such resources and had little difficulty in so doing. So, in order to militarily neutralise the

German base early in the war Japanese intervention was essential. This involvement has not always been perceived in that light. No less an authority than Arthur Marder argued that:

> The Royal Navy had little reason to be grateful to the Japanese in the First World War. Japan refused to send any ships to fight Germany until 1917, when a destroyer flotilla was sent to the Mediterranean, and made hay in the Far East while the British were committed in Europe, as through the seizure of German-occupied Tsingtau and German islands in the Pacific – the Marshalls, Marianas, Carolines, and Palau.[2]

It is self-evidently true that Japan did send ships to fight Germany before 1917 and by so doing freed the Royal Navy from the requirement. It follows that the ability to achieve the Royal Navy's desiderata, of almost overwhelming numerical superiority in the North European theatre, was facilitated by Japanese actions.

The second point made by Marder in terms of 'making hay' has some force, inasmuch as in political-strategic terms Japan had made vast gains for minimal cost including of course acquiring the Kiautschou protectorate. The naval base at Tsingtau may perhaps be compared with the later, and much larger, example that the British constructed at Singapore. In a similar manner Tsingtau was in naval terms more or less useless once it had no fleet. The value of the territory to Japan though wasn't solely based around its position or facilities, but rather the foothold it represented in terms of China.

Indeed it was evident almost from the outset that the Japanese presence was not intended to be greatly limited in either time or space. In respect of Kiautschou, evidence for this may be adduced by noting that, under the mantle of 'military necessity' the Japanese Army had taken over control of the Shantung Railway during the operations against Germany. At the capitulation this control had lengthened to include Tsinan, a distance of nearly 400km, and had broadened to accommodate the Poshan mines.[3] That the occupation was, from the Japanese perspective, less limited than might have been implied by the phrase 'eventual restoration [...] to China' used in the ultimatum of 15 August was evidenced by the response to a Chinese point that the 'war-zone' might be abolished, made on 25 November 1914. The Japanese reply was curt: 'Our military authorities desire no change in the status of the war zone for the time being.' Upon further pursuing the subject, on 2 December, China received much the same response; the invocation of 'military necessity'.[4]

Further indications of Japanese intentions were evidenced by Foreign Minister Kato's 'clarification' in the Japanese Parliament on 8 December. The matter was published in the Japanese press as a question and answer session:

Questions:
(a) Whether Kiautschou will be returned to China?
(b) Whether the Imperial Government of Japan were pledged to China, or to any other Power, in the matter of the final disposition of Kiautschou?
(c) Whether the clause in the ultimatum [to Germany] referring to the final restitution of Kiautschou to China did not bind the action of Japan?

Baron Kato's Replies:
(a) The question regarding Kiautschou was, at present, unanswerable.
(b) Japan had never committed herself to any foreign Power on this point.
(c) The purpose of the ultimatum to Germany was to take Kiautschou from Germany and so to restore peace in the Orient. Restitution after a campaign was not thought of and was not referred in the ultimatum.[5]

That Japan most definitely did not have a benevolent attitude towards China was reemphasised on 18 January 1915. The Chinese government was presented with a secret ultimatum in a note outlining what became known as the 'Twenty-One Demands'. These would, if acceded to in total, have 'reduced China to vassalage'.[6] The Chinese leaked details of the demands to the press and international community, provoking an outburst of nationalism in China and the disapprobation of Woodrow Wilson and the

US government. This remonstration, accompanied by similar protests from the UK, succeeded, in part, in toning down the demands, which had become 'requests' by 21 March.[7] Bruce Elleman has recently demonstrated that the issue of the 'Twenty-One Demands' vis-à-vis Chinese domestic politics was far from straightforward.[8] What is more clear-cut is the suspicion of Japanese motives and ambitions in respect of China and Chinese territory engendered in the US body politic by Japanese behavior. Conversely Japan felt resentment at what they saw as US intervention in an essentially bilateral matter.[9] Consequently the issue delineated Japanese-US differences over China, and though it was not always at the forefront it was a matter that was not to be finally settled until 1945.[10]

It was similar with regard to the Pacific islands; the possession of the formerly German island territory north of the equator. Despite the valueless nature of these islands in economic terms, in the strategic sense they were potentially of great value to their new owners. Their possession advanced Japan's naval perimeter by several thousand kilometres and provided the opportunity for anchorages well outside home waters. This was of particular concern to the US Navy, as it afforded the Japanese Navy a flank position on the line of communication between the continental US and American territory in the western Pacific, primarily the Philippines. That these territories were held under a League of Nations Mandate that precluded fortification was of little consequence to the US; the Japanese kept the islands veiled in secrecy and generally denied all access to foreigners which inevitably fuelled suspicions.[11]

The US Navy's famous War Plan Orange, though subject to various manifestations and updates, had as a core principle that in the event of conflict with Japan the American fleet would project its sea power across the Pacific, relieve American forces at Guam and the Philippines, and then wage a decisive battle close to the Japanese home islands. The Japanese plan to counter this involved weakening the advancing fleet by the use of submarine and aircraft attack, so that when the decisive battle occurred their fleet would be the stronger, nearer to home waters, and thus the likely victor. Both navies were, though US strategy changed over time, in thrall to the Mahanian objective of the decisive battle.[12]

In order to reduce the threat the Japanese flank positions posed to the naval thrust of their war plan, it would be necessary for the US to neutralise them, which would be a task entrusted to the Marine Corps. Accordingly Major General John J. Lejeune, the commanding officer of the Corps in 1920, tasked a Marine Corps staff officer, Major Earl H. Ellis, 'reputed to be the most brilliant planner in the Corps', with studying the problem.[13] Ellis' conclusions were embodied in *Operation Plan 712, Advanced Base Operations in Micronesia*, which was endorsed by Lejeune in July 1921 as the basis for future training and wartime mobilisation planning in the Marine Corps.[14] Ellis succinctly described the problem:

> In order to impose our will upon Japan, it will be necessary for us to project our fleet and land forces across the Pacific and wage war in Japanese waters. To effect this requires that we have sufficient bases to support the fleet, both during its projection and afterwards. As the matter stands at present, we cannot count upon the use of any bases west of Hawaii except those which we may seize from the enemy after the opening of hostilities. Moreover, the continued occupation of the Marshall, Caroline and Pelew Islands by the Japanese [...] invests them with a series of emergency bases flanking any line of communications across the Pacific throughout a distance of 2300 miles. The reduction and occupation of these islands and the establishment of the necessary bases therein, as a preliminary phase of the hostilities, is practically imperative.[15]

So Japan did indeed derive great theoretical advantage from possession of the islands, though the systematic militarisation of them did not actually begin until 1940. Work then advanced on several – Saipan in the Marianas, Truk, Ponape and the Palau Islands in the Carolines and Kwajalein, Wotje, Jaluit and Maloelap in the Marshalls – enough to warrant their inclusion in Yamamoto's 'Combined Fleet Secret Operation Order No. 1' of 5 November 1941. This document formed the blueprint for the offensive phase of the war against the US. Truk in particular became an important base for Japan's Combined Fleet.[16] The strategy of using them as bases to attrite an American advance across the Central Pacific failed however. When the time came the old battle-fleet tactics had been replaced by something much more formidable; the US Navy had developed an operational plan of its own; and the Japanese faced overwhelming materiel and technological superiority.[17]

In the period after the First World War though it was not only the US that was rendered more vulnerable and disadvantaged by the extension of Japanese power. Australia, New Zealand and, by extension, the UK perceived themselves threatened too. Put bluntly the Japanese Navy possessed capabilities far in excess of those of the East Asiatic Cruiser Squadron of 1914. Whilst HMAS *Australia* had been a deterrent to that squadron, a single capital ship was no such thing to the Japanese fleet. Since the Royal Navy was responsible for the maritime defence of the Empire, it followed that it, or the RAN, or both, would have to be greatly reinforced in order to provide an effective defence in the event of a war with Japan. Admiral Jellicoe, former commander of the Grand Fleet, stated it thus in 1919 following study of the matter: 'It must be recognised that Australia is powerless against a strong naval and military power without the assistance of the British Fleet.'[18] The 'strong' power mentioned wasn't named, but there was no doubt as to exactly which country he was referring.

The 'Jellicoe Mission' to Australia from May to August 1919 sought to advise on '(*a*.) Naval strategical problems affecting Australian waters and the Pacific; (*b*.) Future composition of Australian Navy; (*c*.) Naval Base and supply requirements in the Pacific and East Indian waters; (*d*.) General organisation of the Naval Forces and Administration.' Jellicoe concluded that 'the naval interests of the Empire are likely to demand within the next five years, a Far Eastern Seagoing Fleet of considerable strength'.[19] It was indeed a strong fleet that he 'assumed':

8 Battleships of modern 'Dreadnought' type.
8 Battle-cruisers, also of modern type.
30 Light Cruisers.
40 Modern Destroyers.
3 Flotilla Leaders.
2 Depot Ships for Destroyers.
36 Submarines (excluding those stationed in Indian waters).
4 Submarine Parent Ships.

4 Aircraft Carriers.
12 Fleet Minesweepers.
1 Large Seagoing Minelayer.
2 Fleet Repair Ships.[20]

The cost was, in percentage terms, to be split 75:20:5 between the UK, Australia and New Zealand respectively. This was way beyond what could be conceivably afforded and so was totally unrealistic even before the Washington Treaty severely pruned naval strength internationally. Therefore, and being unable to construct and maintain a dedicated Far Eastern Fleet, an alternative strategy was evolved whereby the European based fleet would be enabled to deploy effectively to the Far East should the need arise. For that it needed a fleet base and the site chosen for this was at Singapore.

The purpose of the envisioned deployment, the 'Singapore Strategy' or 'Main Fleet to Singapore' as it also became known, was to defend Imperial 'main interests', defined as trade and territorial integrity.[21] It was calculated that some 23 per cent of the total trade of the British Empire and 60 per cent of Australia's trade passed through the Indian Ocean; a figure vital to the existence of Australia.[22] That severe disturbance to this trade was more likely from Japan in any future conflict, and much more troublesome than it had been from Germany in a previous one, was obvious: 'The "Emden" alone was able to seriously dislocate British trade in the Indian Ocean at the commencement of the last war, although she had no base and no support of any sort. [...] How much greater, therefore, would be the effect of 20 "Emden's"?'[23]

When the British Empire did become embroiled with Japan in the Far East it was with a foe that deployed forces considerably more powerful than the equivalent of '20 "Emden's"' and with more far-reaching intentions than the disruption of trade. Whether or not the Singapore Strategy was, in Admiral Herbert Richmond's retrospective words, based on an 'illusion that a Two-Hemisphere Empire could be defended by a One-Hemisphere Navy' is not a matter it is proposed to go into here in any depth.[24] Suffice to say it failed for a variety of reasons. Amongst these, in naval terms, was the detention of the majority of the British fleet in European waters. This was because there were two main theatres of war, one in Europe and one in the Far East, and the European theatre took precedence. There were simply not enough resources to dispute command of the sea with Japan as well as maintain a powerful enough navy to defend British interests in Europe. This problem had been foreseen. For example, the controversial ex-Royal Naval Commander Russell Grenfell published his contribution to the 'Next War' series, edited by Liddell Hart, in 1938. His logic was persuasive:

> If we send the fleet to the Far East in sufficient strength to dispute the command at sea with the Japanese, what must that strength be? The Japanese capital ships now number nine. In the last war a fifty per cent superiority in capital ships was deemed barely sufficient to ensure our command at sea against the Germans. If we reduce that necessary superiority to as low as thirty per cent, for our Far Eastern force, we should need to send out at the very least twelve capital ships. Two of our fifteen capital ships being under reconstruction, this means that at the moment the whole of our capital ship fleet but one would have to proceed eastward. With the bulk of the fleet 10,000 miles from Europe and only one battleship left to deal with, would it not be a terrible temptation to Italy with four battleships and Germany with three pocket ones to try to get the better of us while our main strength was occupied elsewhere [...].[25]

That the Imperial Japanese Navy had become, in terms of technology and tactics, very much superior to the Royal Navy was not, in 1938, generally known, and if it had been it would certainly not have been admitted or accepted. What actually happened when hostilities with Japan commenced is though very well known. Rather than a fleet, a small unbalanced force of two capital ships, Force Z, was despatched, and this proved fatally vulnerable to attack from land-based aircraft and was swiftly destroyed. In military terms the Singapore Base, which like Tsingtau before it was useless without an adequate fleet, proved highly vulnerable to land attack.[26]

The inability of the British Empire to reconcile means and ends meant that large portions of it in the Far East had their territorial integrity decisively breached. That Australia and New Zealand were, at least in terms of their mainland territory, untouched other than by air raids was due to the involvement of the other Great Power in the Pacific, the US. The Japanese-American struggle in the Pacific during 1942–5 involved many of the former German territories; for example, from early 1942 Rabaul became the headquarters for the Japanese Southeastern Fleet, the 11th Air Fleet and the 8th Area Army, with a combined deployment of some 94,000 personnel.[27] Mention has already been made of the fleet headquarters at Truk in the Carolines, which became, in addition, an advanced Combined Fleet Headquarters.[28] Ultimately one of the most significant events in human history took place on Tinian Island in the Marianas, at *c*. 02:45hr on 6 August 1945, when a B-29 bomber named *Enola Gay* took off; the target being Hiroshima.

On 30 October 1918, Winston S. Churchill is said to have remarked that the end of the First World War saw 'a drizzle of Empires falling through the air'.[29] He was referring to the capitulation of the Ottoman Empire and the imminence of the Austro-Hungarian Empire following suit. The German Empire of Kaiser Wilhelm II was not long to survive, and, if one counts Russia as an imperial power, it was the fourth such polity to collapse since 1917. In the current context the end of the Second World War was to see the destruction of the Japanese Empire, and it registered the beginning of the end for the style of imperialism that had pertained until then. In terms of the Far East, the British Empire was able to reassert itself and reoccupy the territories taken by Japan – and vis-à-vis the French and Dutch the same process was applicable – but not for long.[30]

British prestige had been destroyed by the failure of the Singapore Strategy, and even when the Royal Navy was able to deploy a fleet to the Pacific, nearly at the end of the war, it was subsidiary to the US Navy in every sense.[31] There is perhaps some irony in noting that, with its main base at Sydney, Australia, Task Force 57, as it was designated when operating under the control of the US fleet, used Seeadler Harbour (Port Seeadler), 'one of the best fleet anchorages in the South Pacific,' at Manus Island as its advanced base.[32] Manus, the largest of the Admiralty Islands in the Bismarck Archipelago, was of course former German territory.

However, if the formal empires of France and Britain did not dissolve as drizzle falling through the air, they were certainly melting away. The most notable sign of the decline of the British Empire was the loss of the

'Jewel in the Crown', occurring when the British Raj on the Indian sub-continent was dissolved in 1947.[33] The Great Powers had been replaced by two superpowers, and, post-1945, it became ridiculous for Australia and New Zealand to expect that the UK could, or should, be responsible for their defence.

The reality of British abilities in terms of power projection was reflected in the Security Treaty agreed between Australia, New Zealand and the US [ANZUS] on 1 September 1951. The ANZUS Treaty, as it became known, excluded the UK, much to the discomfiture of the British government. Winston S. Churchill, who had become Prime Minister again in 1951, told his Cabinet he 'greatly regretted the Australian acquiescence in the attempt of the United States to usurp our special position in relation to Australia and New Zealand'.[34] Churchill, who had first entered British political life in the reign of Queen Victoria, was of course famously zealous about the British Empire.[35] He was though undoubtedly representing the feelings of many in the party which he led in deprecating any notion of dilution to the principles of imperialism.[36]

None other than Kaiser Wilhelm II had predicted this situation several decades previously, though for the wrong reasons. In one of the few instances where he got things, more or less, right he opined that the visit of the Great White Fleet to Australia and New Zealand in 1908 presaged a defensive alignment, at the cost of the British connection, between the three states:

When self-interest comes in at the door, sentimental patriotism flies out of the window. Do you know why Australia and New Zealand invited Mr [Theodore] Roosevelt to send the American [Great White] fleet to their shores? [...] That invitation was for the express purpose of serving notice of the government of [Britain] that those colonies understand they have in the United States a friend who understands the white man's duty better than the 'mother country' seems to understand it.[37]

It would hardly do to leave the last word to Kaiser Wilhelm though, so to conclude. Militarily the conflict that erupted between Japan and Germany in 1914 was a sideshow, and the result had virtually no bearing on the course or outcome of the First World War; the loss of its colonial empire in no way incommoded Imperial Germany. The Japanese government declared war because it perceived that it was in the national interest to do so, and membership of the Anglo-Japanese Alliance provided it, if resort to cliché may be forgiven, with the required cloak of respectability.

In the naval context the UK gained; the East Asiatic Cruiser Squadron could not face the Japanese fleet, particularly as it was allied with the Australian and British navies, so was forced to flee the theatre. Maximilian von Spee could have split his command and embarked on commerce raiding à la *Emden*, but decided against; the main reason being the difficulties of coal supply particularly for his heavier ships.

Japan gained the former German territory and, perhaps more importantly, a significant foothold in mainland China. It came to dominate the economic life of the area, and retained control of the railways, despite formally handing Tsingtau back in 1922. The history of later Japanese involvement with China is beyond the scope of this book, but the question of foreign interference in Chinese internal and territorial affairs was only finally resolved on 1 October 1949 when Mao proclaimed the People's Republic.

There were few lessons to be learned in military and naval terms from the German-Japanese War of 1914. The use of aircraft was perhaps novel, certainly in the Asian context, and there were one or two aviation 'firsts'. This was particularly so in terms of naval aviation; the deployment of the seaplane carrier *Wakamiya Maru* was definitely a portent of things to come.

Curiously perhaps the military campaign culminating in the investment and fall of Tsingtau, though essentially rooted in the past, also presaged the future, or the near future at least. The Japanese, through their experiences at Port Arthur in 1904–5, were well aware that Vauban's principles were still applicable and so planned, and equipped themselves, for siege operations and trench warfare to take their goal. Indeed in the massing of heavy guns and howitzers firing high-explosive shells, the use of mortars and grenades, and the provision of other material required for siege and trench warfare they anticipated the techniques that shortly appeared on the Western Front in France, but which the armies of the belligerents had yet to learn in 1914.[38]

One lesson that *wasn't* learned, either from 1914 or even the earlier conflict of 1904–5, relates to the effectiveness of Japanese arms. This is surprising given that the Russo-Japanese War was heavily reported and written about in Europe and the US, and most authors were impressed with the prowess shown by the victors. Though obviously obscured by the far larger and infinitely more consequential events taking place on the other side of the globe, the 1914 Japanese campaign against the German colonies was likewise conducted thoroughly, professionally and, most importantly, effectively. A quarter of a century or so later all this had either been forgotten or unlearned.[39] This brings us neatly to the final words; and those of George Bernard Shaw, which will undoubtedly resonate with all students of history, seem rather apposite: 'We learn from experience that men never learn anything from experience.'[40]

Notes

Introduction

1. 'The wife of the Archduke Francis of Austria, heir to the throne, has petitioned the pope to endeavour to obtain for her the full rank accorded to her husband and the Emperor Francis is to be approached by the Pope on the matter. The lady in question, known as the Duchess of Hohenberg, has been systematically snubbed, and at times even insulted by the ladies of the imperial family. At court functions she has been forced to walk at the extreme end of a procession of 80 Archdukes and Archduchesses, while her husband walked immediately behind the emperor, at the head of the procession, with the Archduchess second in seniority on his arm. It has long been felt in Viennese court circles that the Duchess Hohenberg, who is one of the cleverest and most accomplished women in Austria-Hungary, and has unbounded influence over her husband, would not tolerate her unpleasant position for ever, and that she would undoubtedly claim fuller rights after the death of the Emperor Francis Joseph, if not before.', Emil Andrassy, 'Archduke's Wife Asks Pope's Help: Duchess of Hohenberg Wants to Be Recognized as Heir's Lawful Spouse', a syndicated report from Vienna, 28 June 1912.
2. Official Report of Debates of the House of Commons of the Dominion of Canada, Vol. 98 (Ottawa: S.E. Dawson, 1911), p. 239.
3. Austria-Hungary had no extra-European territory aside from a concession zone of 0.61km² in Tianjin, China. This was acquired following Austria-Hungary's contribution of a warship, the *Zenta*, and seventy-five sailors to the Eight Nation Alliance that defeated the Boxers. A certain Lieutenant Georg Ludwig Ritter von Trapp, of *Sound of Music* fame, was among later reinforcements and was decorated for bravery.
4. **Austria-Hungary**: Declared war with Serbia on 28 July 1914. Declared war with Russia on 6 August 1914. **France**: Invaded by Germany on 2 August 1914. Declared war with Austria-Hungary on 12 August 1914. **Germany**: Declared war with Russia on 1 August 1914. Declared war with France on 3 August 1914. Declared war with Belgium on 4 August 1914. **Japan**: Declared war with Germany on 23 August 1914. Declared war with Austria-Hungary on 25 August 1914. Russia: Declared war with Turkey on 2 November 1914. **Serbia**: Declared war with Germany on 6 August 1914. Declared war with Turkey on 2 November 1914. **United Kingdom**: Declared war with Germany on 4 August 1914. Declared war with Austria-Hungary on 12 August 1914. Declared war with Turkey on 5 November 1914.
5. See Paul G. Halpern, *The Naval War in the Mediterranean: 1914–1918* (Abingdon: Routledge, 2016).

6. The campaigns against German colonial territory in Africa, with the exception of that against Togoland, were more protracted. South West African Campaign: September 1914–July 1915. Cameroon Campaign: August 1914–March 1916. East African Campaign: August 1914–November 1918. See Hew Strachan, *The First World War* (Oxford: Oxford University Press, 2004).

Chapter 1

1. Lord Odo Russell to Lord Granville, 11 February 1873, quoted in Lord Edmond Fitzmaurice, *The Life of Granville George Leveson Gower, Second Earl Granville 1815–1891*, 2 vols (London: Longmans Green, 1905), p. 337.
2. Judith A. Bennett, 'Holland, Britain, and Germany in Melanesia', in K.R. Howe, Robert C. Kiste and Brij V. Lal (eds), *Tides of History: The Pacific Islands in the Twentieth Century* (Honolulu HI: University of Hawaii Press, 1994), p. 53. The reference to 'the dead' is on account of the mortality rate amongst the labourers shipped there to work the plantations. Some 40 per cent of them are reckoned to have perished. Robert J. Foster, *Social Reproduction and History in Melanesia: Mortuary Ritual, Gift Exchange, and Custom in the Tanga Islands* (Cambridge: Cambridge University Press, 1995), p. 42.
3. Terrell D. Gottschall, *By Order of the Kaiser: Otto von Diederichs and the Rise of the Imperial German Navy 1865–1902* (Annapolis MD: Naval Institute Press, 2003), p. 134.
4. Grand Admiral von Tirpitz, *My Memoirs*, 2 vols (London: Hurst & Blacket, 1919), Vol. 1, p. 70.
5. Tirpitz, Vol. 1, pp. 73 and 93.
6. Gottschall, p. 136.
7. Walter Nuhn, *Kolonialpolitik und Marine: Die Rolle der Kaiserlichen Marine bei der Gründung und Sicherung des deutschen Kolonialreiches 1884–1914* (Bonn: Bernard & Graefe, 2003), p. 132.
8. Gottschall, p. 104.
9. The accolade attributed to Richthofen is taken from an invitation by the Gesellschaft für Erdkunde zu Berlin to attend an International Symposium in Honour of Ferdinand von Richthofen. Held at the Humboldt-Universität, 6–8 October 2005, this event commemorated the 100th anniversary of his death.
10. Gottschall, p. 146.
11. Tirpitz, Vol. 1, p. 75.
12. Joseph W. Esherick, *The Origins of the Boxer Uprising* (Berkeley CA: University of California Press, 1987), p. 81.
13. George Steinmetz, '"The Devil's Handwriting": Precolonial Discourse, Ethnographic Acuity, and Cross-Identification in German Colonialism', in *Comparative Studies in Society and History*, Vol. 45, Issue 01, January 2003, p. 26.
14. Lanzin Xiang, *The Origins of the Boxer War* (London: Routledge Curzon, 2002), p. 67.
15. Steinmetz, p. 26.
16. For an account of this incident and the context within which it took place see Esherick, pp. 123–35.

174   The Siege of Tsingtau

17. Kaiser Wilhelm to the Foreign Office, 6 November 1897, quoted in John C.G. Röhl, *Wilhelm II: The Kaiser's Personal Monarchy, 1888–1900*, trans. Sheila de Bellaigue (Cambridge: Cambridge University Press, 2004), p. 955.
18. The Kaiser to Diederichs, telegram, 7 November 1897, quoted in Röhl, *Wilhelm II*, p. 955.
19. Diederichs to Knorr, 8 November 1897, quoted in Gottschall, p. 157.
20. Gottschall, p. 157.
21. Quoted in Röhl, *Wilhelm II*, p. 956.
22. Extract from the Kaiser to Bernhard von Bülow, telegram, 7 November 1897, quoted in E.T.S. Dugdale (ed. and trans.), *German Diplomatic Documents, 1871–1914. Volume III, The Growing Antagonism, 1898–1910* (New York NY: Harper & Brothers, 1930), p. 14.
23. Extract from the Kaiser to Bernhard von Bülow, telegram, 7 November 1897. Dugdale, p. 14.
24. Quoted in Röhl, *Wilhelm II*, p. 956
25. The Kaiser to Bernhard von Bülow, telegram, 7 November 1897. Dugdale, p. 14.
26. Extract from the Kaiser to Bernhard von Bülow, telegram, 7 November 1897. Dugdale, p. 14.
27. Extract from the Kaiser to Bernhard von Bülow, telegram, 7 November 1897. Dugdale, p. 14.
28. http://www.peterhof.org/.
29. Count Witte , *The Memoirs of Count Witte* (London: William Heinemann, 1921), ed. A. Yarmolinsky, p. 410.
30. Rotenhan to the Kaiser. 10 November 1897. Dugdale, p. 14.
31. Holstein to Hohenlohe, 9 November 1897, quoted in Röhl, *Wilhelm II*, p. 957.
32. Hohenlohe to Rotenham, 10 November 1897, quoted in Röhl, *Wilhelm II*, p. 957.
33. Rotenhan to Bülow, 11 November 1897, quoted in Röhl, *Wilhelm II*, p. 957.
34. Captain Bernard Smith, 'The Siege of Tsingtau', *The Coast Artillery Journal*, November–December 1934, p. 405.
35. Information taken from Qingdaoshan Hill Battery Fort Educational Base. This area was visited by Dennis and Adrienne Quarmby in 2006, and I am extremely grateful to them for sharing it with me.
36. Gottschall, p. 160.
37. Feng Djen Djang, *The Diplomatic Relations Between China and Germany since 1898* (Shanghai: Commercial Press, 1936), p. 45.
38. Röhl, *Wilhelm II*, p. 957.
39. Koester to Diederichs, 13 November 1897, quoted in Gottschall, p. 160.
40. Diederichs to Koester, 14 November 1897, quoted in Gottschall, p. 160.
41. Knorr to Diederichs, 15 November 1897, quoted in Gottschall, p. 160.
42. Memo of 15 November 1897, quoted in Röhl, *Wilhelm II*, p. 958.
43. Journal entry, 11 September 1895. Friedrich Curtius (ed.), *Memoirs of Prince Chlodwig of Hohenlohe Schillingsfuerst*, trans. George W. Chrystal, 2 vols (London: William Heinemann, 1906), Vol. II, p. 463.
44. Hohenlohe to Count Hatzfeldt, 16 November 1897. Dugdale, p. 14.

45. Hohenlohe to the Kaiser, 18 November 1897, quoted in Röhl, *Wilhelm II*, p. 958.
46. Marginal annotation by the Kaiser in Hohenlohe to the Kaiser, 18 November 1897, quoted in Röhl, *Wilhelm II*, p. 958.
47. Kaiser Wilhelm to the Foreign Office, 24 November 1897, quoted in Röhl, *Wilhelm II*, pp. 958–9.
48. The Second Division was to consist of: the protected cruiser *Kaiserin Augusta* (1892), name ship of her class; the 'Gefion' class light cruiser *Gefion* (1893); the central battery ironclad *Deutschland* (1874), sister ship to *Kaiser*; and *Cormoran*, which was already on station.
49. Feng, p. 50.
50. Kaiser Wilhelm to Hohenlohe, 26 November 1897, quoted in Röhl, *Wilhelm II*, p. 958.
51. Diary entry, 29 November, quoted in Röhl, *Wilhelm II*, p. 958.
52. Feng, p. 91.
53. King Frederick William of Prussia had constituted the first Naval Battalion in 1852 from the *Marinierkorps*, a body that had itself been created in 1850 as an organic naval replacement for army troops assigned to naval duties. The Battalion had been increased to five companies in 1869 and then six companies in 1871. In 1889 it was divided to form I and II Naval Battalions.
54. C. Hugüenin, Oberleutnant im III. See-Bataillon, *Geschichte Des III. See-Bataillons* (Tsingtaü: Adolf Haupt, 1912), p. 15.
55. The Battalion comprised:
    1 Commander (Major Kopka von Lossow)
    5 Company Commanders
    14 lieutenants
    2 physicians
    1 paymaster
    2 Assistant Paymasters
    3 Armourers
    1117 NCOs and Men
    1 second lieutenant (Marine Artillery).
    1 pioneer section
    1 field telegraphic section
    1 military hospital together with personnel.
    See Hugüenin, p. 13.
56. Feng, p. 70. Taken from *Handbuch far das Schutzgebiet Kiautschou* (this book contains all the Imperial decrees, edicts and laws for the German Protectorate of Kiautschou, compiled by F.W. Mohr, formerly assistant interpreter of the Kiautschou government).
57. Gottschall, p. 176.
58. Feng, p. 70.
59. German Historical Institute, Washington DC, German History in Documents and Images (GHDI), http://germanhistorydocs.ghi-dc.org, Wilhelmine Germany and the First World War, 1890–1918. An 'Unequal Treaty': Lease Agreement between China and the German Empire (March 6, 1898).

60. German Historical Institute, Washington DC, German History in Documents and Images (GHDI), http://germanhistorydocs.ghi-dc.org, Wilhelmine Germany and the First World War, 1890–1918.

61. Eyre Crowe, 'Memorandum on the Present State of British Relations with France and Germany' (1 January 1907), in G.P. Gooch and H.W.V. Temperly (eds), *British Documents on the Origins of the War, 1898–1914*, 11 vols (London: HM Stationery Office, 1926—38), Vol. III, *The Testing of the Entente 1904–6*, Appendix A.

Chapter 2

1. Dewey is quoted in Stuart Creighton Miller, *Benevolent Assimilation: The American Conquest of the Philippines, 1899—1903* (New Haven CT: Yale University Press, 1982), p. 37. Kyle Roy Ward, *In the Shadow of Glory: The Thirteenth Minnesota in the Spanish-American and Philippine-American Wars, 1898—1899* (St Cloud MN: North Star, 2000), p. 9.

2. Sharon Delmendo, *The Star-Entangled Banner: One Hundred Years of America in the Philippines* (New Brunswick, NJ: Rutgers University Press, 2004), p. 45.

3. Terrell D. Gottschall, *By Order of the Kaiser: Otto von Diederichs and the Rise of the Imperial German Navy 1865–1902* (Annapolis MD: Naval Institute Press, 2003), p. 187.

4. Gottschall, pp. 189–94.

5. British naval forces deployed in Manila Bay consisted of one armoured and two light cruisers, as well as six gunboats. France sent one armoured and one protected cruiser, as well as the obsolete barbette ship *Bayard*, whilst four protected cruisers represented the Japanese Navy. Even Austria-Hungary sent along a sloop. Not all of these vessels, including the German contingent, were always present at any one time. See Gottschall, p. 196.

6. See, for example, Thomas A. Bailey, 'Dewey and the Germans at Manila Bay', *The American Historical Review*, Vol. 45, No. 1 (Oct., 1939), pp. 59–81.

7. George Dewey, *Autobiography of George Dewey: Admiral of the Navy* (New York NY: Scribner, 1913), p. 258. The 'Eastern Extension Telegraph Company' had refused the Americans the use of their apparatus, stating 'contractual' reasons. Having been refused permission, Dewey cut the cable and took one end aboard ship, intending to make use of it without the shore-based office. The Spanish government however exercised its rights under the contract it had, and embargoed Dewey's messages at the Hong Kong end. Dewey therefore had to send his messages to Hong Kong via ship for onward transmission. See Severo Gómez Núñez, *The Spanish American War: Blockades And Coast Defense* (Washington DC: Government Printing Office, 1899), p. 57; Gottschall, p. 189.

8. Bernhard von Bülow, *Memoirs of Prince von Bülow: From Secretary of State to Imperial Chancellor 1897–1903*, trans. F.A. Voight (Boston MA: Little, Brown and Co., 1931), p. 481.

9. Bülow to Wilhelm II, 14 May 1898, quoted in Nancy Mitchell, *The Danger of Dreams: German and American Imperialism in Latin America* (Chapel Hill NC: University of North Carolina Press, 1999), p. 27.

10. Bulow to Kruger, 18 May 1898, quoted in Mitchell, *The Danger of Dreams*, p. 27.

11. Knorr to Diederichs, 2 June 1898, quoted in Gottschall, p. 190.

12. Gottschall, p. 193.

13. Gottschall, p. 195.

14. Signed by Austria, France, the UK, Prussia, Russia, Sardinia and Turkey. See Gómez Núñez, p. 19.

15. Douglas Owen, *Declaration of War: a Survey of the Position of Belligerents and Neutrals with Relative Considerations of Shipping and Marine Insurance during War* (London: Stevens and Sons, 1889), p. 27.

16. Elbert Jay Benton, *International Law and Diplomacy of the Spanish-American War* (Baltimore MD: John Hopkins, 1898), pp. 130–1.

17. Coleman Phillipson, *International Law and the Great War* (London: T. Fisher Unwin, 1915), p. 351.

18. The British were extremely concerned that any prolongation of the conflict could lead to it spreading across the Atlantic. See John L. Offner, *An Unwanted War: The Diplomacy of the United States and Spain Over Cuba, 1895–1898* (Chapel Hill NC: University of North Carolina Press, 1992), pp. 195–6.

19. Offner, pp. 195–6.

20. Lawrence Sondhaus, *Naval warfare, 1815–1914* (London: Routledge, 2001), pp. 175–6. Donald H. Dyal, Brian B. Carpenter, Mark A. Thomas, *Historical dictionary of the Spanish American War* (Westport CT: Greenwood Press, 1996), p. 256.

21. Offner, p. 237.

22. Sebastian Balfour, *The End of the Spanish Empire, 1898–1923* (Oxford: Oxford University Press, 1997), p. 46. For the full text of the Protocol see Offner, pp. 237–8.

23. Albert A. Nofi, *The Spanish-American War: 1898* (Conshohocken PA: Combined Books, 1996), pp. 289–90.

24. http://www.yale.edu/lawweb/avalon/diplomacy/spain/sp1898.htm.

25. On 21 November 1899 McKinley had an interview with a group of clergymen and missionaries at the White House, which no doubt accounts for the frequent religious references. In the notes written up by one of the attendees, the accuracy of which was confirmed by others that were present, McKinley had this to say concerning the decision to annexe the Philippines:

> I have been criticized a good deal about the Philippines, but don't deserve it. The truth is I didn't want the Philippines, and when they came to us, as a gift from the gods, I did not know what to do with them. When the Spanish War broke out Dewey was at Hong Kong, and I ordered him to go to Manila and to capture or destroy the Spanish fleet, and he had to; because, if defeated, he had no place to refit on that side of the globe, and if the Dons were victorious they would likely cross the Pacific and ravage our Oregon and California coasts. And so he had to destroy the Spanish fleet, and did it! But that was as far as I thought then.
>
> When next I realized that the Philippines had dropped into our laps, I confess I did not know what to do with them. I sought counsel from all sides – Democrats as

well as Republicans – but got little help. I thought first we would take only Manila; then Luzon; then other islands, perhaps, also.

I walked the floor of the White House night after night until midnight; and I am not ashamed to tell you, gentlemen, that I went down on my knees and prayed to Almighty God for light and guidance more than one night. And one night late it came to me this way – I don't know how it was, but it came:

(1) That we could not give them back to Spain – that would be cowardly and dishonourable;

(2) That we could not turn them over to France or Germany, our commercial rivals in the Orient – that would be bad business and discreditable;

(3) That we could not leave them to themselves – they were unfit for self-government, and they would soon have anarchy and misrule worse than Spain's was; and

(4) That there was nothing left for us to do but to take them all, and to educate the Filipinos, and uplift and civilize and Christianize them and by God's grace do the very best we could by them, as our fellow men for whom Christ also died.

And then I went to bed and went to sleep, and slept soundly, and the next morning I sent for the chief engineer of the War Department (our map-maker), and I told him to put the Philippines on the map of the United States (pointing to a large map on the wall of his office), and there they are and there they will stay while I am President!

Quoted in Charles S. Olcott, *The Life of William McKinley*, 2 vols (Boston MA: Houghton Mifflin, 1916), Vol. II, pp. 110–11. See also Daniel B. Schirmer and Stephen Rosskamm Shalom (eds), *The Philippines Reader: A History of Colonialism, Neocolonialism, Dictatorship, and Resistance* (Boston MA: South End Press, 1987), pp. 22–3.

26. Offner, pp. 195–6.

27. Bülow, *Memoirs*, p. 256.

28. Balfour, pp. 46–7.

29. Robert F. Rogers, *Destiny's Landfall: A History of Guam* (Honolulu HI: University of Hawai'i Press, 1995), p. 112.

30. Manfred Jonas, *The United States and Germany: A Diplomatic History* (Chapel Hill NC: University of North Carolina Press, 1992), pp. 60–2.

31. José María Jover, *Política, diplomacia y humanismo popular: Estudios sobre la vida española en el siglo XIX* (Madrid: Turner, 1976), p. 136.

32. President McKinley's State of the Union Address to the Senate and House of Representatives, 5 December 1899. http://www.thisnation.com/library/sotu/1899 wm.html.

33. Bülow, *Memoirs*, p. 384.

34. John C.G. Röhl, *Wilhelm II: The Kaiser's Personal Monarchy, 1888–1900*, trans. Sheila de Bellaigue (Cambridge: Cambridge University Press, 2004), p. 964.

35. Alessandro Duranti, *A Companion to Linguistic Anthropology* (Malden MA: Blackwell, 2004), p. 97.

36. David L. Hanlon, *Remaking Micronesia: Discourses over Development in a Pacific Territory, 1944–1982* (Honolulu HI: University of Hawai'i Press, 1998), p. 1.

37. Major Earl H. Ellis USMC, *Advanced Base Operations in Micronesia* (Fleet Marine Force Reference Publication (FMFRP) 12–46. Department of the Navy – Headquarters US Marine Corps) (Washington DC: US Government Printing Office, 1992), p. 31.
38. Gerd Hardach, 'Defining Separate Spheres: German Rule and Colonial Law in Micronesia', in Herman J. Hiery and John M. MacKenzie (eds), *European Impact and Pacific Influence: British and German Policy in the Pacific Islands and the Indigenous Response* (London: Tauris, 1997), p. 235.
39. Hermann Joseph Hiery, *The Neglected War: The German South Pacific and the Influence of World War I* (Honolulu HI: University of Hawai'i Press, 1995), p. 12.
40. Hardach, p. 235.
41. Hiery, p. 2.
42. Hardach, p. 234.
43. Hardach, p. 234.
44. Bülow, *Memoirs*, p. 331.
45. For information on Samoa see Lowell D. Holmes (ed.), *Samoan Islands Bibliography* (Wichita KS: Poly Concepts, 1984).
46. President McKinley's State of the Union Address to the Senate and House of Representatives, 5 December 1899. http://www.thisnation.com/library/sotu/1899 wm.html.
47. See Paul M. Kennedy, *The Samoan Tangle: A Study in Anglo-German-American Relations, 1878–1900* (New York NY: Barnes & Noble, 1974).
48. Tirpitz to Bülow, 11 October 1899, quoted in E.T.S. Dugdale (ed. and trans.), *German Diplomatic Documents, 1871–1914, Vol. III, The Growing Antagonism, 1898–1910* (New York NY: Harper & Brothers, 1930), pp. 42–73.
49. Hiery, pp. 20–1.
50. James Wood, *History of International Broadcasting*, 2 vols (London: Peregrinus, 1992), Vol. I, pp. 56–7.
51. Roger Cullis, 'Technological Roulette – A Multidisciplinary Study of the Dynamics of Innovation' (University of London PhD Thesis, 1986), p. 257. For accounts of the German radio system see Erdmann Thiele (ed.), *Telefunken nach 100 Jahren: Das Erbe einer deutschen Weltmarke [The Legacy of a Global Brand]* (Berlin: Nicolai, 2003); Michael Friedewald, 'The Beginnings of Radio Communication in Germany, 1897–1918', *The Journal of Radio Studies*, Vol. 7, No. 2, 2000, pp. 441–63. See also Paul Kennedy, 'Imperial Cable Communications and Strategy, 1870–1914', in Paul Kennedy (ed.), *The War Plans of the Great Powers, 1880–1914* (London: Allen & Unwin, 1979).

Chapter 3

1. For a comprehensive account of the how the alliance came into being from the Japanese perspective see Tatsuji Takeuchi, *War and Diplomacy in the Japanese Empire* (Chicago IL: Allen & Unwin, 1936), Chapter XI.
2. The margin was later defined as being a 10 per cent superiority over the combined strength of the next two strongest navies. D.G. Boyce (ed.), *The Crisis of British Power: The Imperial*

and Naval Papers of the Second Earl of Selborne, 1895–1910 (London: The Historians' Press, 1990), pp. 154–5. http://www.manorhouse.clara.net/book3/chapter1.htm#_ftn53.

3. Balfour to Lansdowne, 12 December 1901 in the Balfour Papers at the British Library, Add MSS 49727.
4. Holger H. Herwig, *'Luxury' Fleet: The Imperial German Navy, 1888–1918* (London: George Allen & Unwin, 1980), p. 43.
5. http://www.firstworldwar.com/source/anglojapanesealliance1902.htm.
6. CID 38/10/79 Memorandum by the General Staff, 4 November 1905.
7. Great Britain, Parliamentary Papers, London, 1908, Vol. CXXV, Cmd. 3750.
8. For an analysis of these matters see Ernest Batson Price, *The Russo-Japanese Treaties of 1907–1916 concerning Manchuria and Mongolia* (Baltimore MD: The John Hopkins Press, 1933).
9. Korea had been a virtual Japanese protectorate since 1905.
10. According to Mahan, writing in 1910, the US had 'two principle and permanent external policies: the Monroe Doctrine and the Open Door', Alfred Thayer Mahan to Philip Andrews, 24 September 1910. Robert Seager II and Doris Maguire (eds), *Letters and Papers of Alfred Thayer Mahan*, 3 vols (Annapolis MD: Naval Institute Press, 1975), Vol. III, p. 353.
11. Theodore Roosevelt had written to Henry Cabot Lodge on 21 September 1897, arguing that if the US fought Spain, 'we would have the [Japanese] on our backs'. Elting E. Morison (ed.), *The Letters of Theodore Roosevelt*, 8 vols (Cambridge MA: Harvard University Press, 1951–4), Vol. I, p. 607.
12. An inversion of the Doctrine, from being reactive to active. Theodore Roosevelt, *Addresses and State Papers: Including the European Addresses*, Executive Edition, 8 vols (New York NY: Collier & Son, 1910), Vol. III, pp. 176–7.
13. William Braisted, *The United States Navy in the Pacific 1897–1909* (Austin TX: University of Texas Press, 1958), p. 4.
14. Richard W. Turk, *The Ambiguous Relationship: Theodore Roosevelt and Alfred Thayer Mahan* (Westport CT: Greenwood Press, 1987), p. 4.
15. Herwig, *'Luxury' Fleet*, p. 45.
16. Alfred Thayer Mahan, *Naval strategy compared and contrasted with the principles and practice of military Operations on land: lectures delivered at U.S. Naval War College, Newport, R.I., between the years 1887 and 1911*, repr. facs. of the 1911 edn (Oxford: Greenwood Press, 1975), p. 6.
17. Theodore Roosevelt to Alfred Thayer Mahan, 3 May 1897. Morison, pp. 685–6. Mahan had himself echoed this sentiment in an undated letter (June 1910) to the *Daily Mail* newspaper, pointing out the 'military check [...] the interests of Canada impose upon Great Britain'. Seager II and Maguire (eds), Vol. III, pp. 342–3.
18. Admiralty Memorandum of February 1905, quoted in Phillips Payson O'Brien, *British and American Naval Power: Politics and Policy, 1900–1936* (Westport CT: Praeger, 1998), p. 28.
19. The Great White Fleet made the following visits: Auckland, New Zealand, 9–15 August 1908; Sydney, Australia, 20–8 August 1908; Melbourne, Australia 29 August–5 September 1908; Albany, Australia, 11–18 September 1908. See A. Trotter, 'Friend

to Foe? New Zealand and Japan: 1900–1937', in Roger Peren (ed.), *Japan and New Zealand: 150 Years* (Palmerston North: New Zealand Centre for Japanese Studies, Massey University, on behalf of the Ministry of Foreign Affairs, Tokyo, in association with the Historical Branch, Dept. of Internal Affairs, Wellington, 1999), pp. 70–1.

20. E.M. Andrews, *The Anzac Illusion: Anglo-Australian relations during World War I* repr. edn (Cambridge: Cambridge University Press, 1994), p. 21.

21. For an account of all these matters see Lionel Curtis, *The Problem of the Commonwealth* (London: Macmillan, 1916).

22. 'In the Navy Bills of 1898 and 1900 augmented by Supplementary Bills in 1906, 1908 and 1912, the Reich proposed to create a modern battle fleet of 41 Battleships, 20 Large Cruisers and 40 Light Cruisers.', Herwig, *'Luxury' Fleet*, p. 1.

23. Quoted in Herwig, *'Luxury' Fleet*, p. 1.

24. Richard H. Gimblett, 'Reassessing the Dreadnought Crisis of 1909 and the Origins of the Royal Canadian Navy', *The Northern Mariner/Le Marin du nord*, IV, No. 1 (January 1994), p. 36.

25. Peter Padfield, *The Great Naval Race: Anglo-German Naval Rivalry 1900–1914* (Edinburgh: Birlinn, 2004), p. 201.

26. W.D. Hancock (ed.), *English Historical Documents* (London: Eyre & Spottiswoode, 1977), p. 414.

27. Hancock, p. 422.

28. Reginald McKenna, Imperial Conference on Defence: Admiralty Memorandum of 20 July 1909, TNA, CAB 37/100/98. This memorandum formed the basis of the British position at the subsequent Conference.

29. McKenna Memorandum.

30. McKenna Memorandum.

31. William Creswell, 'Captain Creswell's Views on Result of Imperial Conference, 16 November 1909', in G.L. Macandie, *The Genesis of the Royal Australian Navy: A Compilation* (Sydney NSW: Government Printer, 1949), p. 252.

32. MacDonald to Grey, 5 April 1911, quoted in G.P. Gooch and H.W.V. Temperly (eds), *British Documents on the Origins of the War, 1898–1914*, 11 vols (London: HM Stationery Office, 1926–38), Vol. VIII, no. 417.

33. Ian Nish (ed.), *Anglo-Japanese Relations 1892–1925*, 6 vols (London: Palgrave Macmillan, 2003), Vol. VI, p. 47.

34. Nish (ed.), *Anglo-Japanese Relations*, p. 51.

35. For an account of this process see Sir Thomas Barclay, *New methods of Adjusting International Disputes and the Future* (London: Constable, 1917), particularly Appendix VII.

36. A.M. Pooley (ed.), *The Secret Memoirs of Count Tadasu Hayashi* (New York NY and London: G.P. Putnam's Sons, 1915), p. 17.

37. Andrews, p. 22.

38. 'Laid down before Dreadnought and intended to carry 12-inch [305mm] guns, she should have been completed as the world's first all-big-gun battleship. However there were not enough Armstrong 1904 pattern 12-inch guns available, and 10-inch [254mm] guns had to be substituted for all but four of the weapons. Thus, it was that

future all-big gun battleships were to be called "dreadnoughts", and not "satsumas".',
Bernard Ireland, *Jane's Battleships of the 20th Century* (New York NY: Harper Collins,
1996). The USS *South Carolina*, laid down in December 1906, might also have pre-
empted Dreadnought.

39. Warren I. Cohen (ed.), *The Cambridge History of American Foreign Relations*, 4 vols,
Vol. II, Walter LaFeber, *The American Search for Opportunity, 1865–1913* (Cambridge:
Cambridge University press, 1993), p. 207.
40. Ian Gow, *Military Intervention in Pre-War Japanese Politics: Admiral Kato Kanji and
the 'Washington System'* (London: Routledge, 2004), pp. 70–1.
41. Edward S. Miller, *War Plan Orange: The U.S. Strategy to Defeat Japan, 1897–1945*
(Annapolis MD: US Naval Institute Press, 2007).

Chapter 4
1. Bismarck is supposed to have predicted that 'some damned silly thing in the Balkans'
would lead to war. The evidence that he did is at several removes, and seems to originate
in a speech made by Winston S. Churchill in the House of Commons on 16 August
1945. According to Churchill: 'I remember that a fortnight or so before the last war,
the Kaiser's friend Herr Ballin, the great shipping magnate, told me that he had heard
Bismarck say towards the end of his life, "If there is ever another war in Europe, it will
come out of some damned silly thing in the Balkans."' Churchill was thus recalling a
second-hand remark made to him some thirty-one years previously, which was itself
a recollection of a comment made around seventeen years before that. Robert Rhodes
James (ed.), *Winston S. Churchill: His Complete Speeches, 1897–1963*, 8 vols (New York
NY: Chelsea House Publishers, 1974), Vol. VII, 1943–9, p. 7214.
2. Winston S. Churchill, *The World Crisis 1911–1918*, 2 vol. edn (London: Odhams,
1938),Vol. 1, p. 103.
3. David Lloyd George, *War Memoirs*, 2 vols (London: Odhams, 1938), Vol. I, pp. 27–8.
4. A.J.P. Taylor, *The Struggle for Mastery in Europe 1848–1915* (Oxford: Oxford University
Press, 1954), p. 437.
5. Viscount Grey of Falloden, *Twenty-Five Years: 1892–1916*, 2 vols (London: Hodder &
Stoughton, 1925), Vol. I, p. 75.
6. Scott D. Sagan, '1914 Revisited: Allies, Offense, and Instability', in Michael E. Brown,
Owen R Coté Jr, Sean M. Lynn-Jones and Steven E. Miller (eds), *Offense, Defense, and
War* (Cambridge MA: The MIT Press, 2004), p. 174.
7. Neville Meaney, *Australia and the World: A Documentary History from the 1870s to the
1970s* (Melbourne: Longman Cheshire, 1985), p. 217.
8. S.S. Mackenzie, *Rabaul: The Australians At Rabaul; The Capture And Administration
Of The German Possessions In The Southern Pacific*, tenth edn (Sydney NSW: Angus
and Robertson, 1941), Vol. X of C.E.W. Bean (ed.), *The Official History of Australia
in the War of 1914–1918*, 12 vols various edns (Sydney NSW: Angus and Robertson,
1941), p. 5. http://www.awm.gov.au/histories/volume.asp?conflict=1.
9. Anon., 'Before Gallipoli-Australian Operations in 1914', *Semaphore: Newsletter of the
Sea Power Centre, Australia*, Issue 7, August 2003, p. 1.

10. The 'armoured' cruiser became a feasible concept only in 1897 when a new hardening process, developed by Germany's Krupp, allowed vessels that had formerly been designated as 'protected' cruisers, having a protective deck covering the machinery and other vitals, to be fitted with side armour. This type of armour was designed to withstand penetration from 6in shells whilst not greatly adding to the displacement, dimensions or cost of the vessels. In the context of the British Royal Navy, the first armoured cruisers formed the 'Cressy' class of 1899–1901 and the design culminated in the 'Minotaur' class of three ships constructed from 1904–5. The Minotaurs were large, 490ft long and displacing 14,600 tons, powerful, 4 × 9.2in and 10 × 7.5in guns, and fast, 23 knots. As a type they were eclipsed by the battlecruiser. For a detailed discussion of the type see William Hovgaard, *Modern History of Warships* (New York NY: Spon & Chamberlain, 1920).

11. Arthur W. Jose, *The Royal Australian Navy 1914–1918*, ninth edn (Sydney NSW: Angus and Robertson, 1941), Vol. IX of Bean (ed.), p. 7.

12. Jerram's entire letter is reproduced in Ian Nish, *Collected Writings (Collected Writings of Modern Western Scholars on Japan)* (London: Routledge Curzon, 2003), pp. 167–8.

13. Nicholas A. Lambert, 'Economy or Empire? The Fleet Unit Concept and the Quest for Collective Security in the Pacific, 1909–1914', in Keith Neilson (ed.), *Far-flung Lines: Studies in Imperial Defence in Honour of Donald Mackenzie Schurman* (London: Frank Cass, 1997), p. 68.

14. Edward Breck, review of *The World Crisis* by Winston S. Churchill, *The American Historical Review*, Vol. 29, No. 1 (October, 1923), p. 139.

15. Jose, p. 5.

16. *Semaphore: Newsletter of the Sea Power Centre Australia*, Issue 10, September 2004.

17. '[…] six companies of the Royal Australian Naval Reserve, a battalion of infantry at war strength (1,023 strong), two machine-gun sections, a signalling section, and a detachment of the Australian Army Medical Corps. The naval reservists were drawn from Queensland, New South Wales, Victoria, and South Australia; but, in view of the imperious necessity for rapid organisation, the infantry battalion, the machine-gun and signalling sections, and the medical complement were enlisted in New South Wales. The unit was under the military command of Colonel William Homes.', Mackenzie, pp. 23–4. The protectorate of German New Guinea consisted of: Kaiser-Wilhelmsland, the Bismarck Archipelago, the German Solomon Islands (Buka, Bougainville and several smaller islands), the Carolines, Palau, the Marianas (except for Guam), the Marshall Islands and Nauru.

18. Sir Ronald Craufurd Munro-Ferguson (created 1st Viscount Novar in 1920) was the sixth Governor-General of Australia, and the most politically active holder of the post. The outbreak of war in 1914 caused an acute crisis in Australian government as Parliament had been dissolved and the government was in caretaker mode. Given also that contemporary Australian politicians were inexperienced in foreign affairs, Munro-Ferguson, who reckoned he had both the constitutional authority and the confidence, took an extremely active role, which included becoming the conduit of communication between the Australian and British governments. See Chris Cunneen, *King's Men: Australia's Governors-General from Hopetoun to Isaacs* (Sydney: Allen

& Unwin Australia, 1984) and David Torrance, *The Scottish Secretaries* (Edinburgh: Birlinn, 2006).

19. Mackenzie, pp. 5–6.
20. Mackenzie, p. 6.
21. It was only on 1 January 1901 that federation of the individual colonies was achieved, and the Commonwealth of Australia came into being as a British Dominion.
22. See, for example, Hew Strachan, *The First World War, Volume One: To Arms* (Oxford: Oxford University Press, 2003), p. 71. The term 'sub-imperialism' was coined by the Marxist writer Ruy Mauro Marini; '"sub-imperialism" is a small-scale parody of the high imperialism of the late 19th century', Jay Lewis, 'Imperialism Yesterday and Today', *Workers' Liberty*, Issue 63, July 2000.
23. Herbertshöhe was the site of the landing by Australian troops on the morning of 11 September 1914. Only twenty-five personnel were landed initially but reinforcements consisting of four companies of infantry, a machine-gun section and a 12-pounder gun were landed later that day. http://www.awm.gov.au/units/place_2439.asp.
24. Mackenzie, pp. 51–2.
25. Quoted in Grey to Greene, 11 August 1914, in Martin Gilbert, *Winston S. Churchill: Companion Volume III, Part 1 July 1914–April 1915* (Boston MA: Houghton Mifflin, 1973), pp. 28–9.
26. Grey to Greene, 1 August 1914, quoted in G.P. Gooch and H.W.V. Temperly (eds), *British Documents on the Origins of the War, 1898–1914*, 11 vols (London: HMSO, 1926–38), Vol. XI *The Outbreak of War: Foreign Office Documents June 28th–August 4th, 1914* (35371), No. 436.
27. Note by Sir Walter Langley (wrongly attributed to Sir William Tyrrell), dated 3 August 1914, quoted in Gooch and Temperley (eds), Vol. XI (35865), No. 534. See also Peter Lowe, *Great Britain and Japan 1911–1915: A Study of British Far Eastern Policy* (London: Macmillan, 1969), p. 180.
28. Note by Sir Walter Langley (wrongly attributed to Sir William Tyrrell) dated 3 August 1914, quoted in Gooch and Temperley (eds), Vol. XI (35865), No. 534. See also Lowe, *Great Britain and Japan*, p. 180.
29. Grey to Greene, 3 August 1914, quoted in Gooch and Temperley (eds), Vol. XI (35865), No. 549.
30. Greene to Grey, 4 August 1914, quoted in Gooch and Temperley (eds), Vol. XI (35666), No. 571.
31. Grey to Greene, 4 August 1914, quoted in Gooch and Temperley (eds), Vol. XI (36531), No. 641.
32. Greene to Grey, 4 August 1914, quoted in Gooch and Temperley (eds), Vol. XI (35937), No. 637.
33. Gooch and Temperley (eds), Vol. X, Pt II, *The Last Years of Peace* (London: HMSO, 1938), Appendix II, p. 823. Also quoted in Nish, *Collected Writings*, pp. 176–7.
34. Greene to Grey, 2 August 1914, quoted in Gooch and Temperley (eds), Vol. XI (35445), No. 499.
35. Nish, *Collected Writings*, p. 177.

36. The *Genro* was an extra-constitutional group composed of specific Japanese elder statesmen. Their function was to serve as informal, learned advisors to the emperor.

37. Communicated by Inouye, 10 August 1914, quoted in Lowe, *Great Britain and Japan*, p. 185.

38. Nish, *Collected Writings*, p. 178.

39. Grey to Greene, 11 August 1914, in Gilbert, *Winston S. Churchill*, pp. 28–9.

40. Nish, *Collected Writings*, p. 180.

41. Nish, *Collected Writings*, p. 178.

42. Martin Gilbert, *The Challenge of War: Winston S. Churchill 1914–1916* (London: Minerva, 1990), p. 42.

43. Churchill to Grey, 11 August 1914, quoted in Gilbert, *Winston S. Churchill*, p. 30.

44. Gilbert, *Winston S. Churchill*, p. 30.

45. Ian Nish, *Japanese Foreign Policy 1869–1942* (London: Routledge and Kegan Paul, 1977), pp. 94–5.

46. Barbara J. Brooks, 'Peopling the Japanese Empire: the Koreans in Manchuria and the Rhetoric of Inclusion', in Sharon A. Minichiello (ed.), *Japan's Competing Modernities: Issues in Culture and Democracy, 1900–1930* (Honolulu HI: University of Hawai'i Press, 1998), p. 36. Assassination was an occupational hazard for Japanese politicians and others thought to be too 'moderate' until after the end of the Second World War. See Ozaki Yukio (trans. Fujiko Hara), *The Autobiography of Ozaki Yukio: The Struggle for Constitutional Government in Japan* (Princeton NJ: Princeton University Press, 2001).

47. W.G. Beasley, *Japanese Imperialism 1894–1945* (Cary NC: Oxford University Press, 1987), pp. 108–9. For biographical details of Makino see Peter Wetzler, *Hirohito and War: Imperial Tradition and Military Decision Making in Prewar Japan* (Honolulu HI: University of Hawai'i Press, 1998), pp. 142–3.

48. Beasley, p. 108.

49. Noriko Kawamura, *Turbulence in the Pacific: Japanese-US Relations During World War I* (Westport CT: Prager, 2000), p. 12.

50. Quoted in Nish, *Collected Writings*, p. 193.

51. Lansing to Bryan, 7 August 1914, quoted in Robert Lansing, *Papers Relating to the Foreign Policy of the United States: The Lansing Papers, 1914–1920*, 2 vols (Washington DC: Government Printing Office, 1939–40), Vol. I, p. 2.

52. Lansing to Bryan, 7 August 1914, quoted in Lansing, *Lansing Papers*, Vol. I, pp. 3–4.

53. Lansing to Bryan, 7 August 1914, quoted in Lansing, *Lansing Papers*, Vol. I, p. 4.

54. http://www.usd.edu/~sbucklin/primary/roottakahira.htm.

55. http://www.firstworldwar.com/source/tsingtau_okuma.htm.

56. Kajima Morinosuke, *The Diplomacy of Japan, 1894–1922*, 3 vols (Tokyo: The Kajima Institute, 1976), Vol. III *The First World War, Paris Peace Conference, Washington Conference*, p. 55.

57. MacMurray to Bryan, 20 August 1914, Joseph V. Fuller (ed.), *Foreign Relations of The United States: 1914 (World War Supplement)* (Washington DC: Government Printing Office, 1928), pp. 173–4.

58. MacMurray to Bryan, 20 August 1914, *Foreign Relations*, p. 174.

59. Nish, *Collected Writings* p. 185.

60. Page to Bryan, 18 August 1914, SD 763.72/508, quoted in Charles B. Burdick, *The Japanese Siege of Tsingtau* (Hamden CT: Archon, 1976), p. 224.
61. Churchill to Grey, 29 August 1914, in Gilbert, *Winston S. Churchill*, p. 65.
62. For an authoritative account of this deployment see David Evans and Mark Peattie, *Kaigun: Strategy, Tactics, and Technology in the Imperial Japanese Navy, 1887–1941* (Washington DC: United States Naval Institute, 1997).
63. Launched in 1912, *Kongō* was the last major Japanese warship to be built abroad, being built by Vickers in the UK, and the world's first to be armed with 14in main guns. Launched in 1907, *Ibuki* had a main armament of four 305mm (12in) guns and as a 1st class heavy cruiser this vessel and her sister *Kurama* were reclassified as battlecruisers in 1912. Regarding the UK's request, see Grey to Greene, 6 August 1914, quoted in Gilbert, *The Challenge of War*, p. 202. Regarding the search for raiders, see 'Operations – Japanese Navy in the Indian and Pacific Oceans during War 1914–1918', Office of Naval Intelligence, Record Group 45, Subject File 1911–1927, WA-5 Japan, box 703, folder 10, NND 913005, p. 98.
64. Regarding the efforts of the *Chikuma*, see 'Japanese Naval Activities during European War', 11 December 1918; Office of Naval Intelligence, Record Group 38.4.3 Communications with Naval Attaches, U-4-B, 11083, National Archives, Washington DC, p. 11. Regarding the ANZAC troop convoys, see C.E.W. Bean, *The Story of Anzac: The First Phase*, 11th edn (Sydney NSW: Angus and Robertson, 1941), Vol. I of Bean (ed.), p. 90.
65. 'Operations – Japanese Navy in the Indian and Pacific Oceans during War 1914–1918', Office of Naval Intelligence, Record Group 45, Subject File 1911–1927, WA-5 Japan, box 703, folder 10, NND 913005, p. 38.
66. 'Operations – Japanese Navy in the Indian and Pacific Oceans during War 1914–1918', Office of Naval Intelligence, Record Group 45, Subject File 1911–1927, WA-5 Japan, box 703, folder 10, NND 913005, pp. 55–8, Vol. I of Bean (ed.), Vol. 1, p. 94.
67. 'Official Report of Japanese Naval Activities during the War', 11 December 1918, translation of official statement issued by Japanese Navy Department on 8 December 1918; Office of Naval Intelligence, Record Group 38.4.3, Communications with Naval Attaches, U-4-B, 11083, National Archives, Washington DC, p. 7.
68. *Ikoma* was launched as a 1st class heavy cruiser of the 'Tsukuba' class in 1906 and reclassified as a battlecruiser in 1912. 'Official Report of Japanese Naval Activities during the War', 11 December 1918, translation of official statement issued by Japanese Navy Department on 8 December 1918; Office of Naval Intelligence, Record Group 38.4.3 Communications with Naval Attaches, U-4-B, 11083, National Archives, Washington DC, p. 6.
69. 'Operations – Japanese Navy in the Indian and Pacific Oceans during War 1914–1918', Office of Naval Intelligence, Record Group 45, Subject File 1911–27, WA-5 Japan, box 703, folder 10, NND 913005, p. 13. Timothy D. Saxon, 'Anglo-Japanese Naval Cooperation, 1914–1918', *Naval War College Review*, Winter 2000, Vol. LIII, No. 1.
70. *Hizen* was the ex-Russian pre-dreadnought *Retvizan*, sunk at Port Arthur in 1904 but subsequently raised and commissioned in the Japanese fleet. A member of the 'Bussard' class of unprotected steel-hulled cruisers (main armament eight 10.5cm.

rapid firers), SMS *Geier* was launched at the Imperial Dockyard, Whilhelmshaven, on 18 October 1894. Designed for extended overseas duties such vessels had a large coal capacity and could be rigged for sail in order to expand their endurance. When the First World War broke out, the *Geier* was in Indonesian waters en route to patrol Germany's island possessions in the Central and South Pacific Ocean, designated the 'Australia Station' by the German Navy. The warship travelled to German colonial possessions in the Bismarck Archipelago and then to the Marshall Islands in an unsuccessful attempt to join with Spee. The *Geier* then attempted to operate against British and Japanese shipping in the Central Pacific, but engine problems compelled her to enter Honolulu, Hawaii, on 15 October 1914. Interned by the US government, *Geier* was, following American entry into the First World War, commissioned in the US Navy on 15 September 1917 as USS *Schurz*. The vessel was lost on 19 June 1918 after being rammed by the merchant ship SS *Florida* off the coast of North Carolina. A sister ship, SMS *Cormoran*, was at Tsingtau when war broke out. See Timothy P. Mulligan, *M2089: Selected German Documents from the Records of the Naval Records Collection of The Office Of Naval Records And Library, 1897–1917* (Washington DC: National Archives and Records Administration, 2006), p. 3.

71. 'Operations – Japanese Navy in the Indian and Pacific Oceans during War 1914–1918', Office of Naval Intelligence, Record Group 45, Subject File 1911–27, WA-5 Japan, box 703, folder 10, NND 913005, p. 9.

72. Mackenzie, p. 150.

73. Mackenzie, pp. 148–9.

74. Bean (ed.),Vol. 1, p. 90.

75. Harcourt to Munro-Ferguson, 10 September 1914, FO 371/2017, quoted in Lowe, *Great Britain and Japan*, p. 201.

76. SMS *Planet*, and her sister *Möwe* (scuttled at Dar es Salaam, German East Africa (now Tanzania) on 9 August 1914), launched 1905 and 1907 respectively, were scientific survey ships displacing some 650 tonnes apiece. Each had a nominal crew of just over a hundred officers and men, and they were very lightly armed. The *Planet* was raised and refloated by the Japanese in 1916. These vessels carried out some significant scientific work. See, for example, Reichs-Marine-Amt, *Forschungsergebnisse S.M.S. 'Planet' 1906/7, Band 1: Reisebeschreibung* (Berlin: Karl Sigismund, 1909).

77. Greene to Grey, 10 October 1914, FO 371/2017, quoted in Lowe, *Great Britain and Japan*, p. 201.

78. Mackenzie, p. 149.

79. Mackenzie, pp. 150–1. HMS *Fantome* was constructed for the Royal Navy Survey Service. Launched in 1901, she displaced 1,070 tonnes and was designated a sloop. She arrived in Australian waters in 1907 to continue the Barrier Reef survey begun in 1905. Rearmed with 3×12-pounder guns, she was manned by and commissioned into the RAN as HMAS *Fantome* on 27 November 1914. Built by Bremer Vulcan in 1911 as a yacht for the Governor of German New Guinea, *Komet* was captured by HMAS *Nusa* (another ex-German vessel commandeered into the RAN) on 11 October 1914 at Talasea on the Willaumez Peninsula, now part of Papua New Guinea. Designated a sloop, she was armed with three 4in guns and renamed HMAS *Una*.

Somewhat astonishingly the vessel survived until 1955, being renamed *Akuna* following the First World War, as the Pilot boat for the Port Phillip Sea Pilot organisation, which provides pilotage services to the ports of Melbourne, Geelong and Westernport. See http://www.deansmarine.co.uk/Productpage/Komet.htm   and   http://www.ppsp. com.au/Bas ic_Hist.htm.

80. Greene to Grey, 12 October 1914, FO 371/2017, quoted in Lowe, *Great Britain and Japan*, p. 202.

81. Churchill to Harcourt, 18 October 1914. Harcourt Papers, Colonial Office 1910-15, Box 6. Quoted in Lowe, *Great Britain and Japan*, p. 204.

82. Ernest Scott, *Australia During The War,* seventh edn (Sydney NSW: Angus and Robertson, 1941), Vol. XI of Bean (ed.), p. 163.

83. Jose, p. 129.

84. Jose, p. 104.

85. Oliver A. Gillespie, *Official History of New Zealand in the Second World War 1939–45: The Pacific* (Wellington: Department of Internal Affairs, War History Branch, 1952), p. 2.

86. Lowe, *Great Britain and Japan*, p. 202.

87. Mackenzie, p. 153.

88. Mackenzie, p. 153.

89. http://www.adb.online.anu.edu.au/biogs/A110216b.htm.

90. Mackenzie, pp. 155–6.

91. Mackenzie, p. 157.

92. Anguar (or Ngeaur) is now a part of the island nation of Palau. It is also known as 'Monkey Island' because of its population of feral macaques, which were released during German occupation.

93. Jose, p. 72.

94. Jose, p. 101.

95. Mackenzie, pp. 157–8.

96. Green to Grey, 21 November 1914, FO 371/2018, quoted in Lowe, *Great Britain and Japan*, p. 202.

97. Mackenzie, p. 158.

98. Mackenzie, p. 158.

99. Harcourt to Munro–Ferguson, 24 November 1914. George Philip (ed.), *British Documents on Foreign Affairs: Reports and Papers from the Foreign Office Confidential Print, Series E, Asia, 1914–1939*, Pt II, *From the First to the Second World War* (Frederick MD: University Publications of America, 1991), p. 136. Jose, p. 136.

100. Mackenzie, p. 159.

101. William Morris 'Billy' Hughes, Attorney-General in the Labour Government of 1914–15, became Prime Minister in October 1915. Hughes was born in London of Welsh parents and, partially at least, raised in Llandudno, North Wales. He thus had somewhat more in common with David Lloyd George than merely being a political maverick. During a visit to London in early 1916 he spoke at length with Sir Edward Grey and various other Foreign Office dignitaries concerning the position vis-à-vis Japan and the German Islands. Hughes was told that acquiescence to Japanese

occupation was determined by the degree of assistance sought by the Allies (Japan was to send naval forces to the Mediterranean the following year), and that the prospect of getting the Japanese to disgorge their conquests after the war would raise great resentment. When asked if he objected to such a situation he is reported to have replied, 'I am confronted with a *fait accompli* and can do nothing.' See Scott, p. 765. See also Brian Carroll, *Australia's Prime Ministers: From Barton to Howard* (Stanmore; Cassell Australia, 1978).

102. Munro-Ferguson to Harcourt, 25 November 1914, quoted in Mackenzie, p. 150.
103. See, for example, the *U.S. Department of State Foreign Affairs Handbook Volume 5 Handbook 1 – Correspondence* for an explanation the various statuses of diplomatic communications. http://foia.state.gov/masterdocs/05fah01/CH0610.pdf.
104. Greene to Grey, 1 December 1914, FO 371/ 2018, quoted in Lowe, *Great Britain and Japan*, p. 206.
105. Greene to Grey, 1 December 1914, FO 371/ 2018, quoted in Lowe, *Great Britain and Japan*, p. 206.
106. Harcourt to Munro-Ferguson, 3 December 1914, quoted in Mackenzie, p. 150.
107. Gillespie, p. 3.
108. Morinosuke, *The Diplomacy of Japan*, Vol. III, p. 30.

Chapter 5

1. Immanuel C.Y. Hsu, *The Rise of Modern China*, sixth edn (New York NY: Oxford University Press USA, 1999), pp. 394–5.
2. Albert Röhr, *Handbuch der deutschen Marinegeschichte* (*Manual of German Naval History*) (Oldenburg: Gerhard Stalling, 1963), p. 130.
3. Charles B. Burdick, *The Japanese Siege of Tsingtau* (Hamden CT: Archon, 1976), p. 30.
4. Reuters Agency quotation from the *Los Angeles Times*, 31 August 1914. I am grateful to the following people and organisations for their assistance in tracing information and material relating to Alfred M. Brace: Sam Markham, Assistant Archivist at Associated Press, Katie Morgan, Beloit College Archives Summer Manager, and, in particular, Carrie Marsh, Special Collections Librarian at the Honnold/Mudd Library, Claremont, California, who very kindly supplied me with some important documentation. Brace's quotation from Alfred M. Brace, 'With the Germans in Tsingtau: an Eye Witness Account of the Capture of Germany's Colony in China', *The World's Work: A History of Our Time*, Vol. XXIX, November 1914–April 1915 (New York NY: Doubleday, Page & Company, 1915), p. 634.
5. Arthur Judson Brown, *New Forces in Old China: An Inevitable Awakening*, second edn (New York NY: F.H. Revell, 1904), p. 176. 'Germany's large expenditure upon fortified works in Kiautschou is exciting considerable interest, amounting, in certain quarters, to suspicion and anxiety concerning the ulterior designs of this country in the Far East.', *International Herald Tribune*, 17 May 1905.
6. The sources for this and other descriptions of the defences, unless otherwise stated, are: Kurt Aβmann, *Die Kämpfe der Kaiserlichen Marine in den deutschen Kolonien* (Berlin: Mittler, 1935), pp. 108–9. This work gives a breakdown of the artillery positions, both permanent and extemporised. A 'Map of Tsingtau showing the Defences During

the Siege', located at The National Archives (TNA), Kew, reference MPI 1/546/16. According to an added inscription, 'The original of this map was taken from a German artillery officer, now a prisoner of war in Hong Kong.' It details the positions of the various batteries and, in general, is in accord with Aβmann's work. Also utilised are Japanese descriptions of what they encountered in Saito Seiji, *Hi Taisho 3-nen Nichi-Doku senshi bekkan 2 Nichi-Doku Chintao Senso* (*A History of the Japanese-German War of 1914*, Appendix 2: *The Battle between Japan and Germany for Qingdao*) (Tokyo: Yumani Shobo, 2001). This draws on the earlier Sanbo hombu (General Staff Office), *Taisho 3-nen Nichi-Doku senshi* (*History of the Japanese-German War of 1914*), 2 vols (Tokyo: Sanbo Honbu, 1916). Further information has been taken from photographs of plaques mounted at Qingdaoshan Hill Battery Fort Educational Base, formerly the Bismarck Hill complex, which was visited by Dennis and Adrienne Quarmby in 2006. Captain Bernard Smith made a 'detailed reconnaissance' of the area *c.* 1929 and discovered that there had been 'comparatively small damage to the works after 72 days of siege and lapse of some fifteen years'. See Captain Bernard Smith, 'The Siege of Tsingtau', *The Coast Artillery Journal*, November–December 1934, pp. 405–19. Commander Charles B. Robbins, 'German Seacoast Defences at Tsingtao, 1914', *The Coast Defence Journal*, May 2007, pp. 85–90. Commander Robbins analyses an earlier article by Philip Sims – 'German Tsingtao Mounts Photographs', *The Coast Defence Journal*, November 2006 – which had attempted to identify a number of photographs of the defences taken by US sailors during the 1920s. As he put it: 'The pictures are prints in scrap books without dates or captions, so which batteries are shown in the pictures is a subject of educated guesswork.'

7. Gruson chilled cast-iron armour was invented at the works of Hermann Gruson, at Magdeburg-Buckau, in 1868. It was extremely hard and thus difficult to penetrate, though more vulnerable to fracture. A potential rival to the giant Krupp corporation, Gruson's company was taken over by Krupp in 1893. See Julius von Schütz (trans. Hubert Herbert Grenfell), *Gruson's Chilled Cast-Iron Armour* (London: Whitehead, Morris & Lowe, 1887).

8. Tirpitz refers to the line of defences as the 'so called Boxer protection' and the 'Boxer line'. Since it does not seem to have been called anything else I have followed his usage. Grand Admiral von Tirpitz, *My Memoirs*, 2 vols (London: Hurst & Blacket, 1919), Vol. I, pp. 79 and 89.

9. The scarp is, from the point of view of the defenders, the inner side of the ditch. The opposite side is termed the counterscarp.

10. In fortification terminology the Covered Way (sometimes referred to as Covert Way) ran along the top of the counterscarp, and was provided with a protective embankment forming the crest of the glacis. Thus soldiers standing on the Covered Way received some protection from enemy fire. A site on the Covered Way where troops might assemble for sorties was dubbed A Place of Arms.

11. A glacis is an artificial slope, usually of earth, in front of fortifications and constructed so as to deprive any assailant of cover and keep them under fire.

12. Walter von Schoen, *Auf Vorposten für Deutschland: Unsere Kolonien im Weltkrieg* (*On Germany's Outposts: Our Colonies in the World War*) (Berlin: Ullstein, 1935), p. 28.

Gunther Plüschow, *Die Abenteuer des Fliegers von Tsingtau: Meine Erlebnisse in drei Erdteilen (The Adventures of the Tsingtau Flier: My Experiences in Three Continents)* (Berlin: Ullstein, 1916), p. 47.

13. Holger H. Herwig *'Luxury' Fleet: the Imperial German Navy, 1888–1918* (London: George Allen & Unwin, 1980), p. 61.

14. Herwig, p. 63.

15. Burdick, p. 23.

16. Burdick, p. 202, n. 11.

17. The *Landwehr* was often made up of men in their 30s and 40s; the upper age limit for service being 45. See Norman Stone, *The Eastern Front 1914–1917* (New York NY: Charles Scribner's Sons, 1975), p. 55.

18. Tirpitz's opposite number politically, Winston S. Churchill, was the prime mover behind the creation of a British equivalent, the Royal Naval Division. See Douglas Jerrold, *The Royal Naval Division* (London: Hutchinson, 1923).

19. This was no real loss; the Fifth Battle Squadron comprised the five pre-Dreadnoughts of the 'Kaiser Friedrich III' class: *Kaiser Friedrich III, Kaiser Wilhelm II, Kaiser Wilhelm der Grosse, Kaiser Karl der Grosse* and *Kaiser Barbarossoa*. Laid down between 1895 and 1898, and armed principally with $4 \times$ 240mm and $15 \times$ 150mm they were obsolete in 1914 and unfit for operations against the Grand Fleet. Of even less utility were the vessels of the Sixth Battle Squadron. This unit consisted of eight Coastal Defence Battleships of the 'Siegfried' and 'Odin' (modified Siegfried) classes: *Siegfried, Beowulf, Frithjof, Heimdall, Hildebrand, Hagen, Odin* and *Agir*. Laid down between 1889 and 1895 their main armament consisted of $3 \times$ 240mm guns with $8 \times$ 88mm as secondary armament.

20. Mark D. Karau, *'Wielding the Dagger': The MarineKorps Flandern and the German War Effort, 1914–1918* (London: Praeger, 200), pp. 7–15. See also Alex Deseyne, *De Kust Bezet 1914–1918 (The Coast Occupied 1914–1918)* (Nieuwpoortsesteenweg, Belgium: Provincial Domain of Raversijde, 2007).

21. H.W. Brands, *Bound to Empire: The United States and the Philippines* (Oxford: Oxford University Press, 1992), p.46.

22. Walter LaFeber, *The Cambridge History of American Foreign Relations*, 4 vols, Vol. II, *The American Search for Opportunity* (Cambridge: Cambridge University Press, 1993), p. 210.

23. For views on Taft's Presidency see David H. Burton, *William Howard Taft, Confident Peacemaker* (Philadelphia PA: Saint Joseph's University Press, 2004); Michael L. Bromley, *William Howard Taft and the First Motoring Presidency, 1909–1913* (Jefferson NC: McFarland & Co., 2003); Paolo E. Coletta, *The Presidency of William Howard Taft* (Lawrence KS: University Press of Kansas, 1973).

24. James D. Startt, *Woodrow Wilson and the Press: Prelude to the Presidency* (New York NY: Palgrave Macmillan, 2004), p. 1.

25. Woodrow Wilson, *Message to Congress*, 63rd Congress, 2nd Session, Senate Doc. No. 566 (Washington DC, 1914), pp. 3–4. Available from: http://net.lib.byu.edu/~rdh7/wwi/1914/wilsonneut.html. Biographies on Wilson include: Mario R. Di Nunzio (ed.), *Woodrow Wilson: Essential Writings and Speeches of a Scholar-President*

(New York NY: New York University Press, 2006); Kendrick A. Clements, *The Presidency of Woodrow Wilson: American Presidency Series* (Lawrence KS: University Press of Kansas, 1992); Arthur Walworth, *Woodrow Wilson*, 2 vols (New York NY: Longmans, Green, 1958); Arthur S. Link, *Woodrow Wilson and the Progressive Era, 1910–1917* (New York NY: Harper, 1954).

26. For an account of the relationship between the two states see Ian Nish, 'German-Japanese Relations in the Taisho Period', in Ian Nish, *Collected Writings of Ian Nish*, 2 vols (Richmond VA: Curzon Press, 2001–2) Vol. I, pp. 188–203.

27. Shunjiro Kurita, *Who's Who in Japan 1913* (Tokyo: The Who's Who in Japan Office, 1913), p. 360.

28. Nebogatov's flagship, *Czar Nicholas I*, a 'Czar Alexander II' class battleship commissioned in 1891, was also captured after Tsushima. Recommissioned as *Iki*, she was used as a gunnery training ship and not deployed with Kato.

29. The *Chiyoda* should probably be classed as a light cruiser.

30. On board was a young naval officer named Onishi Takijiro. During the Second World War he founded the Kamikaze Corps. Walter J. Boyne, *Clash of Wings: World War II In The Air* (New York NY: Simon & Schuster, 1994), pp. 94–5.

31. See David Lyon, *The First Destroyers* (London: Caxton Editions, 2001).

32. See Arne Røksund, *The Jeune Ecole: The Strategy of the Weak* (Leiden, Netherlands: Brill, 2007); Erwin F. Sieche, 'The Kaiser Franz Joseph I Class Torpedo-rams of the Austro-Hungarian Navy', in John Roberts (ed.), *Warship 1995* (London: Conway Maritime Press, 1995); Lawrence Sondhaus, *The Naval Policy of Austria-Hungary 1867–1918: Navalism, Industrial Development and the Politics of Dualism* (West Lafayette IN: Purdue University Press, 1994).

33. Burdick, p. 28.

34. Burdick, pp. 38–9.

35. The primary armament of *S-90* consisted of three torpedo tubes; the *Kennet* had two.

36. Brace, p. 634.

37. British reports of the engagement are at TNA, ADM 137, 'Admiralty: Historical Section: Records used for Official History, First World War'. An account utilising these sources, as well as German documents, can be found in Burdick, pp. 65–7, p. 216, nn. 15–16.

38. The 'finding' of the piece of steel is described in Burdick, p. 67. For a description of British attitudes towards, and equipment for, minelaying see Peter F. Halvorsen, 'The Royal Navy and Mine Warfare, 1868–1914', *The Journal of Strategic Studies*, Vol. 27, No. 4/December 2004, pp. 685–707.

39. Minus the British contingent, which did not join until 12 September.

40. TNA, FO 228/2306, quoted in Burdick, p. 218.

41. Burdick, p. 74.

42. For an account of the storm and its damaging effects see Burdick, pp. 74–5.

43. Shunjiro, p. 334.

44. Sterling Seagrave, *Dragon Lady: The Life and Legend of the Last Empress of China*, repr. edn (London: Vintage, 1993), p. 507.

45. Copies of the campaign plans are at TNA, WO 106/668, 'Japanese and Chinese maps and literature relating to operations at Tsingtau', and these, together with Japanese documents, form the basis of Burdick's work on the subject. See Burdick, pp. 58–127. I have also drawn heavily on the Japanese 'official history' (Sanbo Honbu (General Staff Office), *Taisho 3-nen Nichi-Doku senshi* (*History of the Japanese-German War of 1914*), 2 vols (Toyko: Sanbo Honbu, 1916)) and unless otherwise stated this forms the source for the account of the campaign.

46. Gilbert Reid, 'The Neutrality of China', *The Yale Law Journal*, Vol. 25, No. 2 (December 1915), p. 122.

47. Noriko Kawamura, *Turbulence in the Pacific: Japanese-US Relations During World War I* (Westport CT: Praeger, 2000), p. 18.

48. Burdick, p. 105.

49. Burdick, p. 104.

50. Hans Grade was an engineer and a German aviation-pioneer. On 28 October 1908, at Magdeburg, he successfully conducted the first powered flight in Germany in an aeroplane of his own construction. On 30 October 1909 he won a 40,000 mark prize for being the first German to fly an indigenously constructed and powered aeroplane in a 'figure of eight' around two marker posts set 1km apart. For details on Grade's life and achievements see Ruth Glatzer, *Panorama einer Metropole: Das Wilhelminische Berlin* (Berlin: Siedler, 1997), p. 258; Niels Klußmann and Arnim Malik, *Lexikon der Luftfahrt* (Berlin: Springer, 2004), p. 320; Hans Fabian, 'Aeronautical Research Comes into Being During the Time of Empire', in E.H. Hirschel, H. Prem and G. Madelung, *Aeronautical Research in Germany: From Lilienthal Until Today* (Berlin: Springer, 2004), pp. 38–40.

51. Lila Sumino, 'L'Avion: l'Envol du Japon', *Asia: Journal collégien et lycéen d'établissements français de la zone Asie-Pacifique*, No. 2 December, 2006, p. 4.

52. For the story of early Japanese aviation see Shinji Suzuki and Masako Sakai, 'History of Early Aviation in Japan', a paper (AIAA 2005-118) presented to the 43rd AIAA (American Institute of Aeronautics and Astronautics) Aerospace Sciences Meeting and Exhibit, 10–13 January 2005, Reno, NV.

53. Richard J. Samuels, *'Rich Nation, Strong Army:' National Security and the Technological Transformation of Japan* (Ithaca NY: Cornell University Press, 1994), p. 109.

54. Stéphane Nicolaou, *Flying Boats and Seaplanes: A History from 1905* (Osceola WI: MBI, 1998), p. 48.

55. Tom D. Crouch, *Wings: A History of Aviation from Kites to the Space Age* (New York NY: W.W. Norton, 2003), pp. 137–8.

56. James Davilla and Arthur Soltan, *French Aircraft Of The First World War* (Stratford CT: Flying Machines Press, 1997), p. 218.

57. Plüschow, pp. 3–4.

58. John Killen, *The Luftwaffe: A History* (Barnsley: Pen and Sword, 2003), p. 8.

59. Grand Admiral von Tirpitz, *My Memoirs* (London: Hurst & Blacket, 1919), 2 vols, Vol. I, p. 139.

60. Plüschow, pp. 10 and 20.

61. For a biographical account of Franz Oster see Wilhelm Matzat, 'Franz Oster (1869–1933) – der erste Flieger von Tsingtau' ('Franz Oster (1869–1933) – The First Tsingtau Flier'), available online at: http://www.earlyaviators.com/eoster.htm. For the Ceylon crash see the 'Air Traffic Control Sri Lanka' website at: http://atcsl.tripod.com/1911_1949.htm.

62. Plüschow, pp. 26–8.

63. Plüschow, pp. 38–40.

64. *Flugzeug vollständig zertrümmert. Wiederaufbau lohnt sich nicht mehr*, Gunther Plüschow, diary entry for 27 August 1914, quoted in Matzat.

65. See Carl Johannes Voskamp, *Aus dem belagerten Tsingtau* (Berlin: Society of Evangelical Missions, 1915), p. 60. Also Matzat.

66. Burdick, pp. 93–4.

67. Plüschow, p. 49.

68. Burdick, pp. 88–9.

69. Burdick, p. 97.

70. The Japanese cavalry, like that of European nations, was trained and equipped to fight dismounted when necessary. Edward A. Altham, *The Principles of War Historically Illustrated* (London: Macmillan, 1914), p. 83.

71. Waldemar Vollerthun, *Der Kampf um Tsingtau: eine Episode aus dem Weltkrieg 1914/1918 nach Tagebuchblättern* (*The Battle for Tsingtau: an Episode from the World War of 1914–18 from the Pages of a Diary*) (Leipzig: Hirzel, 1920), p. 98; Burdick, p. 90; H.G.W. Woodhead and H.T.M. Bell, *The China Year Book* (Shanghai: *North China Daily News & Herald*, 1914), p. 623. http://homepage3.nifty.com/akagaki/cyuui3.html.

72. Burdick, pp. 44–5.

73. Burdick, pp. 46–8.

74. Burdick, pp. 61–2.

75. Burdick, p. 96.

76. Otto von Gottberg, *Die Helden von Tsingtau* (Berlin: Ullstein, 1915), p. 147.

77. Burdick, p. 100.

78. These, and similar, works, although hastily constructed would appear to have been robust. James R. Lilley, the US Ambassador to the Peoples Republic of China from 1989–91, spent his early childhood (he was born in 1924) in Tsingtau, and, later, he recalled exploring the 'old German forts' dug into the hillsides in 'Laoshan Mountain'. This must have been in the late 1920s or early 1930s. See James R. Lilley with Jeffrey Lilley, *China Hands: Nine Decades of Adventure, Espionage, and Diplomacy in Asia* (New York NY: PublicAffairs, 2004), p. 12.

79. Burdick, pp. 100–2.

80. The *Mecklenburghaus* opened on 1 September 1904 and was named in honour of the president of the German Colonial Society, Duke Johann Albrecht zu Mecklenburg. See Deutsche Kolonialgesellschaft (German Colonial Society) (eds), *Deutscher Kolonial-Atlas mit Jahrbuch* (*German Colonial Atlas and Yearbook*) (Berlin: Deutsche Kolonialgesellschaft, 1905), p. 22.

81. Burdick, pp. 102–3.

82. Davilla and Soltan, p. 218. Burdick, p. 104.

83. Burdick, pp. 98 and 104–5.

84. A 'Decauville Railway' was a 600mm narrow gauge line made up of easily portable pre-assembled sections. The inventor was French farmer Paul Decauville, who conceived the idea after visiting the narrow gauge Rheilffordd Ffestiniog (Ffestiniog Railway) between Blaenau Ffestiniog and Porthmadog in North Wales. He originally devised it as a means of improving access to his land, but realised that it could be adapted for other purposes. He formed a company to produce track and rolling stock in 1875. The French Army adopted the system in 1888 and it had become standardised equipment for the militaries of several countries by 1914. See 'Portable Railways', *Scientific American Supplement No. 446*, New York, 19 July 1884; Pascal Ory, *1889 La Mémoire des siècles: L'Expo universelle* (Paris: Editions Complexe, 1989), p. 119; Ffestiniog Railway Company, *Rheilffordd Ffestiniog Guide Book* (Porthmadog: Ffestiniog Railway Company, 1997); Jim Harter, *World Railways of the Nineteenth Century: A Pictorial History in Victorian Engravings* (Baltimore MD: John Hopkins University Press, 2005), p. 141.

85. Burdick, pp. 109, 147, 231, n. 42.

86. For a history of the regiment see C.T. Atkinson, *The History of the South Wales Borderers 1914–1918* (Uckfield: Naval & Military Press, 2002).

87. John Albert White, *Transition to Global Rivalry: Alliance Diplomacy and the Quadruple Entente, 1895–1907* (Cambridge: Cambridge University Press, 2002), p. 181. Details of Barnardiston's career and his papers are located at the Liddell Hart Centre for Military Archives at King's College London, Reference code: GB99 KCLMA Barnardiston.

88. Kitchener to General Officer Commanding (GOC) North China, 21 August 1914, quoted in Burdick, p. 82.

89. As well as 970 personnel, Barnardiston commanded 240 Chinese labourers with 98 wagons as well as 200 mules. See TNA, ADM 137/35.

90. Barnardiston to the War Office, 9 October 1914, TNA, WO 106/667, 'Operations at Tsing Tau: Reports by Brig-Gen N.W. Barnardiston MVO'. Also printed in the Supplement to the *London Gazette* of 30 May 1916. Available at http://www.1914-1918.net/barnardistons_first_despatch.htm. Attached to Barnardiston's command as liaison officer was Lieutenant Colonel Everard Ferguson Calthrop of the Royal Artillery. Calthrop was one of the 'Language Officers' attached to the British Legation in Tokyo, a scheme initiated in September 1903 so that British military personnel could learn to communicate with their recent ally. See Sebastian Dobson, *The Russo-Japanese War: Reports from Officers Attached to the Japanese Forces in the Field*, 5 vols, repr. edn with an introduction by Sebastian Dobson (Bristol: Ganesha Publishing, 2000), Vol. I, pp. v–lxii. Calthrop's notes on his attachment are at TNA, WO 106/661, 'Japanese participation in North China (Tsing Tau): Original Transcripts'.

91. In so doing, Barnardiston became the first British commander to set foot on German territory during the First World War. Burdick, p. 111. An excellent work that focuses on the British contribution to the campaign is John Dixon, *A Clash of Empires: The South Wales Borderers at Tsingtao, 1914* (Wrexham: Bridge Books, 2008).

92. Burdick, pp. 113–14.

93. Burdick, pp. 114–18.
94. Burdick, pp. 68 and 71.
95. Burdick, p. 118.
96. Burdick, p. 124.
97. Burdick, p. 23.
98. Burdick, p. 124.
99. Burdick, p. 121.
100. Burdick, p. 122.
101. Plüschow, pp. 52–3.
102. 'Until several years after World War I, Japan had no separate permanent naval landing organization corresponding to the U.S. Marine Corps. Instead, naval landing parties were organized temporarily from fleet personnel for a particular mission and were returned to their ships at its conclusion. This practice was made possible by the fact that every naval recruit was given training in land warfare concurrently with training in seamanship. The results of such training, together with any special skills [...] were noted on the seaman's service record to serve as a basis for his inclusion in a landing party. Normally, the fleet commander designated certain ships to furnish personnel for the landing party. This practice, however, depleted their crews and lowered their efficiency for naval action. Therefore, in the late 1920s Japan began to experiment with more permanent units known as Special Naval Landing Forces (*Rikusentai*).', *Handbook on Japanese Military Forces: War department Technical Manual TM-E 30-480* (Washington DC: War Department, 1944), p. 76.
103. G. Nash and G. Gipps, 'Narrative of the Events in Connection with the Siege, Blockade, and Reduction of the Fortress of Tsingtau', TNA, ADM 137/35; Burdick, p. 231, n. 42.
104. Burdick, p. 123.
105. Plüschow, p. 54; Burdick, pp. 125–6, 235, n. 87.

Chapter 6

1. Peter Overlack, 'The Force of Circumstance: Graf Spee's Options for the East Asian Cruiser Squadron in 1914', *Journal of Military History*, Vol. 60, No. 4 (October 1996), p. 659.
2. Jurgen Tampke (ed.), *Ruthless Warfare: German Military Planning and Surveillance in the Australia-New Zealand Region Before the Great War* (Canberra: Southern Highlands Publishers, 1998), pp. 69–70.
3. See http://web.genealogie.free.fr/Les_militaires/1GM/Allemagne/Marine/Admiral/B.htm for a brief resumé of Bendemann's career. The Certificate conferring the Order of the Rising Sun can be found in the British Library, Ref. Or. 14819.
4. Fisher to Balfour, undated, quoted in Nicholas Lambert, 'Economy or Empire? The Fleet Unit Concept and the Quest for Collective Security in the Pacific, 1909–1914', in Keith Neilson (ed.), *Far-flung Lines: Studies in Imperial Defence in Honour of Donald Mackenzie Schurman* (London: Frank Cass, 1997), p. 58. See also Nicholas Lambert, *Sir John Fisher's Naval Revolution* (Columbia SC: University of South Carolina Press, 1999), pp. 86–7.

5. Lambert, 'Economy or Empire?', p. 57.

6. Lawrence Sondhaus, *Naval warfare, 1815–1914* (London: Routledge, 2001), pp. 175–6. Donald H. Dyal, Brian B. Carpenter, Mark A. Thomas, *Historical dictionary of the Spanish American War* (Westport CT: Greenwood Press, 1996), p. 256.

7. Albert A. Nofi, *The Spanish-American War: 1898* (Conshohocken PA: Combined Books, 1996), pp. 80–2.

8. See Holger H. Herwig, *Politics of Frustration: The United States in German Naval Planning, 1889–1941* (Boston MA: Little, Brown, 1976), p. 90. John A.S. Grenville and George B. Young, *Politics, Strategy, and Diplomacy: Studies in Foreign Policy, 1873–1917* (New Haven CN: Yale University Press, 1966), pp. 306–7. The German Bundesarchiv-Militararchiv (Federal Military Archive), at Freiburg contains correspondence between the principals and updates of versions of the Pacific War Plans, in BA/MA Reichs-Marine 5/v 5955. This was utilised by Peter Overlack for 'German War Plans in the Pacific, 1900–1914', pp. 579–93, available at: http://findarticles.com/p/articles/mi_hb3498/is_199803/ai_n8291670.

9. Klaus-Volker Giessler, *Die Institution des Marineattachés im Kaiserreich (The Institution of the Imperial Marine Attachés)* (Boppard am Rhein: Boldt, 1976), p. 311.

10. Peter Overlack, 'German Commerce Warfare Planning for the Asia-Pacific Region before World War I', available at http://www.geocities.com/peteroverlack/page2.htm.

11. Alfred Thayer Mahan, *The Influence of Sea Power Upon History, 1660–1783* (Boston MA: Adamant Media Corporation, 2002), p. 25.

12. Tampke, p. 191.

13. Tom Frame, *No Pleasure Cruise: The Story of the Royal Australian Navy* (Crows Nest, NSW: Allen & Unwin, 2005), p. 103.

14. Alfred Thayer Mahan, *The Influence of Sea Power upon the French Revolution and Empire, 1793–1812*, 2 vols (Boston MA: Adamant Media Corporation, 2002), Vol. II, p. 217.

15. Sir Cyprian Bridge, *The Art of Naval Warfare: Introductory Observations* (London: Smith, Elder and Co., 1907), pp. 144–5.

16. Winston S. Churchill, *The World Crisis 1911–1918*, 2-vol. edn (London: Odhams, 1938), Vol. 1, p. 177.

17. Tampke, p. 194.

18. There are a huge number of works detailing the fate of Spee and the Cruiser Squadron. One of the best is undoubtedly that by Keith Yates, *Graf Spee's Raiders: Challenge to the Royal Navy 1914–1915* (Annapolis MD: Naval Institute Press, 1995).

19. This prize was sent to Tsingtau, where it was armed with the weaponry from the laid up and unrepairable gunboat *Cormoran* for use as an auxiliary cruiser. Rechristened *Cormoran II*, it met with no success.

20. Dated only 'the end of July', quoted in Arthur W. Jose, *The Royal Australian Navy 1914–1918*, ninth edn (Sydney NSW: Angus and Robertson, 1941), Vol. IX of C.E.W. Bean (ed.), *The Official History of Australia in the War of 1914–1918*, 12 vols, various edns (Sydney NSW: Angus and Robertson, 1941), pp. 26–7.

21. The Australian Centre For Maritime Studies, Submission To The 'Inquiry Into Australia's Maritime Strategy', 4 November 2002, p. 10. http://www.acmarst.com/parl_sub/maritimesub.pdf.

22. Geoffrey Bennett, *Naval Battles of the First World War,* rev. edn (London: Penguin, 2002), p. 40.

23. There have been several excellent accounts of the adventures of the *Emden*. One of the best, and certainly the most accessible, is by Dan Van der Vat, *The Last Corsair: The Story of the Emden*, rev. edn (Edinburgh: Birlinn, 2001). Other works include R.K. Lochner (trans. Thea and Harry Lindauer), *The Last-Gentleman-Of-War: The Raider Exploits of the Cruiser Emden* (Annapolis MD: Naval Institute Press, 1988) and Hugo von Waldeyer-Hartz, *Der Kreuzerkrieg 1914–1918: das Kreuzergeschwader, Emden, Königsberg, Karlsruhe, die Hilfskreuzer* (Oldenburg: Gerhard Stalling, 1931).

24. According to *Merchant Shipping (Losses)*, House of Commons Paper 199, *1919* (London: HMSO, 1919) the following British vessels were captured and sunk by *Emden*: *Indus*, 10 September; *Lovat*, 11 September; *Killin*, 13 September; *Diplomat*, 13 September; *Trabboch*, 14 September; *Clan Matheson*, 14 September; *King Lud*, 25 September; *Tymeric*, 25 September; *Buresk*, 27 September; *Ribera*, 27 September; *Foyle*, 27 September; *Clan Grant*, 16 October; *Benmohr*, 16 October; *Ponrabbel*, 16 October; *Troilus*, 18 October; *Chilkana*, 19 October. To these may be added: *Pontoporus* (Greek), 9 September, captured with a cargo of British coal and impressed; *Kabinga* (British), 12 September, captured with neutral cargo and released; *Loredano* (Italian), 13 September, stopped and released; *Gryfevale* (British), 26 September, captured and released with captured crewmen from previous prizes; *St Egbert* (British), 18 October, captured and released with captured crewmen from previous prizes. See also Van der Vat.

25. On the east wall of the High Court at Parry's Corner, at the intersection of North Beach Road and NSC (Netaji Subhas Chandra) Bose Road, there is a plaque commemorating the shelling. Every 22 September there is a gathering at this site, not to remember the shelling, but rather to commemorate Dr Champakaraman Pillai, a committed anti-imperialist. He is credited with coining the phrase 'Jai Hind' meaning 'Victory for India' which became a nationalist mantra. At the start of the First World War he was in Switzerland, though he shortly moved to Berlin where, with German encouragement, he became a founder member of the Indian Independence Committee. It is said that Champakaraman Pillai was aboard the *Emden* when she raided the city and even helped direct fire onto specific targets. He returned to Germany after the war and was supposedly murdered by the Nazis in 1934. His wife, following Independence, returned his ashes to India. He is today remembered in India as a great freedom fighter. See *The Hindu*, Monday, 1 October 2001 and 19 November 2001, http://www.hinduonnet.com/ and also Sadhu Prof. V. Rangarajan and R. Vivekanandan, *The Saga of Patriotism: Revolutionaries in India's Freedom Struggle* (Bangalore: Sister Nivedita Academy, 2004).

26. The panic in Ceylon resulted in the arrest of a game ranger at what is today Ruhunu (Yala) National Park in Sri Lanka. The ranger, H.H. Engelbrecht, was taken prisoner by the British during the Boer War but was not returned to South Africa on account of

Notes   199

his refusal to swear allegiance to the British monarchy. He became the first ranger of
the forerunner to the National Park, the game sanctuary, in 1908. He was accused, an
accusation completely without foundation, of supplying meat to the *Emden* in 1914 and
incarcerated until after the war. http://padayatra.org/yala.htm.

27. John Ashley Hall, *The Law of Naval Warfare*, rev. and enlarged edn (London: Chapman
    & Hall, 1921), p. 85.
28. *New York Times*, 29 October 1914.
29. Overlack, 'The Force of Circumstance', p. 680.
30. The trans-Pacific cable, linking Vancouver to New Zealand and Australia via Norfolk
    Island, Fiji and Fanning Island, had been completed in 1902.
31. The *Nürnberg*'s boiler problems are discussed in Jose, p. 29.
32. Jose, p. 560.
33. *The Times*, 10 September 1914, p. 7.
34. Jose, p. 181.
35. The adventures of the abandoned landing party constitute a story straight out of
    Boys' Own Adventure Stories. Finding themselves marooned they commandeered the
    Ayesha, a small three-masted schooner, and made for the neutral territory of Padang,
    on Sumatra, in the Dutch East Indies. There they rendezvoused with a German
    merchantman that took them to Ottoman territory on the Red Sea. A nightmare land
    journey then began, and eventually most of them made it to safety and eventually
    back home to Germany and a heroes' welcome. See Van der Vat; also Hellmuth von
    Mücke, *The Emden-Ayesha adventure: German raiders in the South Seas and beyond,
    1914* (Annapolis MD: Naval Institute Press, 2000).
36. HMAS *Sydney*: 4,900 tonnes; 26 knots; 8 × 152mm guns. SMS *Emden*: 3,052 tonnes;
    23 knots; 10 × 105mm guns.
37. Quoted in Martin Gilbert, *The First World War: a Complete History* (New York NY:
    Henry Holt, 1994), p. 110.
38. See, for example, Geoffrey Bennett, *Coronel and the Falklands*, rev. edn (Edinburgh:
    Birlinn, 2001). Barrie Pitt, *Coronel and Falkland: Two Great Naval Battles of the First
    World War* (London: Cassell, 2004).
39. T.B. Dixon, *The Enemy Fought Splendidly* (Poole: Blandford Press, 1983), p. 26.
40. One, *Princess Royal*, went to the Caribbean.
41. The other ships were *Caernarvon*, *Cornwall*, *Glasgow* and *Bristol*.
42. The squadron comprised *Scharnhorst*, *Gneisenau*, *Nürnberg*, *Leipzig* and *Dresden*.

Chapter 7

1. See Georg Kerst, *Jacob Meckel: Sein Leben und sein Wirken in Deutschland und Japan*
   (Göttingen: Musterschmidt, 1970), pp. 54–5. Doris G. Bargen, *Suicidal Honor: General
   Nogi and the Writings of Mori Ogai and Natsume Soseki* (Honolulu HI: University of
   Hawai'i Press, 2006), pp. 49–50.
2. Oe Shinobu, *Nichi-Ro senso no gunjishiteki kenkyu* (Tokyo: Iwanami shoten, 1976),
   p. 130.
3. Endo Yoshinobu, *Kindai Nihon guntai kyoikushi kenkyu* (Tokyo: Aoki shoten, 1994),
   p. 122.

4. All these matters are discussed in Hara Takeshi, *Nichi-Ro senso*, 4 vols (Tokyo: Gunjishi gakkai hen, 2005), Vol. 2, pp. 271–87.
5. Hara, Vol. 2, pp. 272 and 282.
6. Hara, Vol. 2, p. 285. Endo, pp. 116–17.
7. There is a massive canon of work in English concerning the Russo-Japanese War in general and the Siege of Port Arthur in particular. See, for example, B.W. Norregaard, *The Great Siege: The Investment and Fall of Port Arthur* (London: Methuen, 1906); Lieutenant General N.A. Tretyakov, *My Experiences at Nan-Shan and Port Arthur with the Fifth East Siberian Rifles* (London: Hugh Rees, 1911); Reginald Hargreaves, *Red Sun Rising* (London: Wiedenfield & Nicolson, 1962); Richard Connaughton, *The War of the Rising Sun and Tumbling Bear* (London: Routledge, 1991).
8. Barnardiston to the War Office, 10 November 1914, Brigadier General N.W. Barnardiston, 'Operations at Tsing Tau', TNA, WO 106/667; also printed in the Supplement to the *London Gazette* of 30 May 1916; available at: http://www.1914–1918.net/barnardistons_first_despatch.htm.
9. Otto von Gottberg, *Die Helden von Tsingtau* (Berlin: Ullstein, 1915), p. 127; Charles B. Burdick, *The Japanese Siege of Tsingtau* (Hamden CT: Archon, 1976), pp. 134–6. According to Brace the Japanese sent a full list of those they had captured to the defenders by wireless. Alfred M. Brace, 'With the Germans in Tsingtau: an Eye Witness Account of the Capture of Germany's Colony in China', in *The World's Work: A History of Our Time*, Vol. XXIX, November 1914–April 1915 (New York NY: Doubleday, Page & Company, 1915), p. 640.
10. John Ellis, *Eye-Deep in Hell: Trench Warfare in World War I* (Baltimore MD: Johns Hopkins University Press, 1976), p. 76.
11. Nikolas Gardner, *Trial by Fire: Command and the British Expeditionary Force in 1914* (Westport CT: Praeger, 2003), p. 95.
12. The form the German artillery operation would take had been decided at a war council presided over by Meyer-Waldeck on 28 September. Burdick, pp. 128–9.
13. Burdick, pp. 130–1.
14. Gunther Plüschow, *Die Abenteuer des Fliegers von Tsingtau: Meine Erlebnisse in drei Erdteilen* (*The Adventures of the Tsingtau Flier: My Experiences in Three Continents*) (Berlin: Ullstein, 1916), p. 43.
15. E.F. Young, 'Tethered Balloons – Present and Future', a paper (AIAA-1968-941) presented to the Aerodynamic Deceleration Systems Conference of the AIAA (American Institute of Aeronautics and Astronautics), 23–5 September 1968, El Centro, CA, p. 1.
16. Ian Sumner, *German Air Forces 1914–18* (Oxford: Osprey, 2005), p. 29.
17. Brace, p. 637. Burdick, pp. 131–2.
18. Brace, p. 637.
19. Unless otherwise stated, the course of the siege from the Japanese side is taken from Sanbo Honbu (General Staff Office), *Taisho 3-nen Nichi-Doku senshi* (*History of the Japanese-German War of 1914*), 2 vols (Tokyo: Sanbo Honbu, 1916). Plüschow, pp. 57–9.
20. Plüschow, pp. 59–61.
21. TNA, ADM 137/35, attachment to report dated 30 November 1914.

22. Burdick, p. 241, n. 45.
23. Burdick, p. 145.
24. For Japan's occupation of the railway and the political impetus behind it, see Madeleine Chi, *China Diplomacy 1914–1918* (Cambridge MA: Harvard University Press, 1970), pp. 14–25; John T. Pratt, *War and Politics in China* (London: Jonathan Cape, 1943), p. 178.
25. For 'mole warfare' at Port Arthur see Chapter XXX of E.K. Nozhin, A.B Lindsay (trans.) and E.J. Swinton (ed.), *The Truth about Port Arthur* (London: John Murray, 1908), pp. 206–21.
26. Shunjiro Kurita, *Who's Who in Japan 1913* (Tokyo: The Who's Who in Japan Office, 1913), p. 1211.
27. The French military engineer Marquis Sebastien Le Prestre Vauban (1633–1707), in his 1704 treatise *Le Triomph de la Methode*, advised attackers to always dig three wide parallels that enveloped the front under attack and connected to each other. These three parallel trenches ('*places d'armes*') each dug progressively closer to the fortress than the previous one and connected to it by zigzagged communication trenches ('*sapes*' or saps), allowed the besiegers to closely approach the object under attack whilst being sheltered from defensive fire. For a (very) brief summary and a colourful sketch lifted directly from Vauban's work see Charles Stephenson, 'Master of Siegecraft: Seigneur de Vauban, 1633–1707', in Charles Stephenson (consultant ed.), *Castles: A History of Fortified Structures Ancient, Medieval and Modern* (New York NY: St Martin's Griffin, 2011), pp. 234–5.
28. Chinese citizens were also used by the Germans, and not only for carrying out the donkey work. Tsingtau had a contingent of Chinese police, and some of these, prior to the Japanese closing up with the defences, were sent into enemy held territory in civilian guise in order to collect intelligence. Such missions were dangerous in the extreme – the Japanese had no hesitation in shooting those they thought might be spies – and, whilst such men were undoubtedly brave, the effort was, in all likelihood, unproductive. Burdick, pp. 133–4 and 138–9.
29. Burdick, pp. 140–1.
30. Plüschow, p. 68.
31. This has been claimed as an aviation first, but that seems improbable given there were encounters over Europe in August 1914, which is unsurprising given there were far greater number of aircraft deployed there. I have also seen it argued that the first aeroplane-aeroplane aerial combat took place over Mexico the year before during the revolutionary turmoil in that country. Then two American mercenary pilots, Phil Rader and Dean Ivan Lamb who were flying for opposite sides, discharged revolver fire at each other. However according to the later account of one of them, they were merely play-acting and not seriously attempting to shoot at each other at all. Colonel Dean Ivan Lamb, *The Incurable Filibuster: Adventures of Colonel Dean Ivan Lamb* (New York NY: Farrar & Rinehart, 1934), pp. 93–4.
32. Plüschow, p. 70.
33. Burdick, p. 242, n. 58.
34. Barnardiston to the War Office, 9 October 1914.

35. Burdick, pp. 142 and 239, n. 33.
36. Burdick, pp. 144–5 and 151–2.
37. Burdick, pp. 142–3.
38. Barnardiston to the War Office, 29 October 1914.
39. Barnardiston to the War Office, 29 October 1914. Burdick, pp. 146–7.
40. Burdick, pp. 152–3.
41. Plüschow, p. 78.
42. Burdick, pp. 153 and 244, nn. 75–9.
43. Burdick, pp. 148–9 and 160.
44. Burdick, pp. 139 and 158–9.
45. Burdick, pp. 161 and 246, nn. 15–16.
46. *Jinrickisha*, usually spelt *jinrikisha* was a rickshaw. Brace, p. 637.
47. Plüschow, p. 80.
48. Burdick, p. 162.
59. Burdick, pp. 161 and 246, n. 17.
50. Correspondents of *The Times*, *The Times History of the War*, 22 vols (London: *The Times*, 1915), Vol. II, p. 119.
51. During the Battle of the Somme in 1916 the British deployed fifty-four artillery tubes per kilometre. A record at the time, though soon surpassed. See B.H. Liddell Hart, *History of the First World War* (London: Pan Books, 1972), p. 234.
52. Burdick, p. 165; Plüschow, p. 83.
53. Burdick, p. 165. Brace, p. 638. For information on the Asiatic Petroleum Company see Charles van der Leeuw, *Oil and Gas in the Caucasus and Caspian: A History* (Richmond: Curzon Press, 2000), p. 80.
54. A.N. Hilditch, 'The Capture of Tsingtau (Nov. 7) Japan Expels Germany from the Far East', in Charles F. Horne (ed.), *Source Records of World War I*, 7 vols, Vol. II, *1914 – The Red Dawning of 'Der Tag'* (New York NY: Edwin Mellen Press, 1997), p. 402.
55. Burdick, pp. 165 and 247, n. 29. Hilditch, p. 402.
56. Burdick, pp. 166–7.
57. Burdick, pp. 168–9.
58. Sources differ as to who was in charge of the various Infantry Works over the course of the bombardment, and of course personnel and units were rotated. I have chosen to mainly follow Kurt Aßmann, *Die Kämpfe der Kaiserlichen Marine in den deutschen Kolonien* (Berlin: Mittler, 1935), Pt I of which deals with the Tsingtau campaign. Also authoritative at least for the initial deployment is Hans Klehmet, *Tsingtau: Rückblick auf die Geschichte, besonders der Belagerung und des Falles der Festung, mit kritischen Betrachtungen* (Berlin: Georg Bath, 1931).
59. Burdick, pp. 170–1 and 249, n. 46.
60. Anon., 'Notes from Tsingtau', *Journal of the United States Artillery* (Fort Monroe VA: Coast Artillery School Press, 1915), pp. 374–5.
61. Burdick, pp. 170–1. Hilditch, p. 403.
62. Burdick, pp. 170–1.
63. Jefferson Jones, *The Fall of Tsingtau, With a Study of Japan's Ambitions in China* (Boston MA: Houghton Mifflin, 1915). Portions relating to the siege and fall of

Tsingtau are available online at http://www.greatwardifferent.com/Great_War/ Tsing_Tao/Japanese_Orient_01.htm. Jones, who was the Staff Correspondent of the *Minneapolis Journal* and *Japan Advertiser*, had this work added to the UK's proscribed list during the course of the First World War. His study of Japan's ambitions in China was considered to be hostile to Japan, and Britain had no wish to antagonise a valuable ally. For the banning of the book see Peter Fryer, *Private Case-Public Scandal* (London: Seeker & Warburg, 1966), pp. 139–40.

64. Burdick, p. 248, n. 41.
65. Burdick, pp. 172 and 249, n. 53.
66. Burdick, p. 172.
67. Major R.L. McClintock, Royal Engineers, who was at the time attached to the Madras Sappers and Miners, a unit of the Indian Army based at Bangalore, invented the original Bangalore Torpedo in 1912. It consisted of lengths of explosive-filled metal tubing that could be attached end to end to the requisite length. These were then pushed through barbed-wire entanglements and detonated, the resultant explosion cutting a channel through the wire. Major General W. Porter, *The History of the Corps of Royal Engineers*, 11 vols (London: Longmans, Green, 1952), Vol. II, p. 67. Also see the Royal Engineers Museum website http://www.remuseum.org.uk/corpshistory/ rem_corps_part13.htm.
68. Barnardiston to the War Office, 10 November 1914. The British enumerated the infantry works right–left from their perspective. The Germans did the same but from their viewpoint. Therefore what Barnardiston called 1 and 2 Redoubts were, to his opponents, 4 and 5. To add confusion, the Japanese gave each of them individual names. So what was Redoubt Number 1 to the British was Redoubt Number 5 to the Germans and the Seacoast Fort to the Japanese. Starting from the Seacoast Fort, the four works were dubbed the Tai-tung-chen East Fort, Central Fort, Hsiao-chan-shan North Fort and Hsiao-chan-shan Fort respectively.
69. Yoichi Hirama, 'The Anglo-Japanese Alliance and the First World War', in Ian Gow, Yoichi Hirama and John Chapman (eds), *History of Anglo-Japanese Relations, 1600– 2000, Volume III: The Military Dimension* (Basingstoke: Palgrave Macmillan, 2003), p. 51. TNA, FO 371/3816, Japan, Code 23/Code W23 File 86-4026, Document 345 'Abstracts of Newspapers'.
70. Quoted in Burdick, p. 174.
71. Hilditch, p. 403. Burdick, p. 174.
72. Quoted in Burdick, p. 175.
73. Plüschow, pp. 95–6; Isot Plüschow and Gunther Plüschow, *Deutscher Seemann und Flieger* (Berlin: Ullstein, 1933), p. 171.
74. Burdick, p. 176. Barnardiston to the War Office, 10 November 1914.
75. Burdick, pp. 176–7.
76. Burdick, pp. 178 and 251, n. 68; Aβmann, p. 112.
77. For details of the engagements see Nakamura Jekizo (trans. J.A. Irons), 'Assault on the Central Fort, Tsingtao Campaign, 1914', Report in the US Army Military Research Collection at US Army Military History Institute, Carlisle Barracks, PA. Also Anon., 'The Charge against the Central Works at Tsingtau', in *Kaikosha Kiji* (*Army Officers' Journal*), September 1915.

78. Burdick, pp. 180 and 251, n. 71.
79. Brace, p. 639.
80. Quoted in Aβmann, p. 90; quoted in translation in Burdick, p. 181.
81. Regarding Barnardiston's contention that all firing ceased at 07:00hr, see Barnardiston to the War Office, 10 November 1914.
82. Burdick, p. 181.
83. Some British officers were convinced that they had purposely been left 'in ignorance of the fact' that the Japanese intended to force the Boxer Line on the night of 6–7 November, and were therefore deliberately excluded from taking part in the final battle. Dixon quotes one as noting 'It is impossible to believe that when this operation was decided on, the Japanese GHQ inadvertently forgot that we existed.' Given the opportunistic nature of the events leading to the capture of the Central Fort, it can be concluded that these such sentiments were unfounded. For details of the controversy see John Dixon, *A Clash of Empires: The South Wales Borderers at Tsingtao, 1914* (Wrexham: Bridge Books, 2008), p. 240.
84. Barnardiston to the War Office, 10 November 1914.
85. Burdick, p. 182.
86. This was granted by order of the Japanese Emperor on 9 November.
87. Burdick, pp. 185–6; TNA, WO 106/661, 'Japanese participation in North China (Tsing Tau): Original Transcripts'.
88. 'About 50,000 men and 12,000 horses', according to the General Staff history.
89. Burdick, p. 194.
90. The total figure includes thirty-seven 'officials' taken prisoner after May 1915. See also Charles B. Burdick and Ursula Moessner, *The German Prisoners-of-War in Japan, 1914–1920* (Lanham MD: University Press of America, 1984).
91. Burdick and Moessner, pp. 9–11.
92. Welles, the grand-nephew of Senator Charles Sumner, whose wife had, apparently dallied with Holstein in 1866–7, went on to have a glittering career in the US diplomatic service, thanks to his closeness to Franklin D. Roosevelt. He reached the rank of Assistant Secretary of State, but his affinity with the President 'made his diplomatic role often more important than that of Secretary [of State] [Cordell] Hull'. Justus D. Doenecke, 'The United States and the European War, 1939–1941: A Historiographical Review', in Michael J. Hogan (ed.), *Paths to Power: The Historiography of American Foreign Relations to 1941* (Cambridge: Cambridge University Press, 2000), p. 250.
93. Benjamin Welles, *Sumner Welles: FDR's Global Strategist, a Biography* (New York NY: St Martin's Press, 1997), pp. 45–7. There is an excellent German language website devoted to the German prisoners of war and their incarceration at http://www.tsingtau.info/index.html?lager/gefangenenlager.htm.
94. Prior to the Battle of Neuve Chapelle, 10–13 March 1915, Douglas Haig told Hugh Trenchard, 'If you can't fly because of the weather, I shall probably put off the attack.' Rebecca Grant, 'Trenchard at the Creation', *Air Force Magazine*, February 2004, Vol. 87, No. 2, p. 78.
95. Brace, p. 640.

96. Shinji Ishii, 'The Fall of Sei-Tö (Tsing-Tao) and its Aftermath', *The Royal Society for India, Pakistan, and Ceylon, Asian Review: Journal of the Royal Society for India, Pakistan, and Ceylon* (London: The Royal Society) January–May 1915, Nos 13–16, p. 17.

97. Using the Nippon-shiki Romaji system. See J. Marshall Unger, *Literacy and Script Reform in Occupation Japan* (New York NY: Oxford University Press, 1996), p. 147.

Chapter 8

1. According to Winston S. Churchill, the detachment of *Invincible*, *Inflexible* and *Princess Royal* from the Grand Fleet to hunt Spee after the Battle of Coronel produced 'continuous protests' from Sir John Jellicoe. Winston S. Churchill, *The World Crisis 1911–1918*, 2-vol. edn (New York NY: Charles Scribner's Sons, 1928), Vol. I, p. 353.

2. Arthur J. Marder, *Old Enemies, New Friends: The Royal Navy and the Imperial Japanese Navy* (Oxford: Clarendon Press, 1981), p. 5.

3. 'Since the capture of Tsingtau in November 1914 the railway has been controlled and operated by a Japanese administration with strong militaristic tendencies. As the result of the Peace Conference award of May 1919 the railway, with the inheritance of all German concession rights in the province of Shantung was handed over to Japan. China refused to accept this condition and abstained from signing the Peace Treaty. Various attempts have been made by Japan to regularise the position but popular feeling has prevented the opening of negotiations. An agreement made in September 1919 provided for the withdrawal of Japanese garrisons with the exception of those at the termini and for their replacement by a Chinese police force officered by Japanese.', H. Stringer, *The Chinese Railway System* (Shanghai: Kelly and Walsh, 1922), pp. 102–3. See also Thomas F. LaFargue, *China and the World War* (Palo Alto CA: Stanford University Press, 1937), pp. 23–4.

4. Kajima Morinosuke, *The Diplomacy of Japan, 1894–1922*, 3 vols (Tokyo: The Kajima Institute, 1976), Vol. III, *The First World War, Paris Peace Conference, Washington Conference*, pp. 164–6.

5. Thomas F. Millard, *Our Eastern Question* (New York NY: Century, 1916), p. 121.

6. Benjamin Welles, *Sumner Welles: FDR's Global Strategist, a Biography* (New York NY: St Martin's Press, 1997), p. 32.

7. Kendrick A. Clements, *The Presidency of Woodrow Wilson: American Presidency Series* (Lawrence KS: University Press of Kansas, 1992), p. 109.

8. Bruce A. Elleman, *Wilson and China: A Revised History of the Shandong Question* (Armonk NY: Sharpe, 2002), pp. 15–21.

9. Noriko Kawamura, *Turbulence in the Pacific: Japanese-US Relations During World War I* (Westport CT: Praeger, 2000), p. 57.

10. Articles 156 and 157 of the Treaty of Versailles transferred all Germany's 'rights, title and privileges particularly those concerning the territory of Kiaochow, railways, mines and submarine cables … and of all other arrangements relative to the Province of Shandong' to Japan. Also acquired were the 'The movable and immovable property owned by the German State in the territory of Kiaochow … free and clear of all charges

and encumbrances'. As a result, and unsurprisingly, China ended up refusing to sign the Peace Treaty with Germany. However some three years later under the Shantung Treaty of 4 February 1922, negotiated as part of the Washington Conference, Japan agreed to withdraw military forces and restore the former German interests to China. See Paul French, *Betrayal in Paris: How the Treaty of Versailles Led to China's Long Revolution* (Melbourne: Penguin Group Australia, 2016); Elleman; Warren I. Cohen, *America's Response to China: A History of Sino-American Relations* (New York NY: Columbia University Press, 2010).

11. Dirk Anthony Ballendorf, 'Earl Hancock Ellis: A Marine in Micronesia', *Micronesian Journal Of The Humanities And Social Sciences*, Vol. 1, Nos 1–2, December 2002, pp. 9 and 11.

12. A.T. Mahan, *Naval Strategy* (London: Sampson Low, Marston & Company, 1911), p. 199.

13. Anne Cipriano Venzon, *From Whaleboats to Amphibious Warfare: Lt. Gen. 'Howling Mad' Smith and the U.S. Marine Corps* (Westport CT: Praeger, 2003), p. 50.

14. Allan R. Millett, 'Assault From the Sea: The Development of Amphibious Warfare between the Wars – the American, British, and Japanese experiences', in Williamson Murray and Allan R. Millett (eds), *Military Innovation in the Interwar Period* (Cambridge: Cambridge University Press, 1996), p. 72.

15. Major Earl H. Ellis USMC, *Advanced Base Operations in Micronesia* (Fleet Marine Force Reference Publication (FMFRP) 12-46. Department of the Navy – Headquarters US Marine Corps) (Washington DC: US Government Printing Office, 1992), p. 29. Earl H. 'Pete' Ellis is a fascinating, larger than life, character who served in the Philippines during the insurrection and was later stationed at Guam before serving under Pershing in France. Having set out the issues in Advanced Base Operations in Micronesia, he then visited the area to gather detailed information. Ellis perished under what were considered mysterious circumstances whist at Koror in the Pelew Islands on 12 May 1923. However, recent scholarship has revealed that his death was from illness (he was an alcoholic) rather than Japanese intervention. For details of his life and untimely death see Ballendorf, pp. 9–17.

16. Samuel Eliot Morison, *History of United States Naval Operations in World War II*, Vol. 7, *Aleutians, Gilberts and Marshalls, June 1942–April 1944* (Champaign IL: University of Illinois Press, 2002), pp. 66 and 70.

17. See, for example, Clark G. Reynolds, *The Fast Carriers: The Forging of an Air Navy* (Annapolis MD: Naval Institute Press, 2014).

18. Report of Admiral of the Fleet Viscount Jellicoe of Scapa GCB OM GCVO on Naval Mission to the Commonwealth of Australia (May–August 1919), 4 vols, Vol. I, p. 1.

19. Jellicoe Report, Vol. I, p. 5.

20. Jellicoe Report, Vol. I, p. 15.

21. 'An Appreciation of the Value of Singapore to Australia', a document in the Australian Archives, Series: A981/1, Item: DEF 331, Pt 2, Title: Defence Singapore, p. 1. This document is undated, but its contents reveal it was written in 1936.

22. 'An Appreciation of the Value of Singapore to Australia', pp. 1–2.

23. 'An Appreciation of the Value of Singapore to Australia', p. 2.

24. Admiral Sir Herbert Richmond, *Statesmen and Sea Power* (Oxford: Clarendon Press, 1946), p. 328.

25. Commander Russell Grenfell, *Sea Power in the Next War* (London: Geoffrey Bles, 1938), p. 165.

26. Ian Hamill, *Strategic Illusion: Singapore Strategy and the Defence of Australia and New Zealand, 1919–42* (Singapore: Singapore University Press, 1981).

27. Gordon Rottman, *World War II Pacific Island Guide: A Geo-Military Study* (Westport CT: Greenwood, 2002), p. 174.

28. Harry A. Gailey, *Bougainville: The Forgotten Campaign, 1943–1945* (Lexington KY: University of Kentucky Press, 2003), p. 79. Burton Wright III, *Eastern Mandates (US Army Campaigns of World War II)* (Washington DC: US Army Center of Military History, 1993), p. 9.

29. Martin Gilbert, *In Search of Churchill: A Historian's Journey* (London: HarperCollins, 1994), p. 174.

30. See the final chapter of Frederick Quinn, *The French Overseas Empire* (Westport CT: Praeger, 2000), pp. 219–64. See also Bart Luttikhuis and A. Dirk Moses (eds), *Colonial Counterinsurgency and Mass Violence: The Dutch Empire in Indonesia* (Abingdon: Routledge, 2014).

31. See, for example, Peter C. Smith, *Task Force 57: The British Pacific Fleet, 1944–45* (London: William Kimber, 1969). For an American perspective see Samuel Eliot Morison, *History of United States Naval Operations in World War II*, Vol. 14, *Victory in the Pacific 1945* (Champaign IL: University of Illinois Press, 2002), pp. 102–7.

32. Morison, Vol. 14, p. 104. Regarding the quote about Seeadler Harbour, Alan Powell, *The Third Force: ANGUA's New Guinea War, 1942–46* (Melbourne: Oxford University Press, 2003), p. 82. ANGUA was an acronym for the 'Australian New Guinea Administrative Unit'.

33. The term 'Jewel in the Crown' originates, I think, with Benjamin Disraeli, who almost used it at a speech in the Free Trade Hall, Manchester, on 3 April 1878. In criticising his Liberal opponents' policy and attitude towards India, Disraeli argued that it had been proven with 'mathematical demonstration to be the most costly jewel in the Crown of England'. See W.F. Moneypenny and George E. Buckle, *The Life of Benjamin Disraeli: Earl of Beaconsfield*, 6 vols (New York NY: MacMillan, 1920), Vol. IX, pp. 191–2; Sneh Mahajan, *British Foreign policy 1874–1914: The Role of India* (London: Routledge, 2002), p. 34.

34. John Ramsden, *Man of the Century: Winston Churchill and his Legend since 1945* (New York NY: Columbia University Press, 2002), p. 416. The text of the ANZUS Treaty can be found at http://australianpolitics.com/foreign/anzus/anzus-treaty.shtml.

35. Peter Clarke, *The Last Thousand Days of the British Empire* (London: Allen Lane, 2007).

36. See, for example, Philip Murphy, *Party Politics and Decolonisation: The Conservative Party and British Colonial Policy in Tropical Africa, 1951–1964* (Oxford: Clarendon Press, 1995).

37. Peter Winzen, *Das Kaiserreich am Abgrund: Die Daily-Telegraph-Affaere und das Hale-Interview von 1908* (*The Empire at the Abyss: The Daily-Telegraph Affair and the Hale-Interview of 1908*) (Stuttgart: Franz Steiner, 2002), p. 346.

38. Sir James Edmonds, Britain's official historian of the First World War, wrote that although the British Army was well trained, 'In heavy guns and howitzers, high-explosive shell, trench mortars, hand-grenades, and much of the subsidiary material required for siege and trench warfare, it was almost wholly deficient.' Brigadier General Sir James E. Edmonds, *History of The Great War Based on Official Documents by Direction of The Historical Section Of The Committee of Imperial Defence. Military Operations France and Belgium, 1914. Mons, The Retreat To The Seine, The Marne And The Aisne August–October 1914* (London: Macmillan, 1937), pp. 10–11. Anthony Saunders, using Edmonds as his source, put it thus: 'No army went to war in 1914 expecting to conduct trench warfare for four years and, consequently, no army was equipped for such an eventuality.' Anthony Saunders, *Reinventing Warfare 1914–18: Novel Munitions and Tactics of Trench Warfare* (New York NY: Continuum, 2012), p. 1.

39. According to Michael Bess, who is undoubtedly correct: 'Racial prejudices on the Allied side led to a gross underestimation of Japanese capabilities in 1941 – a misperception for which Britain and the United States paid dearly in December 1941 and the early months of 1942.', see Chapter 1 of Michael Bess, *Choices Under Fire: Moral Dimensions of World War II* (New York NY: Alfred A. Knopf, 2006).

40. David Graham, *Inside the Mind of George Bernard Shaw* (UK: Ben Berger, 2014), p. 43.

Bibliography

Documents and Collections
The core of this work, the Japanese military and naval operations against Germany's Kiautschou protectorate, is based largely on four substantial volumes that were published by the General Staff of the Japanese Army (*Rikugun Sanbo Honbu*) for internal use. These are: *Taisho 3 Nen Seneki Shoken Shu* (*Collection of Reports and Observations on the War of 1914*), 2 vols (1915), and *Taisho 3 Nen Nichi-doku Senshi* (*The German-Japanese War of 1914*), 2 vols (1916). These works were put together as staff studies and are incredibly detailed; they give day-to-day accounts of the movements of all the Japanese formations involved and reproduce the various orders issued at all levels. They are not easy reads in any sense of the term, but have been invaluable in providing information on the various operations from the Japanese perspective.
Other archival sources that offer valuable insights into the campaign from British and American perspectives include:

'Japanese and Chinese maps and literature relating to operations at Tsingtau', TNA, WO 106/668.
'Map of Tsingtau showing the Defences During the Siege', TNA, MPI 1/546/16.
'Admiralty: Historical Section: Records used for Official History, First World War', TNA, ADM 137.
'Japanese participation in North China (Tsing Tau): Original Transcripts', TNA, WO 106/661.
Japan, Code 23/Code W23, File 86-4026, Document 345, 'Abstracts of Newspapers', TNA, FO 371/3816.
'Japanese participation in North China (Tsing Tau): Original Transcripts', TNA, WO 106/661.
Japan's Declaration of War against Germany, and Capture of Tsingtao, TNA, FO 228/2306.
Nash, G. and G. Gipps, 'Narrative of the Events in Connection with the Siege, Blockade, and Reduction of the Fortress of Tsingtau', TNA, ADM 137/35.
'Operations – Japanese Navy in the Indian and Pacific Oceans during War 1914–1918', Office of Naval Intelligence, Record Group 45, Subject File 1911–1927, WA-5 Japan, box 703, folder 10, NND 913005, National Archives, Washington DC.
'Japanese Naval Activities during European War', 11 December 1918; Office of Naval Intelligence, Record Group 38.4.3, Communications with Naval Attachés, U-4-B, 11083, National Archives, Washington DC.

'Official Report of Japanese Naval Activities during the War', 11 December 1918, translation of official statement issued by Japanese Navy Department on 8 December 1918; Office of Naval Intelligence, Record Group 38.4.3, Communications with Naval Attachés, U-4-B, 11083, National Archives, Washington DC.

Contemporaneously produced German sources are not so easy to come by; the vast majority of German military and naval personnel were confined as prisoners of war. Their various accounts were later used by Kurt Aβmann, a naval officer who achieved flag rank, in his book *Die Kämpfe der Kaiserlichen Marine in den deutschen Kolonien* (Berlin: Mittler, 1935). I have generally used this as a guide in covering matters from the German perspective. Pre-1914 Pacific War Plans pertaining to the Imperial German Navy can be found in BA/ MA Reichs-Marine 5/v 5955, Bundesarchiv-Militararchiv (Federal Military Archive), Freiburg.

The American journalist, Alfred M. Brace, who observed the conflict from the German side published a detailed account in 1915: 'With the Germans in Tsingtau: an Eye Witness Account of the Capture of Germany's Colony in China', in *The World's Work: A History of Our Time*, Vol. XXIX, November 1914–April 1915 (New York NY: Doubleday, Page & Company, 1915). This has been valuable for providing a little colour to the proceedings, as has been the description of the famous 'Tsingtau Flier' Gunther Plüschow. His account, *Die Abenteuer des Fliegers von Tsingtau: Meine Erlebnisse in drei Erdteilen* (*The Adventures of the Tsingtau Flier: My Experiences in Three Continents*) (Berlin: Ullstein, 1916) has *Boys' Own* elements but is important given the author's unique aerial perspective.

Other documents consulted are:

'An Appreciation of the Value of Singapore to Australia', a document in the Australian Archives, Series: A981/1, Item: DEF 331, Pt. 2, Title: Defence Singapore.

Papers of Alfred Deakin, National Library of Australia, MS 1540, 1804-1973, Item 15/3705-12.

The Balfour Papers (Additional Manuscripts (Add MSS) 49683-49962) at the British Library.

'Memorandum by the General Staff', 4 November 1905, TNA, CID 38/10/79.

Great Britain, Parliamentary Papers, London, 1908.

British *Parliamentary Debates*, 1909.

McKenna, Reginald. Imperial Conference on Defence: Admiralty Memorandum of 20 July 1909, TNA, CAB 37/100/98.

'Notes of the Proceedings of a Conference at the Admiralty On Tuesday, 10th August 1909, between Representatives of the Admiralty and of the Government of the Commonwealth of Australia to Consider a Scheme for the Establishment of an Australian Navy', *Imperial Conference: Proceedings*, Vol. I, TNA, CAB 18/12A.

Merchant Shipping (Losses), House of Commons Paper 199, *1919* (London: HMSO, 1919).

Internet

http://www.1914-1918.net/barnardistons_first_despatch.htm – 'Operations at Tsing Tau: Reports by Brig-Gen N.W. Barnardiston MVO'.

http://www.acmarst.com/parl_sub/maritimesub.pdf – The Australian Centre For Maritime Studies, Submission To The 'Inquiry Into Australia's Maritime Strategy', 4 November 2002.

http://www.alcohol.org.nz/InpowerFiles%5CALACsMagazine%5CDocument WithImage.Document.1359.3d38dc9d-0270-4ca9-9201-6ec734bf4fb8.pdf – Dr Ana Maui Taufe'ulungaki, Director of the Institute of Education at the University of the South Pacific in Fiji, during her keynote address at the Fourth biennial 'Pacific Spirit' conference held at the Waipuna Hotel and Conference Center, Auckland, 3–4 March 2004.

http://atcsl.tripod.com/1911_1949.htm: Franz Oster crash – 'Air Traffic Control Sri Lanka' website.

http://australianpolitics.com/foreign/anzus/anzus-treaty.shtml – The text of the ANZUS Treaty.

http://www.firstworldwar.com/source/parispeaceconf_germanprotest2.htm – Georges Clemenceau's Letter of Reply to the Objections of the German Peace Delegation, May 1919.

http://www.firstworldwar.com/source/anglojapanesealliance1902.htm – Text of the 1902 Anglo-Japanese Alliance.

http://www.firstworldwar.com/source/tsingtau_okuma.htm – Japanese ultimatum to Germany, 15 August 1914.

http://www.firstworldwar.com/audio/loyalty.htm – Gerard's speech, 25 November 1917 to the Ladies Aid Society.

http://foia.state.gov/masterdocs/05fah01/CH0610.pdf – *U.S. Department of State Foreign Affairs Handbook Volume 5 Handbook 1 – Correspondence.*

http://web.genealogie.free.fr/Les_militaires/1GM/Allemagne/Marine/Admiral/B.htm – A brief resumé of Admiral Emil Felix von Bendemann's career.

http://www.hinduonnet.com/ – The *Hindu* online.

http://www.history.navy.mil/index.html – US Naval Historical Center.

http://homepage3.nifty.com/akagaki/cyuui3.html – *The China Year Book.*

http://imperialarmy.hp.infoseek.co.jp/index.html – Kamio's service record.

http://www.lib.byu.edu/~rdh/wwi/1914m/willnick/wilnickc.htm – The 'Willy-Nicky Letters'.

http://marshall.csu.edu.au/Marshalls/html/german/Annex.html – Speech by Rudolf von Bennigsen on the annexation of the Caroline Islands, 12 October 1899.

http://www.micsem.org/photos/sokehs/intro.htm – The Sokehs Rebellion.

http://padayatra.org/yala.htm – Yala National Park, Sri Lanka.

http://www.peterhof.org/ – The Peterhof Palace website.

http://process.portsmouthpeacetreaty.org/process/index.html – The Portsmouth Peace Treaty.

http://www.remuseum.org.uk/corpshistory/rem_corps_part13.htm – Royal Engineers Museum website.

http://www.soilandhealth.org/01aglibrary/010122king/ffc10.html – Text of F.H. King's *Farmers Of Forty Centuries Or Permanent Agriculture In China, Korea And Japan.*

http://www.thisnation.com/library/sotu/1899wm.html – William McKinley, State of the Union Address, 5 December 1899.

http://www.tsingtaobeer.com/index.htm – Tsingtao Brewery site.

http://www.tsingtau.info/index.html?lager/gefangenenlager.htm – German language website devoted to the German prisoners of war.

http://www.usd.edu/~sbucklin/primary/roottakahira.htm – Root-Takahira Agreement.

http://www.yale.edu/lawweb/avalon/diplomacy/spain/sp1898.htm – Treaty of Peace Between the United States and Spain; December 10, 1898.

Books and Published Works

Abelshauser, Werner, Wolfgang von Hippel, Jeffrey Allan Johnson and Raymond G. Stokes. *German Industry and Global Enterprise: BASF: The History of a Company* (Cambridge: Cambridge University Press, 2003).

Aisin-Gioro Pu Yi (trans. W.J.F. Jenner). *From Emperor to Citizen: The Autobiography of Aisin-Gioro Pu Yi* (Peking: Foreign Languages Press, 1964).

Alden, Carroll Storrs and Ralph Earle. *Makers of Naval Tradition* (London: Ginn and Company, 1925).

Alexander, Roy. *The Cruise of the Raider 'Wolf'* (London: Cape, 1939).

Altham, Edward A. *The Principles of War Historically Illustrated* (London: Macmillan, 1914).

Anderson, Eugene N. *The First Moroccan Crisis, 1904–1906* (Chicago IL: University of Chicago Press, 1930).

Andrew, C. *Theophile Delcassé and the Making of the Entente Cordiale: A Reappraisal of French Foreign policy, 1898–1905* (London: Macmillan, 1968).

Andrews, E.M. *The Anzac Illusion: Anglo-Australian relations during World War I,* repr. edn (Cambridge: Cambridge University Press, 1994).

Anon. 'Before Gallipoli-Australian Operations in 1914', *Semaphore: Newsletter of the Sea Power Centre, Australia*, Issue 7, August 2003.

Anon. *Handbook on Japanese Military Forces: War Department Technical Manual TM-E 30–480* (Washington DC: War Department, 1944).

Anon. 'Notes from Tsingtau', *Journal of the United States Artillery* (Fort Monroe VA: Coast Artillery School Press, 1915).

Anon. 'Portable Railways', *Scientific American Supplement*, No. 446, New York NY, 19 July 1884.

Artelt, Jork. *Tsingtau: Deutsche Stadt und Festung 1897–1914 (German city and fortress 1897–1914* (Duesseldorf: Droste, 1984).

Asquith, Herbert Henry. *The Genesis of the War* (New York NY: George H. Doran, 1923).

Atkinson, C.T. *The History of the South Wales Borderers 1914–1918* (Uckfield: Naval & Military Press, 2002).

Aydelotte, William Osgood. *Bismarck and British Colonial Policy: the Problem of South West Africa 1883–1885* (Philadelphia PA: University of Pennsylvania Press, 1937).

Bach, John. *The Australia Station: A History of the Royal Navy in the South West Pacific, 1821–1913* (Kensington NSW: New South Wales University Press, 1986).

Bade, James N. *Von Luckner: A Reassessment. Count Felix von Luckner in New Zealand and the South Pacific. 1917–1919 and 1938* (Frankfurt: Peter Lang, 2004).

Bagby, Wesley M. *The Road to Normalcy: The Presidential campaign and Election of 1920* (Baltimore NJ: Johns Hopkins Press, 1962).

Bailey, Paul John. *China in the Twentieth Century* (Oxford: Blackwell, 2001).

Bailey, Thomas A. 'Dewey and the Germans at Manila Bay', *The American Historical Review*, Vol. 45, No. 1 (October, 1939).

Balfour, Sebastian. *The End of the Spanish Empire, 1898–1923* (Oxford: Oxford University Press, 1997).

Ballendorf, Dirk Anthony. 'Earl Hancock Ellis: A Marine in Micronesia', *Micronesian Journal Of The Humanities And Social Sciences*, Vol. 1, Nos 1–2, December 2002.

Barclay, Sir Thomas. *New Methods of Adjusting International Disputes and the Future* (London: Constable, 1917).

Bargen, Doris G. *Suicidal Honor: General Nogi and the Writings of Mori Ogai and Natsume Soseki* (Honolulu HI: University of Hawai'i Press, 2006).

Barlow, Ima C. *The Agadir Crisis* (Hamden CT: Archon Books, 1971).

Barnardiston, Brigadier General N.W. 'Operations at Tsing Tau', TNA, WO 106/667; also printed in the Supplement to the *London Gazette* of 30 May 1916; available at: http://www.1914-1918.net/barnardistons_first_despatch.htm.

Barraclough, Geoffrey. *From Agadir to Armageddon: Anatomy of a Crisis* (New York NY: Holmes & Meier, 1982).

Barrie, D.S.M. *A Regional History of the Railways of Great Britain: Volume XII South Wales* (Newton Abbot: David & Charles, 1980).

Bauer, Wolfgang. 'Tsingtao's Trade and Economy from the Japanese Occupation in 1914, until the End of the 1920s', *The Asiatic Society of Japan Bulletin No. 1*, January 1996.

Bean, C.E.W. *The Story of Anzac: The First Phase*, 11th edn (Sydney NSW: Angus and Robertson, 1941), Vol. I of C.E.W. Bean (ed.), *The Official History of Australia in the War of 1914–1918*, 12 vols various edns (Sydney NSW: Angus and Robertson, 1941).

Beasley, W.G. *Japanese Imperialism 1894–1945* (Cary NC: Oxford University Press USA, 1991).

Behr, Edward. *The Last Emperor* (New York NY: Bantam Books, 1987).

Bennett, Geoffrey. *Coronel and the Falklands*, rev. edn (Edinburgh: Birlinn, 2001).

Bennett, Geoffrey. *Naval Battles of the First World War*, rev. edn (London: Penguin, 2002).

Bennett, Judith A. 'Holland, Britain, and Germany in Melanesia', in K.R. Howe, Robert C. Kiste and Brij V. Lal (eds), *Tides of History: The Pacific Islands in the Twentieth Century* (Honolulu HI: University of Hawai'i Press, 1994).

Benton, Elbert Jay. *International Law and Diplomacy of the Spanish-American War* (Baltimore MD: John Hopkins Press, 1898).

Beresford, Lord Charles. *The Break-Up of China: With an Account of Its Present Commerce, Currency, Waterways, Armies, Railways, Politics, and Future Prospects* (New York NY: Harper & Brothers, 1900).

Bergere, Marie-Claire (trans. Janet Lloyd). *Sun Yat-sen* (Stanford CA: Stanford University Press, 1998).

Berghahn, V.R. *Germany and the Approach of War in 1914*, second edn (London: Palgrave Macmillan, 1993).

Berghahn, V.R. *Imperial Germany, 1871–1918: Economy, Society, Culture and Politics* (Oxford: Berghahn Books, 2005).

Berman, Sheri. *The Social Democratic Moment: Ideas and Politics in the Making of Interwar Europe* (Cambridge MA: Harvard University Press, 1998).

Bess, Michael. *Choices Under Fire: Moral Dimensions of World War II* (New York NY: Alfred A. Knopf, 2006).

Binder-Krieglstein, E. Baron. *Die Kämpfe des Deutschen Expeditionskorps in China und ihre militärischen Lehren* (Berlin: E.S. Mittler, 1902).

Bismarck, Otto Fürst von. *Die Gesammelten Werke* (*The Collected Works*), 15 vols (Berlin: Stollberg, 1924–35).

Blue, Gregory. 'Opium for China: the British Connection', in Timothy Brook and Bob Tadashi Wakabayashi, *Opium Regimes: China, Britain, And Japan, 1839–1952* (Collingdale PA: Diane, 2000).

Boehmer, Elleke. *Empire Writing: An Anthology of Colonial Literature 1870–1918* (Oxford: University Press, 1998).

Boemeke, Manfred Franz, Roger Chickering and Stig Förster. *Anticipating Total War: The German and American Experiences, 1871–1914* (Cambridge: Cambridge University Press, 1999).

Borkin, Joseph. *The Crime and Punishment of IG Farben* (London: Andre Deutsch, 1979).

Boyce, D.G. (ed.). *The Crisis of British Power: The Imperial and Naval Papers of the Second Earl of Selborne, 1895–1910* (London: The Historians' Press, 1990).

Boyne, Walter J. *Clash of Wings: World War II In The Air* (New York NY: Simon & Schuster, 1994).

Brackman, Arnold C. *The Last Emperor* (New York NY: Charles Scribner's Sons, 1975).

Braisted, William. *The United States Navy in the Pacific 1897–1909* (Austin TX: University of Texas Press, 1958).

Braisted, William R. 'The Evolution of the United States Navy's Strategic Assessments in the Pacific, 1919–31', in Erik Goldstein (ed.), *The Washington Conference 1921–22: Naval Rivalry, East Asian Stability and the Road to Pearl Harbor* (London: Frank Cass, 1994).

Brands, H.W. *Bound to Empire: The United States and the Philippines* (Oxford: Oxford University Press, 1992).

Bredon, Juliet. *Sir Robert Hart: The Romance Of A Great Career* (London: Hutchinson, 1909).

Bridge, Sir Cyprian. *The Art of Naval Warfare: Introductory Observations* (London: Smith, Elder, 1907).

British and Foreign State Papers, 1897–1898, Vol. 90 (London: HMSO, 1901).

Bromby, Robin. *German Raiders of the South Seas* (Sydney: Doubleday, 1985).

Bromley, Michael L. *William Howard Taft and the First Motoring Presidency, 1909–1913* (Jefferson NC: McFarland & Co., 2003).

Brooks, Barbara J. 'Peopling the Japanese Empire: the Koreans in Manchuria and the Rhetoric of Inclusion', in Sharon A. Minichiello (ed.), *Japan's Competing Modernities: Issues in Culture and Democracy, 1900–1930* (Honolulu HI; University of Hawai'i Press, 1998).

Brown, Arthur Judson. *New Forces in Old China: An Inevitable Awakening*, second edn (New York NY: F.H. Revell, 1904).

Brown, D.K. *The Grand Fleet: Warship Design and Development 1906–1922* (Annapolis MD: Naval Institute Press, 1999).

Brownell, Will and Richard N. Billings. *So Close to Greatness: A Biography of William C Bullitt* (New York NY: Macmillan, 1987).

Bülow, Prince Bernhard von (trans. Marie A. Lewenz). *Imperial Germany*, third impression (London: Cassell, 1914).

Bülow, Prince Bernhard von (trans. F.A. Voight). *Memoirs of Prince von Bülow: From Secretary of State to Imperial Chancellor 1897–1903* (Boston MA: Little, Brown and Co., 1931).

Burdick, Charles B. *The Japanese Siege of Tsingtau* (Hamden CT: Archon, 1976).

Burdick, Charles B. and Ursula Moessner. *The German Prisoners-of-War in Japan, 1914–1920* (Lanham MD: University Press of America, 1984).

Burton, David H. *William Howard Taft, Confident Peacemaker* (Philadelphia PA: Saint Joseph's University Press, 2004).

Bywater, Hector C. *Navies and Nations: A Review of Naval Developments Since the Great War* (London: Constable, 1927).

Carroll, Brian. *Australia's Prime Ministers: From Barton to Howard* (Stanmore: Cassell Australia, 1978).

Cavinder, Fred D. *Amazing Tales from Indiana* (Indianapolis IN: Indiana University Press, 1990).

Cecil, Lamar. *Wilhelm II: Emperor and Exile, 1900–1941* (Chapel Hill NC: University of North Carolina Press, 1996).

Chan Lau Kit-Ching, *Anglo-Chinese Diplomacy in the Careers of Sir John Jordan and Yüan Shih-kai 1906–1920* (Hong Kong: Hong Kong University Press, 1978).

Chang Kia-ngau. *China's Struggle for Railroad Development* (New York NY: The John Day Company, 1943).

Charmley, John. *Splendid Isolation?: Britain and the Balance of Power 1874–1914* (London: Hodder & Stoughton, 1999).

Chi, Madeleine. *China Diplomacy 1914–1918* (Cambridge MA: Harvard University Press, 1970).

Chisholm, Geo G. 'The Resources and Means of Communication of China', *The Geographical Journal*, Vol. 12, No. 5 (November 1898).

Choi Jeong-soo. 'The Russo-Japanese War and the Root-Takahira Agreement', *The International Journal of Korean History*, Vol. 7, February 2005.

Churchill, Winston S. *The World Crisis 1911–1918*, 2-vol. edn (London: Odhams, 1938).

Churchill, Winston S. *Great Contemporaries* (London: Odhams Press, 1949).

Clarke, Peter. *The Last Thousand Days of the British Empire* (London: Allen Lane, 2007).

Clements, Kendrick A. *The Presidency of Woodrow Wilson: American Presidency Series* (Lawrence KS: University Press of Kansas, 1992).

Cochrane, Thomas Barnes the 11th Earl of Dundonald and H.R. Fox Bourne. *The Life of Thomas, Lord Cochrane, 10th Earl of Dundonald*, 2 vols (London: Richard Bentley, 1869).

Cocker, Mark. *Rivers of Blood, Rivers of Gold: Europe's Conquest of Indigenous Peoples* (New York NY: Grove Press, 2001).

Cohen, Warren I. *America's Response to China: A History of Sino-American Relations* (New York NY: Columbia University Press, 2010).

Cohen, Warren I. (ed.). *The Cambridge History of American Foreign Relations*, 4 vols (Cambridge: Cambridge University Press, 1993).

Coletta, Paolo E. *The Presidency of William Howard Taft* (Lawrence KS: University Press of Kansas, 1973).

Connaughton, Richard. *The War of the Rising Sun and Tumbling Bear* (London: Routledge, 1991).

Craig, Gordon A. *Germany 1866–1945* (Oxford: Oxford University Press, 1988).

Crankshaw, Edward. *The Fall of the House of Hapsburg* (New York NY: Viking, 1963).

Creswell, William. 'Captain Creswell's Views on Result of Imperial Conference, 16 November 1909', in G.L. Macandie, *The Genesis of the Royal Australian Navy: A Compilation* (Sydney NSW: Government Printer, 1949).

Croft, Henry Page. *The Path of Empire* (London: John Murray, 1912).

Crouch, Tom D. *Wings: A History of Aviation from Kites to the Space Age* (New York NY: W.W. Norton, 2003).

Crowe, Eyre. 'Memorandum on the Present State of British Relations with France and Germany' (1 January 1907), in G.P. Gooch and H.W.V. Temperly (eds), *British Documents on the Origins of the War, 1898–1914*, 11 vols (London: HM Stationery Office, 1926–38), Vol. III, *The Testing of the Entente 1904–6*.

Cullis, Roger. 'Technological Roulette – A Multidisciplinary Study of the Dynamics of Innovation' (University of London PhD Thesis, 1986).

Cunneen, Chris. *King's Men: Australia's Governors-General from Hopetoun to Isaacs* (Sydney: Allen & Unwin Australia, 1984).

Curtis, Lionel. *The Problem of the Commonwealth* (London: Macmillan, 1916).

Curtius, Friedrich (ed.) (trans. George W. Chrystal). *Memoirs of Prince Chlodwig of Hohenlohe Schillingsfuerst*, 2 vols (London: William Heinemann, 1906).

Dahlhaus, Carl. *Nineteenth-Century Music* (Berkeley CA: California University Press, 1989).

Daniels, Josephus. *Annual Report of the Secretary of the Navy, 1916* (Washington DC: Government Printing Office, 1916).

Daunton, M.J. *Coal Metropolis: Cardiff 1870–1914* (Leicester: Leicester University Press, 1977).

Davilla, James and Arthur Soltan. *French Aircraft Of The First World War* (Stratford CT: Flying Machines Press, 1997).

Davis, Clarence B. and Robert J. Gowen. 'The British at Weihaiwei: A Case Study in the Irrationality of Empire', *The Historian*, Vol. 63, 22 September 2000.

Davis, Mike. *Late Victorian Holocausts: El Niño Famines and the Making of the Third World* (New York NY: Verso Books, 2002).

Delmendo, Sharon. *The Star-Entangled Banner: One Hundred Years of America in the Philippines* (New Brunswick NJ: Rutgers University Press, 2004).

Deseyne, Alex. *De Kust Bezet 1914–1918 (The Coast Occupied 1914–1918)* (Nieuwpoort sesteenweg Belgium: Provincial Domain of Raversijde, 2007).

Deutsche Kolonialgesellschaft (German Colonial Society) (eds), *Deutscher Kolonial-Atlas mit Jahrbuch (German Colonial Atlas and Yearbook)* (Berlin: Deutsche Kolonialgesellschaft, 1905).

Dewey, Adelbert M. *The Life and Letters of Admiral Dewey from Montpelier to Manila [...]* (New York NY: Barnes & Noble World Digital Library, 2003).

Dewey, George. *Autobiography of George Dewey: Admiral of the Navy* (New York NY: Scribner, 1913).

Dillon, E.J. 'The Chinese Wolf and the European Lamb', *Contemporary Review*, 79 (May 1901).

Dillon, Michael. *China: A Historical and Cultural Dictionary* (London: Curzon Press, 1998).

Di Nunzio, Mario R. (ed.). *Woodrow Wilson: Essential Writings and Speeches of a Scholar-President* (New York NY: New York University Press, 2006).

Dixon, John. *A Clash of Empires: The South Wales Borderers at Tsingtao, 1914* (Wrexham: Bridge Books, 2008).

Dixon, T.B. *The Enemy Fought Splendidly* (Poole: Blandford Press, 1983).

Dobson, Sebastian. *The Russo-Japanese War: Reports from Officers Attached to the Japanese Forces in the Field*, 5 vols, repr. edn with an Introduction by Sebastian Dobson (Bristol: Ganesha Publishing, 2000).

Doenecke, Justus D. 'The United States and the European War, 1939–1941: A Historiographical Review', in Michael J. Hogan (ed.), *Paths to Power: The Historiography of American Foreign Relations to 1941* (Cambridge: Cambridge University Press, 2000).

Doerries, Reinhard R. 'From Neutrality to War: Woodrow Wilson and the German Challenge', in William N. Tilchin and Charles E. Neu (eds), *Artists of Power: Theodore Roosevelt, Woodrow Wilson, and Their Enduring Impact on US Foreign Policy* (Westport CT: Praeger, 2006).

Dreyer, Edward L. *China at War, 1901–1949* (London: Longman, 1995).

Dryburgh, Marjorie. *North China and Japanese Expansion 1933–1937: Regional Power and the National Interest* (Richmond: Curzon Press, 2000).

Dugdale, E.T.S. (selected and trans.). *German Diplomatic Documents, 1871–1914, Volume III, The Growing Antagonism, 1898–1910* (New York NY: Harper & Brothers, 1930).

Duiker, William J. *Cultures in Collision: The Boxer Rebellion* (San Rafael CA: Presidio Press, 1978).

Dulles, Allen W. *The Craft of Intelligence* (New York NY: Harper & Row, 1963).

Duranti, Alessandro. *A Companion to Linguistic Anthropology* (Malden MA; Blackwell, 2004).

Dyal, Donald H., Brian B. Carpenter and Mark A. Thomas. *Historical dictionary of the Spanish American War* (Westport CT: Greenwood Press, 1996).

Eckart, Wolfgang U. *Medizin und Kolonialimperialismus: Deutschland 1884–1945* (Vienna: Ferdinand Schoeningh, 1997).

Edho Ekoko, A. 'The British Attitude towards Germany's Colonial Irredentism in Africa in the Inter-War Years', *Journal of Contemporary History*, Vol. 14, No. 2 (April 1979).

Edmonds, General Sir James E. *History of The Great War Based on Official Documents by Direction of The Historical Section Of The Committee of Imperial Defence. Military Operations France and Belgium, 1914. Mons, The Retreat To The Seine, The Marne And The Aisne August–October 1914* (London: Macmillan, 1937).

Eksteins, Modris. *Rites of Spring: The Great War and the Birth of the Modern Age* (Boston MA: Houghton Mifflin, 1989).

Elleman, Bruce A. *Wilson and China: A Revised History of the Shandong Question* (Armonk NY: Sharpe, 2002).

Ellis, A.F. *Mid Pacific Outposts* (Auckland: Brown & Stuart, 1946).

Ellis, Major Earl H. USMC. *Advanced Base Operations in Micronesia* (Fleet Marine Force Reference Publication (FMFRP) 12-46. Department of the Navy – Headquarters US Marine Corps) (Washington DC: US Government Printing Office, 1992).

Ellis, John. *Eye-Deep in Hell: Trench Warfare in World War I* (Baltimore MD: Johns Hopkins Press, 1976).

Elman, Benjamin A. *A Cultural History of Civil Examinations in Late Imperial China* (Berkeley CA: University of California Press, 2000).

Endo Yoshinobu, *Kindai Nihon guntai kyoikushi kenkyu* (Tokyo: Aoki shoten, 1994).

Epps, Garrett. *Democracy Reborn: The Fourteenth Amendment and the Fight for Equal Rights in Post-Civil War America* (New York NY: Henry Holt, 2006).

Esherick, Joseph W. *The Origins of the Boxer Uprising* (Berkeley CA: University of California Press, 1987).

Esthus, Raymond A. *Theodore Roosevelt and Japan* (Seattle WA: University of Washington Press, 1966).

Evans, David and Mark Peattie. *Kaigun: Strategy, Tactics, and Technology in the Imperial Japanese Navy, 1887–1941* (Washington DC: United States Naval Institute, 1997).

Evans, Richard J. *The Coming of the Third Reich* (New York NY: Penguin, 2004).

Fabian, Hans. 'Aeronautical Research Comes into Being During the Time of Empire', in E.H. Hirschel, H. Prem and G. Madelung, *Aeronautical Research in Germany: From Lilienthal Until Today* (Berlin: Springer, 2004).

Farrell, Brian and Sandy Hunter (eds). *Sixty Years On: The Fall of Singapore Revisited* (Singapore: Eastern Universities Press, 2002).

Feng Djen Djang, *The Diplomatic Relations Between China and Germany since 1898* (Shanghai: Commercial Press, 1936).

Feuchtwanger, Ed. *Imperial Germany 1850–1918* (London: Routledge, 2001).

Ffestiniog Railway Company. *Rheilffordd Ffestiniog Guide Book* (Porthmadog: Ffestiniog Railway Company, 1997).

Fischer, Gerhard. *Enemy Aliens: Internment and the Homefront Experience in Australia, 1914–1920* (Brisbane QLD: University of Queensland Press, 1989).

✗ Fischer, Steven Roger. *A History of the Pacific Islands* (London: Palgrave Macmillan, 2002).

Fitzmaurice, Lord Edmond. *The Life of Granville George Leveson Gower, Second Earl Granville 1815–1891*, 2 vols (London: Longmans Green, 1905).

Foster, Robert J. *Social Reproduction and History in Melanesia: Mortuary Ritual, Gift Exchange, and Custom in the Tanga Islands* (Cambridge: Cambridge University Press, 1995).

Frame, Tom. *No Pleasure Cruise: The Story of the Royal Australian Navy* (Crows Nest, NSW: Allen & Unwin, 2005).

Franklin, Robert. *The Fringes of History: The Life and Times of Edward Stuart Wortley* (Christchurch: Natula, 2003).

French, David. 'The Royal Navy and the Defence of the British Empire, 1914–1918', in Keith Neilson and Elizabeth Jane Errington (eds), *Navies and Global Defense: Theories and Strategy* (Westport CT: Praeger, 1995).

French, Paul. *Betrayal in Paris: How the Treaty of Versailles Led to China's Long Revolution* (Melbourne: Penguin Group Australia, 2016).

Friedewald, Michael. 'The Beginnings of Radio Communication in Germany, 1897–1918', *The Journal of Radio Studies*, Vol. 7, No. 2, 2000.

Fryer, Peter. *Private Case-Public Scandal* (London: Seeker & Warburg, 1966).

Fuller, Joseph V. (ed.). *Foreign Relations of The United States: 1914 (World War Supplement)* (Washington DC: Government Printing Office, 1928).

Fung, Edmund S.K. *The Military Dimension of the Chinese Revolution: The New Army and Its Role in the Revolution of 1911* (Vancouver: University of British Columbia Press, 1980).

Gailey, Harry A. *Bougainville: The Forgotten Campaign, 1943–1945* (Lexington KY: University of Kentucky Press, 2003).

Gardner, Nikolas. *Trial by Fire: Command and the British Expeditionary Force in 1914* (Westport CT: Praeger, 2003).

Gartzke, Kapitän Leutnant. *Der Aufstand in Ponape und seine Niederwerfung durch S. M. Schiffe 'Emden', 'Nürnberg', 'Cormoran', 'Planet'* (*The Rebellion on Ponape and its Suppression by S. M. S. Emden, Nürnberg, Cormoran and Planet*, Nach amtlichen Berichten zusammengestellt von Kapitän Leutnant Gartzke (From the Official Reports of Lieutenant Captain Gartzke) (Berlin: Marine Rundschau, 1911).

Gates, John Morgan. *Schoolbooks and Krags: The United States Army in the Philippines, 1898–1902* (Westport CT: Greenwood Press, 1973).

Gerard, James W. *Face to Face with Kaiserism* (London: Hodder & Stoughton, 1918).

German Historical Institute, Washington DC. German History in Documents and Images (GHDI), http://germanhistorydocs.ghi-dc.org, Wilhelmine Germany and the First World War, 1890–1918. An 'Unequal Treaty': Lease Agreement between China and the German Empire (6 March 1898).

Gewald, Jan-Bart. 'Learning to Wage and Win Wars in Africa: A Provisional History of German Military Activity in Congo, Tanzania, China and Namibia' (ASC Working Paper

60/2005) (A working paper presented at the conference 'Genocides: Forms, Causes and Consequences' held in Berlin 13–15 January 2005).

Gewald, Jan-Bart. 'Colonial Warfare: Hehe and World War One, the wars besides Maji Maji in south-western Tanzania' (ASC Working Paper 63/2005) (A working paper first presented at the symposium, 'The Maji Maji War 1905–1907: Colonial Conflict, National History and Local Memory', held at the Wissenschaftskolleg zu Berlin, 30 March–1 April 2005.

Gibbon, Edward. *An Essay on the Study of Literature: Written Originally in French, Now First Translated into English* (London: T. Becket and P.A. De Hondt, 1764).

Giessler, Klaus-Volker. *Die Institution des Marineattachés im Kaiserreich* (*The Institution of the Imperial Marine Attachés*) (Boppard am Rhein: Boldt, 1976).

Gilbert, Martin. *Winston S Churchill: Companion Volume III, Part 1 July 1914–April 1915* (Boston MA: Houghton Mifflin, 1973).

Gilbert, Martin. *The Challenge of War: Winston S Churchill 1914–1916* (London: Minerva, 1990).

Gilbert, Martin. *The First World War: a Complete History* (New York NY: Henry Holt, 1994).

Gilbert, Martin. *In Search of Churchill: A Historian's Journey* (London: HarperCollins, 1994).

Gillespie, Oliver A. *Official History of New Zealand in the Second World War 1939–45: The Pacific* (Wellington: Department of Internal Affairs, War History Branch, 1952).

Gimblett, Richard H. 'Reassessing the Dreadnought Crisis of 1909 and the Origins of the Royal Canadian Navy', *The Northern Mariner/Le Marin du nord*, IV, No. 1 (January 1994).

Glad, Betty. *Charles Evans Hughes and the Illusions of Innocence: A Study in American Diplomacy* (Urbana IL: University of Illinois Press, 1966).

Glatzer, Ruth. *Panorama einer Metropole: Das Wilhelminische Berlin* (Berlin: Siedler, 1997).

Godley, Michael R. *The Mandarin-Capitalists from Nanyang: Overseas Chinese Enterprise in the Modernisation of China 1893–1911* (Cambridge: Cambridge University Press, 2002).

Goldstein, Erik. 'The Evolution of British Diplomatic Strategy for the Washington Conference', in Erik Goldstein (ed.), *The Washington Conference 1921–22: Naval Rivalry, East Asian Stability and the Road to Pearl Harbor* (London: Frank Cass, 1994).

Gómez Núñez, Severo. *The Spanish American War: Blockades And Coast Defense* (Washington DC: Government Printing Office, 1899).

Gooch, G.P. and H.W.V. Temperly (eds). *British Documents on the Origins of the War, 1898–1914*, 11 vols (London: HM Stationery Office, 1926–38), Vol. III, *The Testing of the Entente 1904–6.*

Gordon, G.A.H. 'The British Navy, 1918–1945', in Keith Neilson and Elizabeth Jane Errington (eds), *Navies and Global Defence: Theories and Strategy* (Westport CT: Praeger, 1995).

Gottberg, Otto von. *Die Helden von Tsingtau* (Berlin: Ullstein, 1915).

Gottschall, Terrell D. *By Order of the Kaiser: Otto von Diederichs and the Rise of the Imperial German Navy 1865 – 1902* (Annapolis MD: Naval Institute Press, 2003)

Gow, Ian. *Military Intervention in Pre-War Japanese Politics: Admiral Kato Kanji and the 'Washington System'* (London: Routledge, 2004).

Gowen, Herbert H. *An Outline History of China*, 2 vols (Boston MA: Sherman, French & Co., 1913).

Grant, Rebecca. 'Trenchard at the Creation', *Air Force Magazine*, February 2004, Vol. 87, No. 2.

Gray, J.A.C. *Amerika Samoa* (Annapolis MD: United States Naval Institute, 1960).

Greger, Rene. *Die Russische Flotte im Ersten Weltkrieg 1914–1917* (Munchen: J.F. Lehmanns, 1970).

Grenfell, Commander Russell. *Sea Power in the Next War* (London: Geoffrey Bles, 1938).

Grenville, John A.S. and George B. Young. *Politics, Strategy, and Diplomacy: Studies in Foreign Policy, 1873–1917* (New Haven CT: Yale University Press, 1966).

Grey of Falloden, Viscount. *Twenty-Five Years: 1892–1916* 2 vols (London: Hodder & Stoughton, 1925).

Grey, Jeffrey. *A Military History of Australia* (Cambridge: Cambridge University Press, 1999).

Griffiths, Ieuan L. 'African land and Access Corridors', in Dick Hodder, Sarah J. Lloyd and Keith McLachlan (eds), *Land Locked States of Africa and Asia* (London: Frank Cass, 1998).

Hagan, Kenneth J. *This People's Navy: The Making of American Sea Power* (New York NY: Free Press, 1991).

Hall, John Ashley. *The Law of Naval Warfare*, rev. and enlarged edn (London: Chapman & Hall, 1921).

Halpern, Paul G. *The Naval War in the Mediterranean: 1914–1918* (Abingdon: Routledge, 2016).

Halstead, Murat. *Life and Achievements of Admiral Dewey from Montpelier to Manila* (Chicago IL: Dominion, 1899).

Halvorsen, Peter F. 'The Royal Navy and Mine Warfare, 1868–1914', *The Journal of Strategic Studies*, Vol. 27, No. 4/December 2004.

Hamill, Ian. *Strategic Illusion: The Singapore Strategy and the Defence of Australia and New Zealand, 1919–1942* (Singapore: Singapore University Press, 1981).

Hancock, W.D. (ed.). *English Historical Documents* (London: Eyre & Spottiswoode, 1977).

Hanlon, David L. *Remaking Micronesia: Discourses over Development in a Pacific Territory, 1944–1982* (Honolulu HI: University of Hawai'i Press, 1998).

Hannesson, Rögnvaldur. *Investing for Sustainability: The Management of Mineral Wealth* (Boston MA: Kluwer, 2001).

Hara Takeshi, *Nichi-Ro senso*, 4 vols (Tokyo: Gunjishi gakkai hen, 2005).

Hardach, Gerd. 'Defining Separate Spheres: German Rule and Colonial Law in Micronesia', in Herman J. Hiery and John M. MacKenzie (eds), *European Impact and Pacific Influence: British and German Policy in the Pacific Islands and the Indigenous Response* (London: Tauris, 1997).

Hargreaves, Reginald. *Red Sun Rising* (London: Wiedenfield & Nicolson, 1962).

Harter, Jim. *World Railways of the Nineteenth Century: A Pictorial History in Victorian Engravings* (Baltimore MD: Johns Hopkins Press, 2005).

Hattendorf, John B. 'Admiral Prince Louis of Battenberg (1912–1914)', in Malcolm H. Murfett (ed.), *First Sea Lords: From Fisher to Mountbatten* (Westport CT: Praeger, 1995).

Heller, Bernard. *Dawn Or Dusk?* (New York NY: Bookman's, 1961).

Henderson, W.O. *Studies in German Colonial History* (London: Frank Cass, 1962).

Hermann, David G. *The Arming of Europe and the Making of the First World War* (Princeton NJ: Princeton University Press, 1996).

Herring, Peter. *Yesterday's Railways: Recollections of an Age of Steam and the Golden Age of Railways* (Newton Abbot: David & Charles, 2002).

Hershatter, Gail. *Dangerous Pleasures: Prostitution and Modernity in Twentieth-Century Shanghai*, repr. edn (Berkeley CA: University of California Press, 1999).

Herwig, Holger H. *Politics of Frustration: The United States in German Naval Planning, 1889–1941* (Boston MA: Little, Brown 1976).

Herwig, Holger H. *'Luxury' Fleet: The Imperial German Navy 1888–1918* (London: George Allen & Unwin, 1980).

Hevia, James Louis. *English Lessons: The Pedagogy of Imperialism in Nineteenth-Century China* (Durham NC: Duke University Press, 2003).

Hezel, Francis X. *Strangers in Their Own Land: A Century of Colonial Rule in the Caroline and Marshall Islands* (Honolulu HI: University of Hawai'i Press, 1995).

Hiery, Hermann Joseph. *The Neglected War: The German South Pacific and the Influence of World War I* (Honolulu HI: University of Hawai'i Press, 1995).

Hilditch, A.N. 'The Capture of Tsingtau (Nov. 7) Japan Expels Germany from the Far East', in Charles F. Horne (ed.), *Source Records of World War I*, 7 vols, Vol. II, *1914 – The Red Dawning of 'Der Tag'* (New York NY: Edwin Mellen Press, 1997).

Hill, Howard C. *Roosevelt and the Caribbean* (New York NY: Russell and Russell, 1965).

Hinz, Hans-Martin and Christoph Lind (eds), *Tsingtau: Ein Kapitel deutscher Kolonialgeschichte in China 1897–1914* (Berlin: Deutsches Historisches Museum, 1998).

Hoffman, Paul. *Wings of Madness: Alberto Santos-Dumont and the Invention of Flight* (New York NY: Theia Press, 2003).

Holmes, Lowell D (ed.). *Samoan Islands Bibliography* (Wichita KS: Poly Concepts, 1984).

Honan, William H. *Bywater: The Man who Invented the Pacific War* (London: Macdonald, 1990).

Hough, Richard. *The Fleet That Had to Die* (New York NY: Viking Press, 1958).

Hovgaard, William. *Modern History of Warships* (New York NY: Spon & Chamberlain, 1920).

Hsu, Immanuel C.Y. *The Rise of Modern China*, sixth edn (New York NY: Oxford University Press USA, 1999).

Huff, W.G. *The Economic Growth of Singapore: Trade and Development in the Twentieth Century* (Cambridge: Cambridge University Press, 1994).

Hughes, Helga. *Germany's Regional Recipes: Foods, Festivals, Folklore* (Iowa City IA: Penfield, 2002).

Hugüenin, C. Oberleutnant im III. See-Bataillon (First Lieutenant III Naval Battalion). *Geschichte Des III. See-Bataillons* (*History of the III Naval Battalion*) (Tsingtaü: Adolf Haupt, 1912).

Hull, Isabel V. *Absolute Destruction: Military Culture And The Practices Of War In Imperial Germany* (Ithaca NY: Cornell University Press, 2004).

Hunt, Barry D. *Sailor-Scholar: Admiral Sir Herbert Richmond 1871–1946* (Waterloo, Ontario: Wilfrid Laurier University Press, 1982).

Ichisada Miyazaki (trans. Conrad Schirokauer). *China's Examination Hell: The Civil Service Examinations of Imperial China* (New Haven CT: Yale University Press, 1976).

Ikle, Frank W. 'The Triple Intervention: Japan's Lesson in the Diplomacy of Imperialism', *Monumenta Nipponica* 22, Nos 1–2 (1967).

Iikura, Akira. 'The "Yellow Peril" and its Influence on Japanese-German Relations', in Christian W. Spang and Rolf-Harald Wippich (eds), *Japanese-German Relations, 1895–1945: War, Diplomacy and Public Opinion* (London: Routledge, 2006).

International Court of Justice, *The Case Concerning Certain Phosphate Lands in Nauru (Nauru v. Australia), Vol. 1, Application; Memorial of Nauru* (New York NY: United Nations Publications, 2003).

Ireland, Bernard. *Jane's Battleships of the 20th Century* (New York NY: HarperCollins, 1996).

Jäckh, Ernst (ed.). *Kiderlen-Wächter, der Staatsmann und Mensch: Briefwechsel und Nachlaß* (*Kiderlen-Wächter, the Statesman and the Man: Correspondence and Private Papers*), 2 vols (Stuttgart: Deutsche Verlags-Anstalt, 1924).

Jacob, E.A. *Deutsche Kolonialpolitik in Dokumenten: Gedanken und Gestalten der letzten fünfzig Jahre* (*German Colonial Politics in Documents: Thoughts and Patterns from the Last Fifty Years*) (Leipzig: Dieterich, 1938).

Jarausch, Konrad H. *The Enigmatic Chancellor: Bethmann Hollweg and the Hubris of Imperial Germany* (New Haven CT: Yale University Press, 1973).

Jarausch, Konrad H. and Michael Geyer. *Shattered Past: Reconstructing German Histories* (Princeton NJ: Princeton University Press, 2003).

Jefferies, Matthew. *Imperial Culture in Germany, 1871–1918* (New York NY: Palgrave MacMillan, 2003).

Jellicoe, Admiral of the Fleet Viscount. 'Naval mission to Australia May – August 1919', 4-vol. 'Jellicoe Report', National Archives of Australia.

Jerrold, Douglas. *The Royal Naval Division* (London: Hutchinson, 1923).

Jingchun Liang, *The Chinese Revolution of 1911* (Jamaica NY: St John's University Press, 1972).

Johnston, Ian and Rob McAuley. *The Battleships* (Osceola WI: MBI, 2001).

Jonas, Manfred. *The United States and Japan: A Diplomatic History* (Ithaca NY: Cornell University Press, 1984).

Jonas, Manfred. *The United States and Germany: A Diplomatic History* (Chapel Hill NC: University of North Carolina Press, 1992).

Jones, A. Phillip. *Britain's Search for Chinese Cooperation in the First World War* (New York: Garland, 1986).

Jones, Chester Lloyd. *The Caribbean Since 1900* (New York NY: Prentice Hall, 1936).

Jones, Jefferson. *The Fall of Tsingtau, With a Study of Japan's Ambitions in China* (Boston MA: Houghton Mifflin, 1915), portions relating to the siege and fall of Tsingtau are available online at: http://www.greatwardifferent.com/Great_War/Tsing_Tao/Japanese_Orient_01.htm.

Jose, Arthur W. *The Royal Australian Navy 1914–1918*, ninth edn (Sydney NSW: Angus and Robertson, 1941), Vol. IX of C.E.W. Bean (ed.), *The Official History of Australia in the War of 1914–1918*, 12 vols various edns (Sydney NSW: Angus and Robertson, 1941).

Jover, José María. *Política, diplomacia y humanismo popular: Estudios sobre la vida española en el siglo XIX* (Madrid: Turner, 1976).

Kahn, David. *The Reader of Gentlemen's Mail: Herbert O Yardley and the Birth of American Codebreaking* (New Haven CT: Yale University Press, 2004).

Kajima Morinosuke, *The Diplomacy of Japan, 1894–1922*, 3 vols (Tokyo: The Kajima Institute, 1976), Vol. III, *The First World War, Paris Peace Conference, Washington Conference*.

Kane, Robert B. *Disobedience and Conspiracy in the German Army, 1918–1945* (Jefferson NC: McFarland, 2002).

Karau, Mark D. *'Wielding the Dagger': The MarineKorps Flandern and the German War Effort, 1914–1918* (London: Praeger, 2000).

Keegan, John. *The Price of Admiralty: The Evolution of Naval Warfare* (New York NY: Viking, 1989).

Kenji Shimada, *Pioneer of the Chinese Revolution: Zhang Binglin and Confucianism* (Stanford CA: Stanford University Press, 1990).

Kennedy, Paul M. *The Samoan Tangle: A Study in Anglo-German-American Relations, 1878–1900* (New York NY: Barnes & Noble, 1974).

Kennedy, Paul M. *The Rise and Fall of the Great Powers: Economic Change and Military Conflict from 1500–2000* (New York NY: Random House, 1987).

Kennedy, Paul M. 'Imperial Cable Communications and Strategy, 1870–1914', in Paul Kennedy (ed.), *The War Plans of the Great Powers, 1880–1914* (London: Allen & Unwin, 1979).

Kerst, Georg. *Jacob Meckel: Sein Leben und sein Wirken in Deutschland und Japan* (Göttingen: Musterschmidt, 1970).

Killen, John. *The Luftwaffe: A History* (Barnsley: Pen and Sword, 2003).

King, F.H. *Farmers Of Forty Centuries: Organic Farming in China Korea and Japan* (Madison WI: F.H. King, 1911).

Kitchen, Martin. *A History Of Modern Germany 1800–2000* (Oxford: Blackwell, 2006).

Klehmet, Hans. *Tsingtau: Rückblick auf die Geschichte, besonders der Belagerung und des Falles der Festung, mit kritischen Betrachtungen* (Berlin: Georg Bath, 1931).

Klußmann, Niels and Arnim Malik. *Lexikon der Luftfahrt* (Berlin: Springer, 2004).

Koch, H.W. *A History of Prussia* (London: Longman, 1978).

LaFargue, Thomas F. *China and the World War* (Palo Alto CA: Stanford University Press, 1937).

LaFeber, Walter. *The Cambridge History of American Foreign Relations*, 4 vols, Vol. II, *The American Search for Opportunity, 1865–1913* (Cambridge: Cambridge University Press, 1993).

Lamb, Colonel Dean Ivan. *The Incurable Filibuster: Adventures of Colonel Dean Ivan Lamb* (New York NY: Farrar & Rinehart, 1934).

Lambert, Nicholas A. 'Admiral Sir Arthur Knyvett-Wilson, VC (1910–1911)' and 'Admiral Sir Francis Bridgeman-Bridgeman (1911–1912)', in Malcolm H. Murfett (ed.), *First Sea Lords: From Fisher to Mountbatten* (Westport CT: Praeger, 1995).

Lambert, Nicholas A. 'Admiral Sir John Fisher and the Concept of Flotilla Defence, 1904–1909', *The Journal of Military History*, Vol. 59, No. 4 (October 1995).

Lambert, Nicholas A. 'Economy or Empire? The Fleet Unit Concept and the Quest for Collective Security in the Pacific, 1909–1914', in Keith Neilson (ed.), *Far-flung Lines: Studies in Imperial Defence in Honour of Donald Mackenzie Schurman* (London: Frank Cass, 1997).

Lambert, Nicholas A. *Sir John Fisher's Naval Revolution* (Columbia SC: University of South Carolina Press, 1999).

Lamont-Brown, Raymond. *Tutor to the Dragon Emperor: The Life of Sir Reginald Fleming Johnston at the Court of the Last Emperor* (Stroud: Sutton, 1999).

Lampe, Wilhelm Otto. 'The Kiel Canal', in Renate Platzoder and Philomene Verlaan (eds), *The Baltic Sea: New Developments in National Policies and International Cooperation* (The Hague: Kluwer Law International, 1996).

Lansing, Robert. *Papers Relating to the Foreign Policy of the United States: The Lansing Papers, 1914–1920*, 2 vols (Washington DC: Government Printing Office, 1939–40).

Lanzin Xiang, *The Origins of the Boxer War* (London: Routledge Curzon, 2002).

Leibowitz, Arnold H. *Defining Status: A Comprehensive Analysis of United States Territorial Relations* (Dordrecht, Netherlands: Martinus Nijhoff, 1989).

Leonhard, Jörn. 'Construction and Perception of National Images: Germany and Britain, 1870–1914', in Daniel Gallimore and Dimitrina Mihaylova (eds), 'The Linacre Journal: Number 4: "The Fatal Circle": Nationalism and Ethnic Identity Into the 21st Century' (Oxford: Linacre College, 2000).

LePore, Herbert P. *The Politics and Failure of Naval Disarmament 1919–1939: The Phantom Peace* (Lewiston NY: Edwin Mellen Press, 2003).

Lerman, Katharine A. *The Chancellor as Courtier: Bernhard von Bülow and the Governance of Germany, 1900–1909* (Cambridge: Cambridge University Press, 1990).

Lerman, Katherine A. 'Some Basic Statistics for Germany, 1815–1918', in Mary Fulbrook (ed.), *German History Since 1800* (London: Arnold, 1997).

Levene, Mark. *The Rise of the West and the Coming of Genocide*, 4 vols, Vol. II, *Genocide in the Age of the Nation State* (London: Tauris, 2005).

Lewis, Jay. 'Imperialism Yesterday and Today', *Workers' Liberty*, Issue 63, July 2000.

Liddell Hart, B.H. *History of the First World War* (London: Pan Books, 1972).

Lieberthal, Kenneth. *Governing China: From Revolution Through Reform* (New York NY: W.W. Norton, 1995).

Liliencron, Luiz von. *Die Deutsche Marine: Unter Zugrundelegung des neuen Flottengesetzes* (*The German Navy: Using the New Fleet Law*) (Berlin: Mittler, 1899).

Lilley, James R. with Jeffrey Lilley. *China Hands: Nine Decades of Adventure, Espionage, and Diplomacy in Asia* (New York NY: Public Affairs, 2004).

Link, Arthur S. *Woodrow Wilson and the Progressive Era, 1910–1917* (New York NY: Harper, 1954).

Link, Arthur S. (ed.). *The Papers of Woodrow Wilson*, 69 vols (Princeton NJ: Princeton University press, 1966–94), *January–May, 1916*, Vol. 36.

Linn, Brian McAllister. *Guardians of Empire: The U.S. Army and the Pacific, 1902–1940* (Chapel Hill NC: University of North Carolina Press, 1999).

Liu, Gretchen. *Singapore – A Pictorial History 1819–2000* (Abingdon: Routledge, 2001).

Lloyd George, David. *War Memoirs*, 2-vol. edn (London: Odhams, 1938).

Lochner, R.K. (trans. Thea and Harry Lindauer). *The Last-Gentleman-Of-War: The Raider Exploits of the Cruiser Emden* (Annapolis MD: Naval Institute Press, 1988).

Love, Philip H. *Andrew W. Mellon: The Man and His Work* (Baltimore MD: F.H. Coggins, 1929).

Lowe, John. *The Great Powers, Imperialism, and the German Problem 1865–1925* (London: Routledge, 1994).

Lowe, Peter. *Great Britain and Japan 1911–1915: A Study of British Far Eastern Policy* (London: Macmillan, 1969).

Luckner, Graf. *Seeteufels Weltfahrt: Alte und neue Abenteuer* (Gütersloh: Bertelsmann, 1953).

Ludwig, Emil (trans. Ethel Colburn Mayne). *Wilhelm Hohenzollern: The Last of the Kaisers* (Whitefish MT: Kessinger Publishing, 2003).

Luttikhuis, Bart and A. Dirk Moses (eds). *Colonial Counterinsurgency and Mass Violence: The Dutch Empire in Indonesia* (Abingdon: Routledge, 2014).

Lutz, Hermann (trans. E.W. Dickes). *Lord Grey And the World War* (London: Allen & Unwin, 1928).

Lyon, David. *The First Destroyers* (London: Caxton Editions, 2001).

McBeth, Brian S. *Gunboats, Corruption, and Claims: Foreign Intervention in Venezuela, 1899–1908* (Westport CT: Greenwood, 2001).

McClain, James L. *Japan: A Modern History* (New York NY: Norton, 2001).

McCord, Edward A. *The Power of the Gun: The Emergence of Modern Chinese Warlordism* (Berkeley CA: University of California Press, 1993).

Mackenzie, S.S. *Rabaul: The Australians At Rabaul; The Capture And Administration Of The German Possessions In The Southern Pacific*, tenth edn (Sydney NSW: Angus and Robertson, 1941), Vol. X of C.E.W. Bean (ed.), *The Official History of Australia in the War of 1914–1918*, 12 vols various edns (Sydney NSW: Angus and Robertson, 1941).

Mackey, Richard William. *The Zabern Affair 1913–1914* (New York NY: University Press of America, 1991).

MacIntyre, W. David. *The Rise and Fall of the Singapore Naval Base* (Hamden CT: Archon, 1979).

MacKinnon, Stephen R. *Power and Politics in Late Imperial China: Yuan Shi-kai in Beijing and Tianjin, 1901–1908* (Berkeley CA: University of California Press, 1980).

Mahajan, Sneh. *British Foreign policy 1874–1914: The Role of India* (London: Routledge, 2002).

Mahan, Alfred Thayer. *Naval Strategy* (London: Sampson Low, Marston, 1911).

Mahan, Alfred Thayer. *Naval strategy compared and contrasted with the principles and practice of military operations on land: lectures delivered at U.S. Naval War College, Newport, R.I., between the years 1887 and 1911*, repr. facs. 1911 edn (Oxford: Greenwood Press, 1975).

Mahan, Alfred Thayer. *The Influence of Sea Power Upon History, 1660–1783* (Boston MA: Adamant Media Corporation, 2002).

Mahan, Alfred Thayer. *The Influence of Sea Power upon the French Revolution and Empire, 1793–1812*, 2 vols (Boston MA: Adamant Media Corporation, 2002).

Mamdani, Mahmood. *When Victims Become Killers: Colonialism, Nativism, and the Genocide in Rwanda* (Princeton NJ: Princeton University Press, 2002).

Marder, Arthur J. *From the Dreadnought to Scapa Flow: The Royal Navy in the Fisher Era*, 5 vols, Vol. I, *The Road to War 1904–1914* (New York NY: Oxford University Press, 1961).

Marder, Arthur J. *Old Enemies, New Friends: The Royal Navy and the Imperial Japanese Navy* (Oxford: Clarendon Press, 1981).

Martin, W.A.P. *The Awakening of China* (New York NY: Doubleday, Page, 1907).

Massie, Robert K. *Dreadnought: Britain, Germany and the Coming of the Great War* (New York NY: Random House, 1991).

Matzat, Wilhelm. 'Franz Oster (1869–1933) – der erste Flieger von Tsingtau' ('Franz Oster (1869–1933) – The First Tsingtau Flier'), available online at: http://www.tsingtau.info/index.html?geschichte/oster1.htm.

Meaney, Neville. *Australia and the World: A Documentary History from the 1870s to the 1970s* (Melbourne: Longman Cheshire, 1985).

Meleisea, Malama, Donald Denoon, Stewart Firth, Jocelyn Linnekin and Karen Nero. *The Cambridge History of the Pacific Islanders* (Cambridge: Cambridge University Press, 1997).

Millard, Thomas F. 'Punishment and Revenge in China', *Scribner's Magazine*, 29 (February 1901).

Millard, Thomas F. *Our Eastern Question* (New York NY: Century, 1916).

Miller, Edward S. *War Plan Orange: The U.S. Strategy to Defeat Japan, 1897–1945* (Annapolis MD: US Naval Institute Press, 2007).

Miller, Geoffrey. *Superior Force: The Conspiracy Behind the Escape of Goeben and Breslau* (Hull: Hull University Press, 1996).

Miller, J. Martin. *China: The Yellow Peril at War With the World* (n.p.: 1900).

Miller, Stuart Creighton. *Benevolent Assimilation: The American Conquest of the Philippines, 1899–1903* (New Haven CT: Yale University Press, 1982).

Millett, Allan R. 'Assault From the Sea: The Development of Amphibious Warfare between the Wars – the American, British, and Japanese experiences', in Williamson Murray and Allan R. Millett (eds), *Military Innovation in the Interwar Period* (Cambridge: Cambridge University Press, 1996).

Mitchell, Nancy. 'The Height of the German Challenge: The Venezuela Blockade, 1902–03', *Diplomatic History*, 1996, 20(2).

Mitchell, Nancy. *The Danger of Dreams: German and American Imperialism in Latin America* (Chapel Hill NC: University of North Carolina Press, 1999).

Mombauer, Annika. *Helmuth von Moltke and the Origins of the First World War* (Cambridge: Cambridge University Press, 2001).

Mombauer, Annika. 'Wilhelm, Waldersee, and the Boxer Rebellion', in Annika Mombauer and Wilhelm Deist (eds), *The Kaiser: New Research on Wilhelm II's Role in Imperial Germany* (Cambridge: Cambridge University Press, 2003).

Mommsen, Wolfgang J. (trans. Michael S. Steinberg). *Max Weber and German Politics, 1890–1920* (Chicago IL: University of Chicago Press, 1984).

Moneypenny, W.F. and George E. Buckle. *The Life of Benjamin Disraeli: Earl of Beaconsfield*, 6 vols (New York NY: MacMillan, 1920), Vol. IX.

Moretz, Joseph. *The Royal Navy and the Capital Ship in the Interwar Period: An Operational Perspective* (London: Frank Cass, 2002).

Morison, Elting E. (ed.). *The Letters of Theodore Roosevelt*, 8 vols (Cambridge MA: Harvard University Press, 1951–4).

Morison, Samuel Eliot. *History of United States Naval Operations in World War II*, Vol. 7, *Aleutians, Gilberts and Marshalls, June 1942–April 1944* (Champaign IL: University of Illinois Press, 2002).

Morison, Samuel Eliot. *History of United States Naval Operations in World War II*, Vol. 14, *Victory in the Pacific 1945* (Champaign IL: University of Illinois Press, 2002).

Morris, Edmund. '"A Matter Of Extreme Urgency": Theodore Roosevelt, Wilhelm II, and the Venezuela Crisis of 1902', *Naval War College Review*, Spring 2002, Vol. LV, No. 2.

Morse, Hosea Ballou. *The International Relations of the Chinese Empire: The Period of Subjection 1894–1911* (London: Longmans, Green, 1918).

Morton, W. Scott and Charlton M. Lewis. *China: Its History and Culture*, fourth edn (New York NY: McGraw-Hill, 2005).

Mosse, W.E. *The German-Jewish Economic Elite, 1820–1935: A Socio-Cultural Profile* (Oxford: Clarendon Press, 1989).

Moynihan, Daniel Patrick. *Secrecy: The American Experience* (New Haven CT: Yale University Press, 1999).

Mücke, Hellmuth von. *The Emden-Ayesha adventure: German raiders in the South Seas and beyond, 1914* (Annapolis MD: Naval Institute Press, 2000).

Mulligan, Timothy P. *M2089: Selected German Documents from the Records of the Naval Records Collection of The Office Of Naval Records And Library, 1897–1917* (Washington DC: National Archives and Records Administration, 2006).

Munro, Dana G. *Intervention and Dollar Diplomacy in the Caribbean, 1900–1921* (Princeton NJ: Princeton University Press, 1964).

Murphy, Philip. *Party Politics and Decolonisation: The Conservative Party and British Colonial Policy in Tropical Africa, 1951–1964* (Oxford: Clarendon Press, 1995).

Mutsu, Munemitsu (ed. and trans. Gordon Mark Berger). *Kenkenroku: A Diplomatic Record of the Sino-Japanese War, 1894–95*, repr. edn (Tokyo: University of Tokyo Press, 1995).

Nakamura Jekizo (trans. J.A. Irons), 'Assault on the Central Fort, Tsingtao Campaign, 1914', Report in the US Army Military Research Collection at US Army Military History Institute, Carlisle Barracks, PA.

Nerger, Karl August. *SMS Wolf* (Berlin: Scherl, 1918).

Newbolt, Henry. *History of the Great War Based on Official Documents by Direction of the Historical Section of the Committee of Imperial Defence*, Vol. IV, *Naval Operations* (London: Longmans, Green, 1928).

Ngoh, Victor Julius. *History of Cameroon Since 1800* (Limbé, Cameroon: Presbook, 1996).

Nicolaou, Stéphane. *Flying Boats and Seaplanes: A History from 1905* (Osceola WI: MBI, 1998).

Nish, Ian. *Japanese Foreign Policy 1869–1942* (London: Routledge and Kegan Paul, 1977).

Nish, Ian. 'German-Japanese Relations in the Taisho Period', in Ian Nish, *Collected Writings of Ian Nish*, 2 vols (Richmond: Curzon Press, 2001–2).

Nish, Ian (ed.). *Anglo-Japanese Relations 1892–1925*, 6 vols (London: Palgrave Macmillan, 2003).

Nish, Ian. *Collected Writings (Collected Writings of Modern Western Scholars on Japan)* (London: Routledge Curzon, 2003).

Nofi, Albert A. *The Spanish-American War: 1898* (Conshohocken PA: Combined Books, 1996).

Noriko Kawamura. *Turbulence in the Pacific: Japanese-US Relations During World War I* (Westport CT: Prager, 2000).

Norregaard, B.W. *The Great Siege: The Investment and Fall of Port Arthur* (London: Methuen, 1906).

Noyes, J.K. *Colonial Space: Spatiality in the Discourse of German South West Africa 1884–1915* (Reading: Harwood, 1992).

Nozhin, E.K., A.B. Lindsay (trans.), E.J. Swinton (ed.). *The Truth about Port Arthur* (London: John Murray, 1908).

Nuhn, Walter. *Kolonialpolitik und Marine: Die Rolle der Kaiserlichen Marine bei der Gründung und Sicherung des deutschen Kolonialreiches 1884–1914 (Colonial Policy and the Navy: The Role of the Imperial Navy in the Establishment and Protection of the German Colonial Empire 1884–1914)* (Bonn: Bernard & Graefe, 2003).

Ober, W.B. 'Obstetrical events that shaped Western European history', *Yale Journal of Biology and Medicine*, 65, May–June 1992.

O'Brien, Phillips Payson. *British and American Naval Power: Politics and Policy, 1900–1936* (Westport CT: Praeger, 1998).

Oe Shinobu, *Nichi-Ro senso no gunjishiteki kenkyu* (Tokyo: Iwanami shoten, 1976).

Offner, John L. *An Unwanted War: The Diplomacy of the United States and Spain Over Cuba, 1895–1898* (Chapel Hill NC: University of North Carolina Press, 1992).

Oksiloff, Assenka. *Picturing the Primitive: Visual Culture, Ethnography, and Early German Cinema* (New York NY: Palgrave, 2001).

Olcott, Charles S. *The Life of William McKinley*, 2 vols (Boston MA: Houghton Mifflin, 1916).

Olivier, David H. *German Naval Strategy, 1856–1888: Forerunners of Tirpitz* (London: Frank Cass, 2004).

O'Reilly, Bernard. *Life of Leo XIII from an Authentic Memoir Furnished by His Order; Written with the Encouragement, Approbation and Blessing of His Holiness the Pope* (Sydney: Oceanic Publishing, 1887).

Ory, Pascal. *1889 La Mémoire des siècles: L'Expo universelle* (Paris: Editions Complexe, 1989).

Otte, T.G. '"The Baghdad Railway of the Far East:" the Tientsin-Yangtze Railway and Anglo-German Relations, 1898–1911', in T.G. Otte and Keith Neilson, *Railways and International Politics: Paths of Empire, 1848–1945* (Abingdon: Routledge, 2006).

Overlack, Peter. 'The Force of Circumstance: Graf Spee's Options for the East Asian Cruiser Squadron in 1914', *Journal of Military History*, Vol. 60, No. 4 (October 1996).

Overlack, Peter. 'German War Plans in the Pacific, 1900–1914', *The Historian* (Michigan State University Press, 1998), Vol. 60, No. 3, pp. 579–93, available at: http://www.highbeam.com/doc/1G1-20649396.html.

Overlack, Peter. 'German Commerce Warfare Planning for the Asia-Pacific Region before World War I', available at: http://www.geocities.com/peteroverlack/page2.htm.

Owen, Douglas. *Declaration of War: a Survey of the Position of Belligerents and Neutrals with Relative Considerations of Shipping and Marine Insurance during War* (London: Stevens and Sons, 1889).

Ozaki Yukio (trans. Fujiko Hara). *The Autobiography of Ozaki Yukio: The Struggle for Constitutional Government in Japan* (Princeton NJ: Princeton University Press, 2001).

Padfield, Peter. *The Great Naval Race: Anglo-German Naval Rivalry 1900–1914* (Edinburgh: Birlinn, 2004).

Padje, Willem-Alexander van't. 'The "Malet Incident," October 1895: A Prelude to the Kaiser's "Kruger Telegram" in the Context of the Anglo-German Imperialist Rivalry', in Geoff Eley and James Retallack (eds), *German Modernities, Imperialism, and the Meanings of Reform, 1890–1930: Essays for Hartmut Pogge von Strandmann* (Oxford: Berghahn, 2003).

Paine, Lauran. *Britain's Intelligence Service* (London: Hale, 1979).

Paine, S.C.M. *The Sino-Japanese War of 1894–1895: Perceptions, Power, and Primacy* (Cambridge: Cambridge University Press, 2002).

Pakenham, Thomas. *The Scramble for Africa* (London: Abacus, 1992).

Palmer, Alan. *The Kaiser: Warlord of the Second Reich* (London: Wiedenfield & Nicolson, 1978).

Palmer, Niall A. *The Twenties in America: Politics and History* (Edinburgh: Edinburgh University Press, 2006).

Pardoe, Blaine. *The Cruise of the Sea Eagle: The Amazing True Story of Imperial Germany's Gentleman Pirate* (Augusta GA: Lyons Press, 2005).

Perkins, Dexter. *The Monroe Doctrine 1867–1907* (Baltimore MD: Johns Hopkins Press, 1937).

Perras, Arne. *Carl Peters and German Imperialism 1856–1918: A Political Biography* (Oxford: Clarendon Press, 2004).

Peterson, V.G. and Tseng Hsiao. 'Kiao-chau', in Robert V. Andelson (ed.), *Land-Value Taxation Around the World* (Malden MA: Blackwell, 2000).

Philbin, Tobias R. *The Lure of Neptune: German-Soviet Naval Collaboration and Ambitions, 1919–1941* (Columbia SC: University of South Carolina Press, 1994).

Philip, George (ed.). *British Documents on Foreign Affairs: Reports and Papers from the Foreign Office Confidential Print, Series E, Asia, 1914–1939 Part II, From the First to the Second World War* (Frederick MD: University Publications of America, 1991).

Phillips, Kevin P. *The Cousins' Wars: Religion, Politics, and the Triumph of Anglo-America* (New York NY: Basic Books, 1999).

Phillipson, Coleman. *International Law and the Great War* (London: T. Fisher Unwin, 1915).

Pitt, Barrie. *Coronel and Falkland: Two Great Naval Battles of the First World War* (London: Cassell, 2004).

Pleshakov, Constantine. *The Tsar's Last Armada: The Epic Voyage to the Battle of Tsushima* (New York NY: Basic Books, 2002).

Plüschow, Isot and Gunther Plüschow. *Deutscher Seemann und Flieger* (Berlin: Ullstein, 1933).

Pomerantz-Zhang, Linda. *Wu Tingfang (1842–1922): Reform and Modernization in Modern Chinese History* (Hong Kong: Hong Kong University Press, 1992).

Ponsonby, Sir Frederick (ed.). *Letters of the Empress Frederick* (London: Macmillan, 1929).

Pooley, A.M. (ed.). *The Secret Memoirs of Count Tadasu Hayashi* (New York NY and London: G.P. Putnam's Sons, 1915).

Porter, Major General W. *The History of the Corps of Royal Engineers*, 11 vols (London: Longmans, Green, 1952), Vol. II.

Powell, Alan. *The Third Force: ANGUA's New Guinea War, 1942–46* (Melbourne: Oxford University Press, 2003).

Pratt, John T. *War and Politics in China* (London: Jonathan Cape, 1943).

Prentiss, Augustin M. *Chemicals in War: A Treatise in Chemical Warfare* (New York NY: McGraw-Hill, 1937).

Price, Ernest Batson. *The Russo-Japanese Treaties of 1907–1916 Concerning Manchuria and Mongolia* (Baltimore NJ: Johns Hopkins Press, 1933).

Putnam, William Lowell. *The Kaiser's Merchant Ships in World War I* (Jefferson NC: McFarland, 2001).

Quinn, Frederick. *The French Overseas Empire* (Westport CT: Praeger, 2000).

Ramsden, John. *Man of the Century: Winston Churchill and his Legend since 1945* (New York NY: Columbia University Press, 2002).

Rangarajan, Sadhu Professor V. and R. Vivekanandan. *The Saga of Patriotism: Revolutionaries in India's Freedom Struggle* (Bangalore: Sister Nivedita Academy, 2004).

Ransom, Harry H. 'The Battleship Meets the Airplane', *Military Affairs*, Vol. 23, No. 1 (Spring 1959).

Reichs-Marine-Amt, *Forschungsergebnisse S.M.S. 'Planet' 1906/7, Band 1: Reisebeschreibung* (Berlin: Karl Sigismund, 1909).

Reid, Gilbert. 'The Neutrality of China', *The Yale Law Journal*, Vol. 25, No. 2 (December 1915).

Reynolds, Clark G. *The Fast Carriers: The Forging of an Air Navy* (Annapolis MD: Naval Institute Press, 2014).

Reynolds, David. *Britannia Overruled; British policy and World Power in the Twentieth Century* (Harlow: Pearson, 2000).

Rhodes James, Robert (ed.). *Winston S Churchill: His Complete Speeches, 1897–1963*, 8 vols (New York NY: Chelsea House Publishers, 1974).

Rice, Howard. *The Fire of Komwonlaid Cape: the Story of Sokehs Rebellion* (Pohnpei, FSM: Division of Historic Preservation & Cultural Affairs, 1998).

Rich, Norman. *Friedrich von Holstein: Politics and Diplomacy in the Era of Bismarck and William II*, 2 vols (Cambridge: Cambridge University Press, 1965).

Richmond, Admiral Sir Herbert. *Statesmen and Sea Power* (Oxford: Clarendon Press, 1946).

Robbins, Commander Charles B. 'German Seacoast Defences at Tsingtao, 1914', *The Coast Defence Journal*, May 2007.

Rodwell, C.H. Review of 'The German Colonial Claim by L S Amery', in *International Affairs* (Royal Institute of International Affairs, 1931–9), Vol. 18, No. 5 (September–October 1939).

Rogers, Robert F. *Destiny's Landfall: A History of Guam* (Honolulu HI: University of Hawai'i Press, 1995).

Röhl, John C.G. *Germany Without Bismarck: The Crisis of Government in the Second Reich, 1890–1900* (Berkeley CA: University of California Press, 1967).

Röhl, John C.G. (trans. Terence F. Cole). *The Kaiser and his Court: Wilhelm II and the Government of Germany* (Cambridge: Cambridge University Press, 1994).

Röhl, John C.G. *Young Wilhelm: The Kaiser's Early Life, 1859–1888* (Cambridge: Cambridge University Press, 1998).

Röhl, John C.G. (trans. Sheila de Bellaigue). *Wilhelm II: The Kaiser's Personal Monarchy, 1888–1900* (Cambridge: Cambridge University Press, 2004).

Röhr, Albert. *Handbuch der deutschen Marinegeschichte* (*Manual of German Naval History*) (Oldenburg: Gerhard Stalling, 1963).

Røksund, Arne. *The Jeune Ecole: The Strategy of the Weak* (Leiden: Brill, 2007).

Roosevelt, Theodore. *Addresses and State Papers: Including the European Addresses*, executive edn, 8 vols (New York NY: Collier & Son, 1910).

Rose, Inbal. *Conservatism and Foreign Policy During the Lloyd George Coalition 1918–1922* (Abingdon: Taylor & Francis, 1999).

Roth, Guenther. *The Social Democrats in Imperial Germany: A Study in Working-Class Isolation and National Integration* (Totowa NJ: Bedminster Press, 1963).

Rottman, Gordon. *World War II Pacific Island Guide: A Geo-Military Study* (Westport CT: Greenwood, 2002).

Rubinger, Richard. 'Education in Meiji Japan', in Wm Theodore de Bary, Carol Gluck and Donald Keene (eds), *Sources of Japanese Tradition*, 2 vols (New York NY: Columbia University Press, 2003).

Sack, Peter. 'The "Ponape Rebellion" and the Phantomisation of History', *Journal de la Société des océanistes* (1997), Vol. 104, No. 1.

Sagan, Scott D. '1914 Revisited: Allies, Offense, and Instability', in Michael E. Brown, Owen R. Coté Jr, Sean M. Lynn-Jones and Steven E. Miller (eds), *Offense, Defense, and War* (Cambridge MA: The MIT Press, 2004).

Saito Seiji, *Hi Taisho 3-nen Nichi-Doku senshi bekkan 2 Nichi-Doku Chintao Senso* (*A History of the Japanese-German War of 1914*, Appendix 2: *The Battle between Japan and Germany for Qingdao*) (Tokyo: Yumani Shobo, 2001).

Salesa, Damon. 'Samoa's Half-Castes and Some Frontiers of Comparison', Ann Laura Stoler, *Haunted by Empire: Geographies of Intimacy in North American History* (Durham NC: Duke University Press, 2006).

Sanbo Honbu (General Staff Office), *Taisho 3-nen Nichi-Doku senshi* (*History of the Japanese-German War of 1914*), 2 vols (Tokyo: Sanbo Honbu, 1916).

Samuels, Richard J. '*Rich Nation, Strong Army:*' *National Security and the Technological Transformation of Japan* (Ithaca NY: Cornell University Press, 1994).

Saunders, Anthony. *Reinventing Warfare 1914–18: Novel Munitions and Tactics of Trench Warfare* (New York NY: Continuum, 2012).

Saxon, Timothy D. 'Anglo-Japanese Naval Cooperation, 1914–1918', *Naval War College Review*, Winter 2000, Vol. LIII, No. 1.

Schiefel, Werner. *Bernhard Dernburg 1865–1937: Kolonialpolitiker und Bankier im wilhelminischen Deutschland* (Zurich: Atlantis, 1974).

Schirmer, Daniel B. and Stephen Rosskamm Shalom (eds), *The Philippines Reader: A History of Colonialism, Neocolonialism, Dictatorship, and Resistance* (Boston MA: South End Press, 1987).

Schmidt, Hans. *Maverick Marine: General Smedley D Butler and the Contradictions of American Military History* (Lexington KY: University Press of Kentucky, 1987).

Schoen, Walter von. *Auf Vorposten für Deutschland: Unsere Kolonien im Weltkrieg On Germany's Outposts: Our Colonies in the World War*) (Berlin: Ullstein, 1935).

Schoenbaum, David. *Zabern 1913: Consensus Politics in Imperial Germany* (London: George Allen & Unwin, 1982).

Schoonover, Thomas. *Uncle Sam's War of 1898 and the Origins of Globalization* (Lexington KY: University Press of Kentucky, 2003).

Schrecker, John E. *Imperialism and Chinese Nationalism: Germany in Shantung* (Cambridge MA: Harvard University Press, 1971).

Schriffin, Harold Z. *Sun Yat-sen and the Origins of the Chinese Revolution* (Berkeley CA: University of California Press, 1970).

Schroeder, Wilhelm (ed.) (trans. Richard S. Levy). *Das persönliche Regiment: Reden und sonstige öffentliche Äusserungen Wilhelms II* (Munich: Birk, 1912).

Shunjiro Kurita. *Who's Who in Japan 1913* (Tokyo: The Who's Who in Japan Office, 1913).

Schütz, Julius von (trans. Hubert Herbert Grenfell). *Gruson's Chilled Cast-Iron Armour* (London: Whitehead, Morris & Lowe, 1887).

Schwabe, Kurd. *Dienst und Kriegsführung in den Kolonien und auf überseeischen Expeditionen* (*Service and war guidance in the colonies and on overseas expeditions*) (Berlin: Mittler, 1903).

Schweinitz, Hans Lothar von. *Briefwechsel des Botschafters (Exchange of letters of Ambassador) General von Schweinitz* (Berlin: Reimar Hobbing, 1928).

Scott, Ernest. *Australia During The War*, seventh edn (Sydney NSW: Angus and Robertson, 1941), Vol. XI of C.E.W. Bean (ed.), *The Official History of Australia in the War of 1914–1918*, 12 vols various edns (Sydney NSW: Angus and Robertson, 1941).

Seager II, Robert and Doris Maguire (eds). *Letters and Papers of Alfred Thayer Mahan*, 3 vols (Annapolis MD: Naval Institute Press, 1975).

Seagrave, Sterling. *Dragon Lady: The Life and Legend of the Last Empress of China*, repr. edn (London: Vintage, 1993).

Seeley, Sir John Robert. *The Expansion of England: Two Courses of Lectures* (Boston MA: Little, Brown & Company, 1883).

Seligmann, Matthew S. *Rivalry in Southern Africa, 1893–99: The Transformation of German Colonial Policy* (London: Palgrave Macmillan, 1998).

Semenoff, Vladimir. *Rasplata (The Reckoning)* (London: John Murray, 1909).

Semenoff, Vladimir. *The Battle of Tsushima Between the Japanese and Russian Fleets, Fought on 27th May 1905* (New York NY: E.P. Dutton, 1912).

Shinji Ishii, 'The Fall of Sei-Tö (Tsing-Tao) and its Aftermath', *The Royal Society for India, Pakistan, and Ceylon, Asian Review: Journal of the Royal Society for India, Pakistan, and Ceylon* (London: The Royal Society), January–May 1915, Nos 13–16.

Shinji Suzuki and Masako Sakai, 'History of Early Aviation in Japan', a paper (AIAA 2005-118) presented to the 43rd AIAA (American Institute of Aeronautics and Astronautics) Aerospace Sciences Meeting and Exhibit, 10–13 January 2005, Reno NV.

Sieche, Erwin F. 'The Kaiser Franz Joseph I Class Torpedo-rams of the Austro-Hungarian Navy', in John Roberts (ed.), *Warship 1995* (London: Conway Maritime Press, 1995).

Sims, Philip. 'German Tsingtao Mounts Photographs', *The Coast Defence Journal*, November 2006.

Smith, Alson J. *A View of the Spree: The Extraordinary Career of the American Grocer's Daughter Who Became a 'Sanctified Pompadour* (New York NY: John Day Company, 1962).

Smith, Captain Bernard. 'The Siege of Tsingtau', *The Coast Artillery Journal*, November–December 1934, p. 405.

Smith, Peter C. *Task Force 57: The British Pacific Fleet, 1944–45* (London: William Kimber, 1969).

Snyder, Louis L. (ed.), *Documents of German History* (New Brunswick NJ: Rutgers University Press, 1958).

Sobel, Robert. *Biographical Directory of the United States Executive Branch, 1774–1989* (New York NY: Greenwood Press, 1990).

Solzhenitsyn, Alexander. *August 1914: The Red Wheel*, third printing (New York NY: Farrar, Straus and Giroux, 2000).

Sondhaus, Lawrence. *Naval Warfare, 1815–1914* (London: Routledge, 2001).

Smith, Arthur H. *China in Convulsion*, 2 vols (New York NY: F.H. Revell, 1901).

Sondhaus, Lawrence. *The Naval Policy of Austria-Hungary 1867–1918: Navalism, Industrial Development and the Politics of Dualism* (West Lafayette IN: Purdue University Press, 1994).

Sösemann, Bernd. 'Forms and Effects of Public Self-Display in Wilhelmine Germany', in Annika Mombauer and Wilhelm Deist, *The Kaiser: New Research on Wilhelm IIs Role in Imperial Germany* (Cambridge: Cambridge University Press, 2003).

Sowell, Thomas. *Ethnic America: A History* (New York NY: Basic Books, 1981).

Spender, J.A. *Fifty Years of Europe: A Study in Pre-War Documents* (London: Cassell, 1933).

Spennemann, Dirk H.R. *Centenary of German Annexation of the Carolines* (2000), http://marshall.csu.edu.au/Marshalls/html/german/Annex.html.

Sprigade, P. and M. Moisel (eds). *Deutscher Kolonialatlas mit Jahrbuch. Herausgegeben auf Veranlassung der Deutschen Kolonialgesellschaft* (Berlin: Ernst Vohsen, 1905–18); the German Colonial Society published a Yearbook, complete with Atlas, annually between 1905 and 1914, and a final edition in 1918 detailing the loss of the colonies.

Staatsarchiv, Das (trans. Adam Blauhut), *Sammlung der offiziellen Aktenstücke zur Geschichte der Gegenwart (Collection of Official Documents Relating to Contemporary History)* (Leipzig: Duncker and Humblot, 1891).

Startt, James D. *Woodrow Wilson and the Press: Prelude to the Presidency* (New York NY: Palgrave Macmillan, 2004).

Steele, David. *Lord Salisbury: A Political Biography* (London: Routledge, 2005).

Steinberg, John W., Bruce W. Menning, David Schimmelpenninck van der Oye, David Wolff and Shinji Yokote (eds). *The Russo-Japanese War in Global Perspective: World War Zero* (Leiden: Brill Academic Publishers, 2005).

Steinmetz, George. 'Precoloniality and Colonial Subjectivity: Ethnographic Discourse and Native Policy in German Overseas Imperialism. 1780s–1914', in Diane E. Davis (ed.), *Political Power and Social Theory, Volume 15* (Oxford: Elsevier Science, 2002).

Steinmetz, George. '"The Devil's Handwriting": Precolonial Discourse, Ethnographic Acuity, and Cross-Identification in German Colonialism', *Comparative Studies in Society and History*, Vol. 45, Issue 01, January 2003.

Steinmetz, George. 'From "Native Policy" to Exterminationism: German Southwest Africa, 1904, in Comparative Perspective', in Paper 30, *Theory and Research in Comparative Social Analysis*, Department of Sociology, UCLA (Los Angeles CA: University of California, 2005).

Stephenson, Charles, 'Master of Siegecraft: Seigneur de Vauban, 1633–1707', in Charles Stephenson (consultant ed.), *Castles: A History of Fortified Structures Ancient, Medieval and Modern* (New York NY: St Martin's Griffin, 2011).

Stevens, David. 'HMAS Australia: a Ship for a Nation', in David Stevens and John Reeve (eds), *The Navy and the Nation: The Influence of the Navy on Modern Australia* (Crows Nest NSW: Allen & Unwin, 2005).

Stevenson, Robert Louis. *A Footnote to History: Eight Years of Trouble in Samoa* (New York NY: Charles Scribner's Sons, 1892).

Stevenson, Robert Louis. *Vailima Letters: Being Correspondence Addressed by Robert Louis Stevenson to Sidney Colvin. November 1890–October 1894* (London: Methuen, 1895).

Stoecker, Helmuth. 'Cameroon 1906–1914', in Helmuth Stoecker (ed.) (trans. Bernd Zöllner), *German Imperialism in Africa: From the Beginnings Until the Second World War* (London: Hurst, 1986).

Stoecker, Helmuth and Helmut Nimschowski. 'Morocco 1898–1914', in Helmuth Stoecker (ed.) (trans. Bernd Zöllner), *German Imperialism in Africa: From the Beginnings Until the Second World War* (London: Hurst, 1986).

Stone, Norman. *The Eastern Front 1914–1917* (New York NY: Charles Scribner's Sons, 1975).

Strachan, Hew. *The First World War, Volume One: To Arms* (Oxford: Oxford University Press, 2003).

Strachan, Hew. *The Outbreak of the First World War* (Oxford: Oxford University Press, 2004).

Stringer, H. *The Chinese Railway System* (Shanghai: Kelly and Walsh, 1922).

Sumida, Jon Tetsuro. 'British Naval Operational Logistics, 1914–1918', *The Journal of Military History* (Lexington VA: Virginia Military Institute, 1993), Vol. 57, No. 3.

Sumino, Lila. 'L'Avion: l'Envol du Japon', *Asia: Journal collégien et lycéen d'établissements français de la zone Asie-Pacifique*, No. 2, December 2006.

Sumner, Ian. *German Air Forces 1914–18* (Oxford: Osprey, 2005).

Taliaferro, Jeffrey W. *Balancing Risks: Great Power Intervention in the Periphery* (Ithaca NY: Cornell University Press, 2004).

Tampke, Jurgen (ed.). *Ruthless Warfare: German Military Planning and Surveillance in the Australia-New Zealand Region Before the Great War* (Canberra: Southern Highlands Publishers, 1998).

Tatsuji Takeuchi. *War and Diplomacy in the Japanese Empire* (Chicago IL: Allen & Unwin, 1936).

Taylor, A.J.P. *The Struggle for Mastery in Europe 1848–1915* (Oxford: Oxford University Press, 1954).

Terrill, Ross. *The New Chinese Empire* (Sydney NSW: University of NSW Press, 2003).

Thiele, Erdmann (ed.). *Telefunken nach 100 Jahren: Das Erbe einer deutschen Weltmarke* (*The Legacy of a Global Brand*) (Berlin: Nicolai, 2003).

Times, The, Correspondents of. *The Times History of the War*, 22 vols (London: *The Times*, 1915), Vol. II.

Tirpitz, Grand Admiral von. *My Memoirs*, 2 vols (London: Hurst & Blacket, 1919).

Tomes, Jason. *Balfour and Foreign Policy: The International Thought of a Conservative Statesman* (Cambridge: Cambridge University Press, 2002).

Torrance, David. *The Scottish Secretaries* (Edinburgh: Birlinn, 2006).

Townsend, Mary E. 'The German Colonies and the Third Reich', *Political Science Quarterly*, Vol. 53, No. 2 (June 1938), p. 187.

Trani, Eugene P. and David L. Wilson. *The Presidency of Warren G. Harding* (Lawrence KS: Regents Press of Kansas, 1977).

Trask, David F. *The War with Spain in 1898* (New York NY: Simon & Schuster, 1981).

'Treaty Between Japan and China for the Settlement of Outstanding Questions Relative to Shantung', *The American Journal of International Law*, Vol. 16, No. 2, Supplement: Official Documents (April 1922).

Tretyakov, Lieutenant General N.A. *My Experiences at Nan-Shan and Port Arthur with the Fifth East Siberian Rifles* (London: Hugh Rees, 1911).

Trotter, A. 'Friend to Foe? New Zealand and Japan: 1900–1937', in Roger Peren (ed.), *Japan and New Zealand: 150 Years* (Palmerston North: New Zealand Centre for Japanese Studies, Massey University, on behalf of the Ministry of Foreign Affairs, Tokyo, in association with the Historical Branch, Department of Internal Affairs, Wellington, 1999).

Tuchman, Barbara W. *The Zimmerman Telegram* (New York NY: Viking Press, 1956).

Tucker, Spencer C. *The Great War 1914–18* (Bloomington IN: Indiana University Press, 1999).

Tucker, Spencer C. (ed.) *Who's Who in Twentieth Century Warfare* (London: Routledge, 2001).

Tunnicliffe, M.D. 'The Fleet We Never Had', *Canadian Naval Review*, Vol. 2, Number 1 (Spring 2006).

Turk, Richard W. *The Ambiguous Relationship: Theodore Roosevelt and Alfred Thayer Mahan* (Westport CT: Greenwood Press, 1987).

Unger, J. Marshall. *Literacy and Script Reform in Occupation Japan* (New York NY: Oxford University Press, 1996).

Van der Leeuw, Charles. *Oil and Gas in the Caucasus and Caspian: A History* (Richmond: Curzon Press, 2000).

Van der Vat, Dan. *The Last Corsair: The Story of the Emden*, rev. edn (Edinburgh: Birlinn, 2001).

Venzon, Anne Cipriano (ed.). *General Smedley Darlington Butler: The Letters of a Leatherneck, 1898–1931* (New York NY: Praeger, 1992).

Venzon, Anne Cipriano. *From Whaleboats to Amphibious Warfare: Lt. Gen. 'Howling Mad' Smith and the U.S. Marine Corps* (Westport CT: Praeger, 2003).

Vercamer, Arvo. *German Military Mission to China 1927–1938*, available at: www.feldgrau. com/articles.php?ID=11.

Vollerthun, Waldemar. *Der Kampf um Tsingtau: eine Episode aus dem Weltkrieg 1914/1918 nach Tagebuchblättern* (*The Battle for Tsingtau: an Episode from the World War of 1914–18 from the Pages of a Diary*) (Leipzig: Hirzel, 1920).

Voskamp, Carl Johannes. *Aus dem belagerten Tsingtau* (Berlin: Society of Evangelical Missions, 1915).

Waldeyer-Hartz, Hugo von. *Der Kreuzerkrieg 1914–1918: das Kreuzergeschwader, Emden, Königsberg, Karlsruhe, die Hilfskreuzer* (Oldenburg: Gerhard Stalling, 1931).

Walters, R.H. *The Economic and Business History of the South Wales Steam Coal Industry, 1840–1914* (New York NY: Arno Press, 1977).

Walton, Joseph. *China and the Present Crisis: With Notes on a Visit to Japan and Korea* (London: Sampson Low, Marston, 1900).

Walworth, Arthur. *Woodrow Wilson*, 2 vols (New York NY: Longmans, Green, 1958).

Ward, Kyle Roy. *In the Shadow of Glory: The Thirteenth Minnesota in the Spanish-American and Philippine-American Wars, 1898–1899* (St Cloud MN: North Star, 2000).

Warner, Marina. *The Dragon Empress: The Life and Times of Tz'u-hsi, Empress Dowager of China, 1835–1908* (New York NY: MacMillan, 1972).

Weisman, Steven R. *The Great Tax Wars: Lincoln to Wilson – The Fierce Battles over Money and Power That Transformed the Nation* (New York NY: Simon and Shuster, 2002).

Welles, Benjamin. *Sumner Welles: FDR's Global Strategist, a Biography* (New York NY: St Martin's Press, 1997).

Wertheimer, Mildred S. *The Pan-German league, 1890–1914* (New York NY: Columbia University Press, 1923).

Wetzler, Peter. *Hirohito and War: Imperial Tradition and Military Decision Making in Prewar Japan* (Honolulu HI: University of Hawai'i Press, 1998).

White, John Albert. *Transition to Global Rivalry: Alliance Diplomacy and the Quadruple Entente, 1895–1907* (Cambridge: Cambridge University Press, 2002).

Wilbur, C. Martin. 'The Nationalist Revolution: from Canton to Nanking, 1923–28', in John K. Fairbank and Denis Twitchett (eds), *The Cambridge History of China, Volume 12, Republican China, 1912–1949* (Cambridge: Cambridge University Press, 1983).

Wilhelm II, Emperor of Germany, 1888–1918 (trans. Thomas R. Ybarra), *The Kaiser's Memoirs* (New York NY: Harper & Brothers, 1922).

Wilson, Michael. *Royal Australian Navy Major Warships: Profile No. 1* (Marrickville NSW: Topmill, n.d).

Wilson, Woodrow. Message to Congress, 63rd Congress, 2d Session, Senate Doc. No. 566 (Washington DC: 1914), pp. 3–4, available at: http://net.lib.byu.edu/~rdh7/wwi/1914/wilsonneut.html.

Winzen, Peter. *Das Kaiserreich am Abgrund: Die Daily-Telegraph-Affaere und das Hale-Interview von 1908* (*The Empire at the Abyss: The Daily-Telegraph Affair and the Hale-Interview of 1908*) (Stuttgart: Franz Steiner, 2002).

Witcover, Jules. *Sabotage at Black Tom: Imperial Germany's Secret War in America, 1914–1917* (Chapel Hill NC: Algonquin, 1989).

Witte, Count (ed. A. Yarmolinsky). *The Memoirs of Count Witte* (London: William Heinemann, 1921).

Wood, James. *History of International Broadcasting*, 2 vols (London: Peregrinus, 1992).

Woodhead, H.G.W. and H.T.M. Bell. *The China Year Book* (Shanghai: *North China Daily News & Herald*, 1914), available at: http://homepage3.nifty.com/akagaki/cyuui3.html.

Worth, Richard. *Fleets of World War II* (Cambridge MA: Da Capo, 2001).

Wright, Burton III. *Eastern Mandates (US Army Campaigns of World War II)* (Washington DC: US Army Center of Military History, 1993).

Yang Xiao. 'Liang Qichai's Political and Social Philosophy', in Chung-Yin Cheng and Nicholas Bunnin, *Contemporary Chinese Philosophy* (Malden MA: Blackwell, 2002).

Yardley, Herbert O. *The American Black Chamber* (Laguna Hills CA: Aegean Park, 1931).

Yates, Keith. *Graf Spee's Raiders: Challenge to the Royal Navy 1914–1915* (Annapolis MD: Naval Institute Press, 1995).

Yoichi Hirama. 'The Anglo-Japanese Alliance and the First World War', in Ian Gow, Yoichi Hirama and John Chapman (eds), *History of Anglo-Japanese Relations, 1600–2000, Volume III: The Military Dimension* (Basingstoke: Palgrave Macmillan, 2003).

Yongling Lu and Ruth Hayhoe. 'Chinese Higher Learning: the Transition Process from Classical Knowledge Patterns to Modern Disciplines, 1860–1910', in Christopher Charle, Jürgen Schriewer, Peter Wagner (eds), *Transitional Intellectual Networks: Forms of Academic Knowledge and the Search for Cultural Identities* (Frankfurt: Campus, 2004).

Young, E.F. 'Tethered Balloons – Present and Future', a paper (AIAA-1968-941) presented to the Aerodynamic Deceleration Systems Conference of the AIAA (American Institute of Aeronautics and Astronautics), 23–5 September 1968, El Centro, CA.

Young, William. *German Diplomatic Relations 1871–1945: The Wilhelmstrasse and the Formulation of Foreign Policy* (New York NY: iUniverse, 2006).

Zarrow, Peter. *China in War and Revolution, 1895–1949* (London: Routledge, 2005).

Index